Antranig Azhderian

The Turk and the Land of Haig

Descriptive, Historical and Picturesque

Antranig Azhderian

The Turk and the Land of Haig
Descriptive, Historical and Picturesque

ISBN/EAN: 9783337293390

Printed in Europe, USA, Canada, Australia, Japan

Cover: Foto ©ninafisch / pixelio.de

More available books at **www.hansebooks.com**

AND

THE LAND OF HAIG

OR

TURKEY AND ARMENIA

DESCRIPTIVE, HISTORICAL, AND PICTURESQUE

BY

ANTRANIG AZHDERIAN

NEW YORK
THE MERSHON COMPANY
PUBLISHERS

In compliance with current
copyright law, LBS Archival
Products produced this
replacement volume on paper
that meets the ANSI Standard
Z39.48-1984 to replace the
irreparably deteriorated original.

1989

To the
Memory of my home across the sea
This first fruit of my youthful pen is
Tenderly Inscribed.

PREFACE.

THE late Armenian tragedies have claimed a large share of the world's attention, and have occasioned the publication of a great deal of literature on the subject; thanks to modern facilities of communication, which have brought mankind everywhere into such close relations that each now studies the other's condition and movements with more interest, and each has a mutual feeling for the other's welfare and destiny. Yet with all the information of the present situation of affairs in the Turkish Empire, there is still a manifest lack of knowledge of the land, its historical associations, the relations which its people sustain one to the other, and their character and home life. Travelers in foreign lands, no matter how keen in their observation, attain, as to the inner real life of the people, ideas very unsatisfactory, and what they say is ofttimes of little worth, not being the true condition of things. They have seen "through a glass darkly." I claim that seeing is not knowing. Often many things, after some time spent in careful observation and study, seem entirely different from our first impressions. To look at the window is a different thing from looking through the window. A great many travelers during their flying trips know things only as they appear to them, and often are deceived; but a native looks not at the things, but through the things; he takes them not as they appear, but as they *are*. The language, religious ceremonies, manners, and customs, the social and moral conditions, and the very atmosphere of the country itself are familiar to a native from his cradle.

The mission of this book, therefore, is not simply to set forth the causes and the development of the late tragedies in Armenia; but, from the standpoint of a native, one who is born and reared in the country, to portray, as accurately as possible, the varied phases of the social, religious, and political customs and institutions of the Armenians and the Turks; and to give some account of their history, past and present, with an earnest desire to bring the life of the country clearly before the minds of the American people, in the hope that a better understanding of my fatherland by Americans may arouse intelligent and practical sympathy, and thus may reflect upon that country some of those blessings which have distinguished America in the march of modern civilization.

THE AUTHOR.

CONTENTS.

	PAGE
PREFACE,	3
INTRODUCTION,	11
THE LAND OF HAIG—ARMENIA,	13
THE CHILDREN OF HAIG—THE ARMENIANS,	35
ARMENIAN LITERATURE,	74
THE ARMENIAN CHURCH,	109
THE EVANGELICAL CHURCH,	129
SOCIAL AND HOME LIFE,	156
THE TURKS,	220
THE RELIGION OF THE TURKS—MOHAMMEDANISM,	248
THE TURKISH GOVERNMENT,	284
THE EASTERN QUESTION,	318
THE CHRONIC CONDITION OF ARMENIA, AND THE CAUSES OF HER TRAGEDIES,	353
THE TURKISH CAMPAIGN OF BUTCHERY,	370

ILLUSTRATIONS.

	PAGE
ANTRANIG AZHDERIAN, THE AUTHOR,	*Frontispiece*
MOUNT ARARAT,	24
RUINS OF ANCIENT ARMENIAN MONASTERIES AND PALACES,	29
REMAINS OF ARMENIAN ANTIQUITY,	33
TRADITIONAL PORTRAIT OF HAIG,	37
LEGENDARY HEROES OF ARMENIA,	43
KINGS OF ANCIENT ARMENIA AND THE CONVERSION AND BAPTISM OF KING TIRIDATES,	49
COAT OF ARMS AND FLAGS OF ANCIENT ARMENIA,	57
JOHN AYVAZOVSK, THE ARMENIAN PAINTER,	67
H. E. DAUD PASHA, LATE ARMENIAN GOVERNOR OF MOUNT LEBANON,	71
EARLY ARMENIAN MONASTERIES—REPOSITORIES OF LEARNING,	83
THE SCENE OF ARMENIAN POETS' FANCY,	95
THE LITTLE LAKE,	100
RAPHAEL PATKANIAN,	105
LEGENDARY PORTRAIT OF VARTAN MAMIGONIAN,	114
MONASTERY OF ETCHMIADZIN,	117
RT. REV. MIGRDITCH KHIRIMIAN, THE ARMENIAN CATHOLICOS,	121
EARLY MONASTERIES AND CHURCHES OF ARMENIA,	127
REV. CYRUS HAMLIN, D. D., LL. D.,	137
ARMENIAN TEACHERS,	141
AMERICAN MISSIONARIES TRANSLATING THE BIBLE AT CONSTANTINOPLE,	145
ANATOLIA COLLEGE,	147
PRESIDENT C. C. TRACY AND STUDENTS OF ANATOLIA COLLEGE,	149

ILLUSTRATIONS.

	PAGE
AMERICAN MISSIONARIES AT MARSOVAN,	153
AN ARMENIAN FAMILY—RELATIVES OF THE AUTHOR,	157
ARMENIAN CHILDREN,	157
A CHARACTERISTIC STREET SCENE,	159
SCHOOLGIRLS IN ARMENIA,	163
TEACHERS AND PUPILS OF AN ARMENIAN SCHOOL,	167
A TURKISH SCHOOL,	174
AN ADVANCED MOSLEM TEACHER AND HIS PUPILS,	177
THE BAZAAR DE DOERKLER-ALTI IN CONSTANTINOPLE,	181
A TURKISH LADY OF RANK,	185
A MOSLEM SLAVE GIRL OF THE HAREM,	188
THE FAIR WOMEN OF THE HAREM,	191
SULTAN'S HAREM ON THE BOSPHORUS,	191
A TURKISH YOUNG LADY,	195
AN ARMENIAN MERCHANT AND FAMILY IN MARSOVAN, TURKEY,	199
AN ARMENIAN FAMILY,	202
A CARAVAN,	207
ON THE ROAD IN TURKEY,	213
A TURKISH PLOW AND PLOWMAN,	218
SOME OF THE SULTANS OF TURKEY,	225
SOLDIERS OF THE OLD MILITARY SYSTEM—JANIZARIES,	229
MOHAMMED II. WITHIN THE WALLS OF CONSTANTINOPLE,	233
SULTAN ABDUL-HAMID II.,	237
SULTAN ABDUL-AZIZ,	239
GATE OF IMPERIAL SERAGLIO IN CONSTANTINOPLE,	241
IMPERIAL PALACE OF DOLMA-BAYTCHE ON THE BOSPHORUS,	243
ARCH IN RUINS IN ASIA MINOR,	245
THEATER IN RUINS,	245
MOSQUES OF THE MOSLEM FOUNDERS, BRUSA,	251
THE MOSQUE OF AHMET IN CONSTANTINOPLE,	255
THE MOSLEM AT PRAYER IN THE DESERT,	261
COURT OF A MOSQUE,	265
THE MOSQUE OF SULEYMAN IN CONSTANTINOPLE,	271
A DERVISH BEGGAR,	277
DANCING DERVISHES,	277

ILLUSTRATIONS.

	PAGE
Public Reading of the Sultan's Firman Regarding the Appointment of a Pasha,	287
A Vali and Suite,	291
A Turkish Judge,	295
A Modern Turkish General,	301
A Turkish Landlord of the Highest Type,	307
Firemen and Fire Engine in Turkey,	309
A Hot Bargain in the Horse Market,	313
Santa Sophia in Constantinople,	321
Constantinople and the Golden Horn,	327
Nicholas I., Emperor of Russia,	329
Lord Salisbury, Prime Minister of Great Britain,	349
Moslem Cutthroats in Armenia,	356
The City of Marsovan,	359
A Group of Armenian Huntchagians,	365
Seven Towers of Constantinople,	367
Moslem Robbers Dividing Spoils,	373
The Ambassadors of the Great Powers at Constantinople,	383
The Late Rt. Hon. W. E. Gladstone, the Great English Friend of the Armenians,	385
An Armenian Massacre,	389
The Costume of a Turkish Highwayman,	391
Armenian Children,	401

INTRODUCTORY.

BY

RT. REV. F. D. HUNTINGTON, LL. D.,

Bishop of the Diocese of Central New York.

It is a pleasure for me to place my name among those of the friends of Mr. Antranig Azhderian in this country. With those who may have but a slight acquaintance with him there can be no occasion for any testimonial to his noble character, his accomplishments, his high aim, or his patriotic devotion to his native land and its institutions.

The many tributes which Mr. Azhderian has in his possession are so explicit, so emphatic, so cordial, so laudatory in terms, and so disinterested in their motive, that I could, even apart from my personal acquaintance with him, feel no hesitation in giving him both confidence and unqualified commendation. These documents are made weighty by the character and standing of men whose signatures they bear, including international officials, scholars, authorities in Oriental literature, educators in this country, Christian missionaries, and ministers of the Gospel. They relate to different periods of Mr. Azhderian's life, his birth and superior breeding, his social position in the Orient, his habits and studies. They bear striking testimony to his unusual gifts as a public speaker, his judgment and taste, his command of languages, his eloquence in oratory.

Any introduction bespeaking favorable attention in behalf of this work would be needless for those who may begin to read it. The qualities as to which the author has been most careful to make his treatise strong and secure in the face of criticism are accuracy, fairness, historical impartiality, and intelligent sympathy with the best institutions and movements of our time, in the Old World and the New. It would not be enough for a patriotic Armenian to revere the venerable antiquities and sacred traditions of his people, or plead for justice and mercy toward them on the ground of what they have been and have done in the romantic past. He must, as a son of a robust and pure ancestry, desire to serve the highest civil and intellectual moral interests of his kindred and his nation, by sending back to them the fruits of his observation among the free, republican, progressive communities of the West. It was this aspiration, and not an idle curiosity, that brought Mr. Azhderian as an independent traveler, young but not immature, to a close acquaintance with the colleges, political systems, industries, and religion of the United States. The presentation of his purpose has naturally led him into wider fields than he at first contemplated entering.

Such a survey, with its attendant argument and appeal, could not have been accomplished at any epoch since the Christian era so suitable as this, when the struggles and tragedies of suffering millions of his fellow-countrymen are uttering their cry to a singularly regardless and unhelpful Christendom.

THE TURK AND THE LAND OF HAIG.

THE LAND OF HAIG—ARMENIA.

> "It would be difficult to point out a more delightful, soul-inspiring, mysteriously fascinating country on the surface of the globe than Armenia. . . Whithersoever we turn our steps, to the north, south, east, or west, the ground we tread is holy. It is history—stratified."—E. H. B. LANIN, London, England.

TRADITIONS OF ANTIQUITY.

ARMENIA, now for the most part subject to the Turkish Empire, is the fountain-head of antiquity. She is most ancient among the ancient—a land whose marvels excite the wonder of the beholder. Her shrines, rocks, rivers, valleys, and mountains—silent witnesses of prehistoric contentions and changing fortunes—are replete with memorials which date back to the beginning of the life and growth of infant humanity. The murmuring of her soft breezes wafts to the listening ear the sweet strains which once rose from the terrestial paradise to mingle with the melodies of the celestial—a land where man first communed with his God!

In the earliest ages of the world, long before the nations and peoples of recorded history existed and flourished, the human race had its home in Armenia. Here was spoken a common language, here was the origin of civil government and monotheistic religion, and from here, when the race grew and multiplied, the people spread over all Asia and Europe.

The position of central Armenia, between the Caspian and Black seas, facilitated the immediate dispersion of the post-diluvian people. Some writers claim that the Hindu-Kush mountains were the oldest home and the distributing center. We contend that geographical position, Holy Writ, modern history, tradition, and scientific research unite in favoring Armenia as the primitive home from which the eastern and western Aryans originated. Mt. Ararat, where, according to the Scriptures, Noah's ark rested, is in the central province of Armenia, although there are some still who question whether the mountain of the flood is the Ararat of Armenia, and who would locate the resting place of the ark in various other places, some at Mount Meirû of India, some in the Kurdish Mountains of central Asia.

Our traditions as to Noah are exceedingly interesting. The name of the village at the entrance to the glen on the northeast foot of Mount Ararat is *Arghuri*, meaning "he planted the vine," and here Noah's vineyard is still pointed out. In 1840 a catastrophe buried the oldest village and the vineyard; but it is alleged that a vine stock planted by the patriarch's hand (Gen. iv. 2) still bears grapes. Not far from *Arghuri*, is *Manard*, "the mother lies here," referring to the burial place of Noah's wife. At a little distance is the city of *Eravan*, "visible," where the legend is that the saved remnant first beheld the dry land when the waters subsided. Nearby is the town of *Nakchvan*, "first habitation," indicating the primeval dwelling of men.

The simple and credulous Christian of Armenia implicitly believes that these traditional spots are veritable relics of the diluvian period. Mount Ararat is known among us as *Massis*, or "the mother of the world." It was also held by the ancient geographers that this was the center of the world. The Persian traditions in regard to this mountain are quite like those of the Armenian. They call it *Kuhi-Nuh*, "the mountain of Noah." Thus not only have we the evidence of the Bible, but our traditions and the testimony of the oldest geographers are in favor of our belief that Armenia was the center for the dispersion of the human race.

But we may even trace our country to still earlier biblical periods. It was a prevailing view among the ancient Latin and Greek interpreters of the Bible, that after the flood the human race, led by Noah, found a safe home in the very region which had been its cradle. Surely the Divine Wisdom had a lesson to teach erring man in restoring him to the same abode whence he was once banished. And how closely, again, does the topography of Eden, as given in the second chapter of Genesis, coincide with the natural characteristics of this region to-day! Notwithstanding some obvious mixture of error in these traditions, they doubtless have a basis in reality, and bear the marks of essential truth. Streams of tradition flowing from a common source have been transmitted from generation to generation, and upon them some of the greatest events in the history of humanity have been inscribed as upon the solid rock. One person, such as Lamech the son of Methuselah, who lived from the days of Adam to those of Noah, would have been sufficient to communicate the story of antediluvian days to Eber, Isaac, and Levi, and from these patriarchs the story may easily have reached Moses himself. May not the Armenians, then, who sprung from the most remote ancestry, rightfully suppose such a chain among their progenitors as would justify their historical traditions, especially in view of the harmony of these traditions with the Bible?

We find various views as to the location of the Garden of Eden. The latest and wildest theory is of its location at the North Pole, upon the assumption that in the lapse of ages the earth has gradually cooled so that the first suitable place for man to live was in the Arctic zone. Armenia, however, has the earliest and most reasonable of all claims. Our land is a natural center. The Tigris, Euphrates, and other rivers of the Paradise of Eden still flow, and the identity of these streams alone should banish all doubt. The very odors of the forest are of singular fragrance. Here bloom indigenous plants of great variety and hue, which refuse to lend their beauty and fragrance to any foreign clime. Numerous birds, too, of peculiar beauty adorn and enliven the enchanting landscapes. Robert Curzon gives us a list of over one hundred and seventy kinds of birds in an Armenian city, enumerating them by their particular names and families. He says: " I have no power to do them justice. The number of various kinds of birds which breed on the great plain is so prodigious as to seem almost incredible to those who have not seen them, as I often have, covering the earth for miles and miles so completely that the color of the ground could not be seen." Do not all these natural and scenic characteristics, coupled with Bible documents and native traditions, bear evidence of these primitive ages? Surely the Armenians are justified in their claim that the beautiful landscape which was twice selected by the Omnipotent as the cradle of the human race was in Armenia; that here was embowered the original Eden, and here the ark rested after the Deluge.

Armenians are thus ever proud of their land of fragrant memories. But what comfort can we obtain from a home made desolate? Paradise has been transformed into a habitation of fallen humanity, and her most enlightened descendants have long since removed to the remoter parts of the world. Some nations glory in their many achievements and in their monuments of antiquity. Rome, in her universal dominion, in her patriotism and statescraft; Greece, in her precious legacy of art and letters; Egypt, in her awe-inspiring ruins of ancient grandeur; Palestine, in her lofty sentiments of religious truths; and the glory of Armenia is her prehistoric legends and the bloom of her sacred memories. But of what value is all this past greatness in itself? The Holy Land has abandoned her Christ. The dust of time and modern traffic has covered the exquisite monuments of Greek culture. They lie buried in ruins, and slumber mute and silent in the eternal death whence there is no resurrection. All roads no longer lead to Rome. And the past is as dead in Armenia as elsewhere. It is the disposition of the nineteenth century to look forward to the glories of the future rather than backward to a glorious past. The soil enriched by the past must bear fruit in the present. And yet there must ever be an inspiration for the patriotic heart in looking back upon the glory of his fatherland; and as I gaze upon the great green hills, blooming valleys, venerable mountains, luxuriant pastures, rippling waters, the banks of the Tigris and Euphrates, and the slope of Ararat, the scene thrills my heart with a deep pride for my native country. There our Armenian fathers bravely fought at the altar of civil and religious liberty; there many noble sons, valiant soldiers of the Cross, stood firm for centuries against the sword and fire of avenging heathenism. Armenia, the mother of nations, the theater of human achievement and divine providence!

The genius of modern investigation has been developed so far from Armenia that here is left to-day the richest and most profitable field that can reward scholarship in every department of human knowledge. The geologist has yet to trace the changes that turned rivers from their courses and have created lakes where cities once stood. The botanist can here add to the world's knowledge of beautiful and useful plants. Here philology has an ample field for the acutest intellect. The antiquarian can delve amid the ruins of cities that were great when Egypt was young. Ere Babylon was built the men whose names these cities bore were fireside heroes in the most civilized regions of the globe.

Dr. George Smith of the British Museum, after an

extensive exploration in the valley of the Euphrates, gathered tons of tablets covered with inscriptions, which he translated into English and published, carefully arranged and classified, in a large volume. He places in parallel columns the Bible text and the text of the tablets, showing their remarkable agreement, and proving that modern scientific research constantly corroborates the assertions of the Scriptures. I am proud to think that my native land has been, and will ever be, a growing witness to the veracity of the Mosaic record. Should the reader be disposed to doubt, let him read Smith's "Chaldean Accounts of Genesis" or, indeed, any of the modern works that treat of the recent researches about the Tigris and Euphrates—Layard's "Nineveh," or Bishop Newman's "Thrones and Palaces," or the "Records of the Past" published by the authorities of the British Museum.

PHYSICAL CHARACTERISTICS.

Armenia is an inland region of Western Asia, lying directly north of the Mesopotamian plain, between the Black and Caspian seas. Like all lands of prehistoric renown, it is a small country, being a little larger than the State of Pennsylvania. Its geographical boundaries, though changed at different periods, became most extensive under the administration of our kings Aram and Tigranes II., when they reached to the Caucasus on the north, to Asia Minor on the west, to Mesopotamia on the south, and to the Caspian Sea and Media on the east. In the earliest periods our country was divided into Armenia Major and Armenia

Minor. The former, known as Armenia Proper, was divided into fifteen provinces, the central being the district of Ararat.

The Armenian highlands are the most elevated region of western Asia, consisting of a succession of rolling plateaus. The mean altitude is from 5000 to 7000 feet above the sea level, culminating in Mount Ararat, the loftiest peak in western Asia, which forms the center of the system, with an elevation of 17,210 feet above the level of the sea, or 10,210 feet above the Plain of Araxes. The surface of the country is broken by upheavals, and consists of a series of terraces, deep valleys, mountain masses, and bleak plateaus; while here and there the dislocation of rocks and the irregularity of the strata afford convincing evidences of volcanic eruption.

From the Armenian plateau at the foot of Mount Ararat arise the sources of the rivers of western Asia— the Tigris, the Euphrates, the Aras or Araxes, the Cyrus (Kur), the Acampis, and the Halys. The first two, with deep and rapid waters, flow southeast into the Persian Gulf. The Acampis, supposed by some to be the Pison of the Bible, rising from the southwest of Erzrum and fed by various streamlets, sweeps with a strong and smooth current toward the Black Sea. The Araxes (perhaps the Gihon of the Bible) takes its rise about thirty miles south of Erzrum from the side of Bingol, or the "mountain of one thousand lakes," winds through fertile regions, and mingles with the Cyrus; and then both, sweeping northward and again southward through the plain of Moghan, discharge eastward into the Caspian Sea by three mouths, being navigable up to the point of junction. The name of the river is supposed to commemorate Araxes, whose son was drowned in the rapid waters. Xenophon, however, traces its derivation to *Ar-ax*, or "holy water," its water being sacred to the sun. This stream possessed different names at different periods, commemorative of various events. The Halys, or the modern *Kizil-Irmak*, is the most westerly of the rivers. It springs from a verdant region at no great distance from the Euphrates, and flows with rapid volume into the Black Sea.

The volcanic soil of the country is of surpassing fertility, and yields abundant crops of wheat, barley, apricots, maize, tobacco, rice, and other minor products. Here are raised also the mulberry, cotton, grapes, and a dye called yellow-berry. Beautiful vineyards, smiling gardens, orchards, and groves abound in many parts of the country, especially in the valleys, where luxuriant vegetation gladdens the heart of the lover of nature. Melons, figs, granates, and trees of oak, pine, ash, walnut, apple, peach, and chestnut abound. Its natural wealth and resources are greater than those of any other province of Asia Minor. There are gold mines on the line of communication between Erzrum and Trebizond. The river Acampis, which "compasseth the whole land of Havilah where there is gold," runs through that section of the country now. The mountains abound in silver, copper, iron, lead, antimony, sulphur, and sulphates, especially in the west and among the hills of the Euphrates. The export minerals comprise salt from Lake Van, sulphur, iron, and alum. There are stones of syenite, jasper, marble, granite, and porphyry. Sandstone and limestone are the prevailing geological formations of the country, and out of these have been quarried the materials for our royal palaces and ecclesiastical edifices.

The climate is healthful, and varies according to altitude. The long winter, extending from October to May, is severe, while the summers are short and pleasant. The air is pure and delicious and the sky clear and bright.

Like all mountain regions, Armenia abounds in lakes. Among them Van, Sevan, and Ormi, or Ormuiah, are the most noteworthy. All these are saline but Sevan, which is called the "sweet lake," and reposes near the city of Erevan. Ormi lies in the southern part of the country, within the territory of the Shah. Lake Van, on the east of the city bearing its name, is by far the largest and most beautiful in all western Asia. Its triangular surface of 14,000 square miles, 5000 feet above the sea level, is in the very center of ancient Armenia in a rich and verdant valley surrounded by forest-clad mountains. Its romantic beauty, the sluggish surge of its deep blue waters, its associations so famed in history and fiction, have been the inspiration of many a poet. The petrified lakes of Armenia are particularly interesting, being the result of evaporation. During the warmest season of the year the water becomes crystallized like ice with deposits of salt about an inch thick, which the neighboring people gather in boats and carry away. Strangely enough, the crust does not appear in cold summers.

Mineral springs, both cold and hot, abound. In my travels through the country I have seen many of them gushing from the ground with great force from between the strata of limestone. These hot springs are another evidence of the subterranean activity of the region. From all over the country people who suffer from any ailment repair to these waters, whose medicinal properties are of great reputation. Sometimes the waters are conducted to city bathing houses or basins by means of pipes.

ARARAT.

As has been mentioned, Mount Ararat is the nucleus of the river and mountain systems, standing high and hoar midway between the Black and the Caspian seas. It is the center of the world. It is a mountain rich with events of undying significance to mankind. Around its base legends and traditions, true and fabulous, hold perpetual sway. To-day it is a mighty boundary stone of three great empires—the Turkish, Russian, and Persian. It has two summits, seven miles apart, the greater at the northwest extremity and the lesser toward the southeast. The snow-clad summit of the greater Ararat is wrapped in clouds during most of the day. These float away at nightfall and leave the snowy crown clear and distinct against the starry sky. A more rugged and awe-inspiring view is obtained from the northeast than from any other point.

No one can do Ararat justice; every turn gives a new picture. It beauty is unrivaled by any other mountain on earth. It is truly "the sublimest object in nature." Its snow-crowned peak, rising from the plain of Araxes, rears itself in solemn majesty above the sea of vapor into the regions of eternal winter, perpetually covered with ice and snow, and ruling over the clouds and the storms. It is a picture of mingled sublimity and beauty, calm, cold, majestic.

One is filled with awe as he watches the mellow radiance of the moon, the changing hues and shadows

MOUNT ARARAT.

of the venerable mountain, or hears the thundering sound of falling ice and rocks from its stupendous heights. The mass of snow on its summit, 14,000 feet above the sea, never dissolves, and is one of the phenomenal features of this mountain, exceeding in quantity that of either the Alps or the Caucasus, as the former average 9000 feet, and the latter from

10,000 to 12,000 feet, in height. The people consider the ascent of Ararat a miracle. They regard the mountain with superstitious awe, and believe that it still contains the relics of the ark, unchanged by time or decay, and that in order to insure their preservation a divine decree has made it inaccessible to mortal approach. The Tartars and the Turks of the neighborhood imagine its summit to be the abode of the " devil" and of wild ghosts, and they fear to approach too near its top. Morier himself declares, "No one appears to have reached the summit of Ararat since the Flood." However, Dr. Friedrich Parrot of the University of Dorpat, after several unsuccessful attempts, finally gained the summit in September, 1829. He is considered the first mortal since the Deluge who has ever ventured amid the ice and snow of the isolated peak.

The name "Ararat" is of the remotest antiquity. It has been known for 3000 years. We find in the most ancient annals of the Mosaic record of creation the expression, "Upon the mountains of Ararat." Moses of Clorene, the father of our history, traces the origin of the word *Ararat* or *Arardhi* to our Armenian patriarch, Ara or Arai, the beautiful, who lived eighteen centuries before Christ. At his fall, in a bloody conflict, the Armenian plain was called after him *Arai-Arat*, "the fall of Arai." Some others advance the theory that the word is composed of *Ar* and *Arah* —*Ar* (Sanskrit), the root of Aryan or "nobles," and *Arah* (classical Armenian), "plains" or "fields," hence meaning "the plains of the Aryans" or "nobles."

The antiquity of the name Ararat antedates by a

few centuries even the time of Moses. "An ancient bilingual tablet makes Urdhu the equivalent of Tilla, of which the Accadian pronunciation is given as Tillā, the latter, as Sir H. Rawlinson long ago pointed out, being probably a Semitic loan word, and meaning the 'highlands.' Tilla, the equivalent of Urdhu, usually signifies the land of Accad or northwestern Babylonia, but since it is not glossed in this passage and stands, moreover, between Akharrue, or Palestine, and Kutu Kurdistan, it would seem that it is employed to mean Armenia. Urardhu, therefore, contracted into Urdhu, would have been the designation of the highlands of Armenia among the Babylonians as early as the sixteenth and seventeenth centuries B. C."*

The term Ararat is used in ancient annals of sacred and secular history for the entire country of Armenia, and not for the mountain itself. Anciently even the inhabitants were known as the people of Ararat. It was not till late years that the name came to be limited to the mountain itself. This misunderstanding has led some to erroneous conclusions and superstitions. Nothing could be more absurd to a native of Armenia than the idea that the ark rested on the very top of Mount Ararat. A well-known American traveler, for instance, after describing the first impression of the mountain, goes on to say : "I could not help thinking what a hard time the mighty line of living things had when marching by twos, male and female, from those cold, bleak heights down into the plains below, after the great flood had subsided, and what a time good old Noah must have had to keep some of his warm-

---

* "Cuneiform Inscriptions of Van," in "Journal R. A. S.," vol. xiv. p. 392.

blooded pets from freezing on that lofty, sixteen-thousand-feet-high pinnacle." Many similar criticisms have been made concerning the ark on Mount Ararat, as though that historic craft had actually rested on its very peak. Such absurd ideas indicate a lack not only of knowledge, but of a proper and common-sense understanding of a simple biblical narrative. The geographical unit is the mountain range, and with the mountain ranges the study of geography should begin. From them a scientific nomenclature can most easily be constructed. How precise and clear is the statement of the Book of Genesis! "The ark rested upon the *mountains of Ararat.*"—not upon Mount Ararat. There are scriptural references in 2 Kings xix. 37; Isaiah xxxvii. 38. In these parallel passages allusion is made to Adrammelech and Sharezer, who, having assassinated their father Sennacherib, "escaped into the land of Ararat." The prophet Jeremiah (in Jeremiah ii. 27), summoning the nations for the overthrow of Babylon, calls "together against her the kingdoms of Ararat, Minni, and Ashchenaz." Thus sacred and secular writers concur in speaking of not only a mountain, but of *a range, a land, a kingdom, an army,* and *a people* of "Ararat." Does the critic suppose that the horses and mules of Ararat were reared on the icebergs of an isolated peak? They were seen in the markets of Syria. Had they wings, that they could fly where a donkey could not climb? An army of Araratians helped Cyrus in the overthrow of Babylon. Did they come on a toboggan slide from the regions of everlasting snow?

Moses of Chorene's appellation, "Arred" or

"Ayrarad," coincides with the Armaniyn or Armenia of the Persian text, which is frequently employed in ancient historical documents, denoting that the name Ararat was identical with the whole country of Armenia. St. Jerome himself always identified Ararat with the plain of Araxes, where the mountain reposes.

Again, the window of the ark is described in Genesis as being above; so that when " on the first day of the tenth month the top of the mountains came forth," Noah would most naturally have been looking upward to see what was above the ark. Therefore, the extreme cone, the highest pinnacle of Ararat, was not the resting place of the diluvian ark, but in all probability a much lower part of the Ararat range.

ANCIENT CITIES.

In Armenia are many once famous cities, unknown to Americans because the hand of time has shorn them of their former splendor and many of them are buried beneath the accumulations of centuries. The largest of these were situated on the fair banks of the Tigris, comparatively few on the Euphrates. Some cities had their streets paved with fragments of sculpture when Moses was with Pharaoh on the throne of Egypt. Some of the walls, thirty or forty feet high, still remain, with solid foundations and towers rising at regular intervals with large arched gateways.

Ani, the glittering city of gold and silver, was the imperial pride of Armenian sovereigns, whose pearly palaces shone with beauty in the dazzling glare of the sunlight. Its streets were clean and richly adorned

RUINS OF ANCIENT ARMENIAN MONASTERIES AND PALACES.

with decorations of nature and art. This ideal city is to-day a heap of colossal ruins.

The venerable city of Van, anciently the city of Semiramis, embowered on the eastern bank of the lake of that name, commanded a view of the wondrous citadel towering on a rugged rock with a natural amphitheater surrounding it and buried amid the loveliest vegetation and vineyards. Its cuneiform inscriptions are famous in history, as they have revealed the secrets of the centuries to modern research. Professor A. H. Sayce of Oxford, England, in his Journal gives the translations of these venerable inscriptions along with other Armenian antiquities.

Artaxata was once the capital of Armenia, where King Tiridates received his crown from Rome. After seeking for years to stifle the incipient Church, he too bowed before the cross of Christ and, like Saul of Tarsus, became the ardent advocate of what he had once endeavored to overthrow.

The holy city of Vagharshabad was built by King Erovant, but all its pomp and glory have faded away except the monastery of Etchmiadzin. This most ancient Episcopal seat of the Armenians still remains as a mighty bulwark, against which the heathen cannon of all ages have thundered in vain. This mother church of Ararat contains a number of holy relics, among them the head of the spear by which the side of the Saviour was wounded, and the hand of St. Gregory, the founder of the monastery, who laid the first stone in the year 302—the hand that baptized King Tiridates, from whom he suffered unimaginable persecutions. The traditions in this Episcopal seat are also rich in apostolic legends. Of these none is more singular that the reputed correspondence of Christ with our King Abgar of Edessa. The story is that the messengers of this sovereign, having some business transaction with the Roman nobility in Palestine, heard of the miracles of Jesus of Nazareth and on their return related them to their sovereign, who was convinced that either Jesus was "that Christ" or else that God had come to dwell on earth. As the king was suffering from a serious disease, he sent a letter to Christ with a company of messengers imploring Him to repair to his court and graciously cure him. An artist was also sent, so that if the Lord should fail to come, he might at least have His portrait. The painter, being at work one day endeavoring to fulfill the royal commission, was observed by the Saviour, who passed a handkerchief over His countenance and handed it to the artist with a perfect likeness of Himself upon it. A reply to the King's letter was written by St. Thomas, commending his faith in an unseen Christ, and informing him that the Divine Master's mission was more urgent elsewhere than in Armenia, but that after His ascension disciples would be sent to enlighten the king's people and relieve him of his sufferings. It has been stated that a papyrus has been discovered in an Egyptian tomb containing the reputed letter of our king.

Erzrum, on the main line of communication between Persia and the Euxine, still survives as a populous military post and commercial *entrepôt*. It reposes in a lovely district about one hundred miles southeast of Trebizond. The extent of its fortifications was so great in Erzrum that twenty-two thousand men were required to defend it. In 415 A. D. the city was fortified by Antolius and became a stronghold of the Roman Empire, its ancient name, Karin, being changed to Theodosiopolis, in honor of the emperor. During the Middle Ages, the city was an object of jealousy and contentions between the Moslems and the Greeks. By those who dwell in the vicinity the city is thought to be the very spot where the garden of Eden was located. They claim that for many a century the flowers of Paradise bloomed around the source of the Euphrates. Tradition says that Nature herself was so horrified at the sacrilegious conduct of a Persian king that she refused to produce those rare beauties any longer, and even changed the source of the river itself. Local accounts of Adam's fall show how a frail, sympathetic man will follow a woman into any kind of a trap. He did not eat of the fruit, they say, until he saw the fatal effect on lovely Eve. Then, concluding that the Creator would have compassion if He saw them both in the same sad plight and restore them to their former estate, he decided to follow her example; reasoning thus, he indulged. We know the result! Restoration did not occur in accordance with his logical reasoning. There was something wrong with the premises. Logic was not taught, except objectively, in his day. Who can blame Adam? "The Lord cursed the serpent, and Eve and I were doomed between the two" was the sad refrain.

There are also Armavir, Ardashed, Kemak, and other cities, whose past associations are inspiring to an

REMAINS OF ARMENIAN ANTIQUITY.

Armenian, although their present state is little more than the shadow of their former grandeur.

The Babylonians and Assyrians have become, like their cities, only a name ; but though conquered and dispersed, with their once proud cities destroyed, the Armenians still remain, and we shall speak of their past and present in succeeding pages.

THE CHILDREN OF HAIG—THE ARMENIANS.

"The Armenians are the representatives of one of the oldest civilized Christian races, and, beyond all doubt, one of the most pacific, one of the most industrious, and one of the most intelligent races in the world."—GLADSTONE.

"Their national character is a powerful one, and will exercise a marked influence in determining the future of the East."—PROFESSOR HENRY F. TOZER, Exeter College, Oxford, England.

THE beginning of our national history, like that of all races of antiquity, is mingled with much of myth and legend. Our father, according to tradition, is Togarmah, the son of Gomer, who was the son of Japheth of the Scriptures (Genesis x. 3). Some of our historians allude to our country as Askhanzian, certainly derived from Askenaz, the brother of Togarmah and the son of Gomer.

Our traditional history, according to the accounts of Chorene, our national historian, dates back twenty-three centuries before Christ, when Haig, the son of Togarmah, began his political career as our first ruler, from whom the appellations Haigian, our national name, and Hayasdan, our country's name, are derived. He was one of the many who were busily engaged on the Plains of Shinar in the construction of the Tower of Babel; but the insatiable ambition of Belus, who sought supremacy, constrained Haig to flee from Babylon to the land of Ararat, where he proposed to plant his own dominion in the vicinity of Lake Van, an enchanting land of glen and valley, rivers and lakes. Belus, the sovereign of Assyria, sending messengers to Haig, commanded him to surrender his power and return to his former subjection. This haughty demand, however, was promptly refused, and war was the consequence.

Belus, at the head of a mighty army, marched to the land of Ararat, and Haig met him with his patriarchal force of numerous sons, grandsons, and servants. It was a crisis which decided the future of his posterity. There the first Armenian hero displayed his valor, and our legendary songs still sing his triumphant praise. He slew the Hamitic giant with his dart, and buried him on the spot where he fell, scattering his army in great confusion. Haig lived the long life of four hundred years with a flourishing dominion, and established a pure monotheistic worship and a patriarchal government. The first dynasty bearing his name had a long genealogy of fifty-nine kings, with the capital at Armavir, to the north of Araxes. Here grew sacred forests, the rustle of whose leaves was held to be the voice of God whispering to men of welfare and peace. It must be remembered that these so-called "kings" were nothing but hereditary rulers who occupied the position of patriarchs.

Haig's son Armenag was the next sovereign. Some suppose that Armenia derived her name from him. His reign is followed by a dim period in the annals of our country, which mention a succession of Armenian princes until Aram, the seventh in the dynasty of Haig, who came to his father's throne about two thou-

TRADITIONAL PORTRAIT OF HAIG.

sand years before Christ. Aram was a king of unusual military and executive attainments. Contemporary with the biblical patriarchs, he so diffused his reputation in the neighboring provinces and countries, through his conquests and magnetic power, that foreign nations from his day to this have associated his name with our country and people in the appellation of Armenia and Armenian.

In ancient accounts Tiglath-Pileser speaks of "the mountains of Aruma," while the inscriptions of Shalmaneser mention "The royal city of Arrame of the land of Unardhians."

This "Aruma" of Tiglath-Pileser and "Arrame" of Shalmaneser coincide with the name "Aram" of the Armenian historians. Different spellings of the same name account for its varied transformations into foreign languages, while they both refer to the "Arram" of the natives, the first referring to the country and the latter to the sovereign. The derivation Togarmah is believed by some scholars to be from *Toka*, the Sanskrit for "race," and *Armah* of the classical Armenian. Thus Aram, Arama, Arrama, and Armah, though differently spelled by different people, are all derived from Aram, the name of the ruler and his province. Anciently the country was known as Aramenia, but it has been contracted into Armenia.

Aram greatly extended the boundaries of his kingdom by conquering large portions of Media, Assyria, and the eastern part of Asia Minor. Nor did he neglect the internal improvements of his growing realm. Among the cities he built Mazaca, or the modern Cæsarea in Cappadocia, is a living monument to his active energy.

Ara, "the Beautiful," who sat upon his father's throne, embellishes the pages of Armenian history with romance not unlike that of Cleopatra. He must have possessed excellence of character along with his great physical beauty, for the blending of these two alone forms the requisite of true beauty. And the embodiment of these two qualities seems to have been the ideal of the fair Assyrian queen Semiramis, who in her infatuated frenzy saw in Ara the fairest of mortals. However, Ara refused to be bound in marriage with an idolatrous ruler, who worshiped not the true God of his fathers. She resolved to win him, if not by will, at least by force of arms. She advanced upon the forces of the youthful Armenian patriarch, but the clash of her conquering arms sounded his death knell, for her long coveted prize was first among the slain. As the stricken king was laid low at the queen's feet, she burst into a frenzy of grief. In vain were all endeavors of magic art to bring him back to life. The spot where he was buried in a coffin of gold is still pointed out as *Ara Seni, i. e.,* " Ara is sacrificed."

After her disappointing adventure in the land of Ara, the semi-mythical queen chose the vernal banks of Lake Van for her summer residence. On such an immense scale were the proportions of the building that its construction required six hundred architects and one thousand two hundred workmen. She named the city after herself "Shamiramaguerd." In later years, however, King Van of the Haigazian dynasty, having rebuilt the city, called it Van, which name it bears to the present day.

With the death of Ara, our land was unable to oppose an effectual barrier to Assyrian progress and sadly dwindled into oblivion for a period of nearly three centuries, as a tributary province to this alien power. The rule of the Haigazian dynasty, though not altogether destroyed, was reduced to utter insignificance beneath the mighty hand of Assyria. The long sway of Semitic rule was not without its detrimental results to our national character. It supplanted the pure monotheism of our fathers, and substituted in its stead the worship of Bel. With this religious change, the social aspects, race, and language, as a natural result, bore the indelible impress of Assyrianism.

Our meager history of this period is engraved in cuneiform characters on monuments distributed throughout the region. The inscriptions of both Armenian and Assyrian kings are vainglorious and self-praising, a characteristic of the ancients. Neither were the deities forgotten in these inscriptions. Curses of the air- and sun-gods are commonly called down on him who should dare to mar these monumental records. However, some of the stones thus inscribed are now found in the walls of Christian churches with the continuity of their records broken. In some other cases they are still legible. Though religion, manners, and customs in the region of Ararat during this era were Assyrian, and though their inscriptions were cuneiform, still the Armenians had a language of their own in which they preserved their identity.

After three hundred years of servitude Armenia once again rose Phœnix-like from its ashes, under

Barvir, who successfully raised the standard of rebellion against Sardanapalus. From this period our people enjoyed a line of independent rulers.

Dikran the Mighty, or Tigranes I., was one of the most notable sovereigns of this dynasty. He was a man of great administrative capacity. He united firmness and courage with sound judgment in all his deliberations and activities. His magnetic influence was not confined to his own country, but was felt far and wide throughout the East. As a friend and colleague of Cyrus, he aided him in the overthrow of Babylon (528 B. C.), in fulfillment of prophecy (Jeremiah ii. 27). He instituted mighty reforms in public improvements, education, and morals. His country, whose boundaries were greatly extended under his military power and statecraft, enjoyed unparalleled prosperity in commerce. An extension of trade navigation on lakes and rivers was also introduced. His deeds of prowess and his vigor truly made his land a star among nations. Vahakn, who succeeded his father Dikran, was so renowned for his physical strength and matchless daring that, after his death, his people, who were fast lapsing into the heathenism of contemporary nations, worshiped his monument. Vahe, the last king of the Haigazian dynasty, in his efforts to aid Darius against the invasions of Alexander the Great, fell with the Persian king before the long spears, splendid discipline, and unquestioned bravery of the Macedonian phalanxes in 328 B. C. Having existed 1922 years, thus ended the first and the longest of the Armenian dynasties.

ARSACID DYNASTY. 149 B. C.–428 A. D.

This dynasty, beginning about a century and a half before Christ, fills by far the most eventful and brilliant centuries in the annals of Armenian history. Having emerged from the hovering mists and clouds of the Haigazian legends, here we are brought into closer proximity to the star of authentic history. Classical names of deathless renown shine out with brilliant radiance. It is during this dynasty that we look upon the Son of Man, the Saviour of the race, to whom our country and nation open their hearts and homes. It is a fact worthy of note that through a multitude of fortunes of war, conflicting armies, incursions, and national calamities far beyond those of former years, our fathers through faith in Christ have remained a national unit. It should not be supposed that during the interval between the Haigazian and Arsacid dynasties our people were in utter servitude, as they are to-day under Turkish despotism. Our country was simply in a state of ignominious vassalage under governors of the Macedonian Empire; for we find in 317 B. C., after the death of Alexander, Armenia, under the leadership of Ardvates, struck a blow for freedom, and thus regained her independence.

Upon his death, after thirty-three years of great prosperity, Ardvates left no competent successor to resist foreign aggressions. Thus Armenia submitted to the Seleucus of Syria, who reduced the country to a tributary state. For a hundred years in vain the Armenians revolted and struggled under the firm grasp of Syrian satraps. About 210 B. C. Antiochus the

LEGENDARY HEROES OF ARMENIA.

Great divided the country into Eastern and Western Armenia, or Armenia Major and Lesser Armenia—the former east of the river Euphrates and the latter west of it. Having thus divided the country he appointed a separate governor over each. But no sooner had Antiochus sustained a crushing defeat by the Romans than Artaxias proclaimed Armenia Major independent, and offered it as an asylum to Hannibal, the greatest strategist of all times, who had sworn to his father, when a boy of twelve years, "eternal enmity to Rome," and for forty years had kept the field against the imperial eagles. It must have required courage of the highest order in Artaxias to harbor the greatest enemy of Rome at his court. Lesser Armenia soon followed the example of the Greater and successfully revolted under Zadriades, whose descendants kept the throne for nearly a hundred years, until the time of Tigranes II., when it became a part of Armenia Major.

Scarcely had Armenia Major been free half a century when the Parthian king, Mithridates I., having vanquished Syria, extended his mighty hand upon the Armenian affairs, and placed his brother, Valarsaces, on the throne. Under his rule the country flourished, laws were established, personal merit among his subjects was rewarded, and great cities were founded. His wise policy laid a good foundation for the great Arsacid family. In 94 B. C. Tigranes II. took the reins of the government with such firmness and ability that his eminence caused wonder and dread to all neighboring nations. Possessed with martial courage, he entered upon a career of mighty conquest. After uniting Lesser Armenia with Armenia Major, he made himself master of Syria; he brought to his subjection many provinces of the Parthian Empire; he conquered Media and annexed Mesopotamia. It was during his early sway that our country reached its meridian of power and popularity. It would, no doubt, have been destined to still brighter prospects had it not been for the unwise promptings of his father-in-law, Mithridates of Pontus, who led him into a disastrous conflict with the conquering legions of Pompey. Great Tigranes, under whose victorious tramp Eastern thrones had once shaken to their foundations, had to bow in humble submission and surrender to Rome, with pledges of allegiance and tribute-paying. In turn, a compromise was effected by the terms of which the provinces of Sophene and Gordyene were made into a separate kingdom for his son, while he himself was permitted to retain the remainder of his lost kingdom as a loyal Roman governor, in which capacity, with his martial ardor tamed by misery, he acted until the time of his death, 55 B. C., when another son, Artavasdes, taking the lead of the government, resolved to bring back to Armenia the brighter days of his father's early career. In his idea to successfully accomplish the cherished end, he denied obligation and governmental allegiance to Rome. Meanwhile, Rome and Parthia, in their contentions for Oriental empire, were alternately irresistible in the East. For Artavasdes neutrality with these powers was impossible; hence his perfidy and independent policy of single-handed government was both imprudent and detrimental. The Armenians looked to Parthia as their ally, while the events of history prove that it would have been wiser to follow the policy of Great Tigranes II. and remain loyal to Rome. In the subsequent conquest, Mark Antony, having seized Artavasdes, occupied the country, while the unfortunate Armenian prince was carried to Alexandria and there beheaded by Cleopatra in the year 30 B. C.

In the same year of this event Artaxes II., the son of Mark Antony's victim, aided by Parthians, in a successful rebellion massacred all the Romans found in Armenia. This event was followed by a long period of anarchy, which is one of the darkest pages in our history. Poor Armenia was between two millstones, Rome on the west and Parthia on the east. The latter was desperate in the throes of declining power, with Persia crowding hard for supremacy in the region of Ararat. These rival powers, in their bloody duel for the mastery of our country, wrought their worst upon our people. Both set their own rulers in our land, separately and alternately as the wave of their strength permitted them. Nor was our land free from broils within its own borders. Over one hundred and seventy of our nobles broke through the restraints of monarchy, set up claims to principalities, and many of them erected independent governments, each reigning supreme in his own district as a petty king. While liberty thus grappled with tyranny for existence, in their helplessness our people did not know where to turn. They had no friendly harbor in which to refit; they rode out of one storm only to enter another more violent. In the midst of such foreign contentions and feudal anarchy, a strong and daring usurper, Erovant by name, with legal claims to the throne on the female line of succession, became a sort of king, 58 A. D., and kept in power until his overthrow by Ardashes, closer to the direct Arsacid line. In spite of Roman and Parthian interference with his right to the throne, he earnestly endeavored to better the condition of his people.

About two centuries of comparative peace gleamed over our unhappy land. Before the next tragic adversities had clouded Armenia's ever-changing skies, the great and serene Prophet of Nazareth had been born, to build upon earth the eternal foundations of a new kingdom that was destined to tower above the ages, the only example in human history which has given itself all-conqueringly to the principle of divine love, teaching men universal fraternity under a spiritual kingdom of a common Father. What a sense of mingled pride and thankfulness fills the heart of an Armenian at the happy thought that his fathers were the first among all nations to welcome Christ's kingdom, and that their posterity would be the last to furnish martyrs for her sake!

As to the authority of our king Abgar's reputed correspondence with Christ, and his subsequent conversion to Christ's religion, we may not wholly subscribe ; for at this point history and fable, poetry and legend, hold eternal and indisputable carnival. Yet, as we advance from the possible twilight of tradition and fable to the broad daylight of history, we find our king Tiridates and his people receiving Christian baptism in 276 A. D., thirty-seven years before Constantine ventured to issue even the Edict of Toleration.

Ever since that time our religious life has been linked with the Church of the Crucified, and our martyr-roll has grown with every century; for with the introduction of Christianity among our people, there was added to political ambition of contending pagan powers a fierce religious hatred, whose flames of persecution have not yet been extinguished.

Let us return to our chronicle. Early in the second century A. D. under Trajan, and later under his successor Hadrian, our land was in a state of relative tranquillity, yet in the course of another century Armenia became once more the theater of almost uninterrupted combat between Persia and Rome. The origin of the struggle was Arsacid's deposition from the Persian throne by the Sassanid Artaxerxes (Ardeshir). Our king Chosroes the Great, in due sense of justice took up arms in defense of Persia's cause, in retaining the Arsacids in power. In the subsequent struggle he maintained the contest with such an indomitable courage and success that the Sassanid usurper, utterly incapable of exertion in open battle, resorted to treacherous methods in inducing Anag, one of his emissaries, to secretly assassinate his valiant adversary. Anag, in the guise of a fugitive from the neighboring court, entered Armenia, was welcomed by our king to the royal city of Vagharshabad, where he stabbed Chosroes to the heart. His crime was punished by Heaven, for while on his flight from threatened vengeance, he was drowned in the river Aras, and his entire family was at once butchered by the soldiery. Immediately upon this event Artaxerxes entered Armenia and massacred all the members of Chosroes' family save an infant, Tiridates, who was secretly conveyed to the Roman court, where the child-prince was educated under

KINGS OF ANCIENT ARMENIA AND THE CONVERSION AND BAPTISM OF KING TIRIDATES.

the faithful guardianship of the emperors. He certainly derived from supposed misfortunes, as Gibbon has said, "such advantages as he could never have obtained on the throne of Armenia—the early knowledge of adversity, of mankind, and of the Roman discipline."

Valerian, in his struggle against Sapor, championing the cause of Armenia, sustained much loss to himself and accomplished nothing for his ally.

Finally the emperor Diocletian, with better success, restored the throne to Tiridates, who was at full manhood of nearly fifty years of age. In due recognition the new king made an alliance of loyalty to Rome, taking upon himself the obligation of Tigranes the Great, which was broken by Tigranes' son to the sad undoing of Armenia for three hundred years. Upon his accession, he enjoyed the good will and the inestimable support of both nobles and populace. Surrounded with such favorable auspices, his military genius had full scope for action. He vanquished Assyria and drove away all foes from the borders of his land. As romantic as fiction is the reign of this able ruler. In the first acts of his reign he persecuted the Christians with fiery intolerance, verily believing, like Paul, that he was right in so doing. Gregory, the saint of Armenia, reared in the Christian faith from childhood, preached the gospel in his native land; but the king imprisoned him for fifteen years in a pit. The light of truth could not be imprisoned, and, beginning with the king himself and the nobles, it soon won the hearts of nearly all the people. The eventful reign of Tiridates lasted nearly half a century. His brave stand against adversaries, his heroic courage in battle, power of conviction, firmness of character, and keen sense of justice—all unite in making him one of the greatest and most beloved of our rulers.

The true greatness of the father was not inherited by the son, Chosroes II., under whose incompetent, weak, and unprincipled administration calamities and disasters cursed our unhappy land and people. Provinces which the valor of his father had annexed to Armenia he failed to firmly retain. Nor is this all; he himself, debauched and utterly void of religious sense, readily yielded to the polytheistic agitation of Persia in the persecution of his Christian subjects; and thus breaking the double ties of policy and religion by which Armenia was bound to Rome, he went on the Persian side, and with a degrading humiliation he acceded to almost every ignominious demand of Sapor. Meanwhile Rome and Persia with redoubled vigor renewed their rival contentions, to the overthrow of the Armenian king and kingdom. While with melancholy interest we gaze upon the fair valleys and plains of Haig thus bathed in blood, with Armenia's sun fast sinking in thickest darkness, let it be remembered that the most efficient cause of such a threatening result was not altogether to be found in foreign despotisms, but in internal strifes and insubordination. Pagan Armenians, with a firm stand against incipient Christianity, united their arms with the Persian forces in ravaging their own country and fighting their own nation. Traitors were common, even among the princes. On the other hand, some Armenian nobles, without religious affinity either to Christ or Zoroaster, were clamoring for their own feudal independence. Such shameful lack of unity on the part of the natives, I dare affirm, was the chief cause of the disintegration and partition of their own fatherland.

Upon the death of Sapor in 379 there was an entire change in the Persian policy toward Rome, and at the accession of Bahram IV. in 390 A. D., by a treaty Theodosius the Great ceded the eastern part, hence called Pers-Armenia, to Persia; while the western part was annexed to the Roman empire. Upon this final disruption of Armenia, to conciliate the people Arsaces IV., then the reigning king, was made a governor in the name of the Roman emperor; while the Persian monarch appointed Chosroes, a descendant of another branch of the Arsacids, governor of the eastern part. At length, in 428 A. D., upon Bahram V.'s substitution of Persian *Marzbans, i. e.*, governor, with Ardashes IV., the Arsacid sway of 580 years was brought to an end forever. Though the Persians were untiring in their efforts to subvert Christianity, their supremacy over Armenia was marked by sanguinary but unsuccessful attempts to overthrow its firmly established and all-conquering power.

In the year 450 A. D. was the most notable of Armenia's contests for religious freedom against the fire-worshipers of Persia. It was led by Prince Vartan Mamigonian, the mighty defender of the faith. This battle was preceded by the massacre of our bishops and priests, whose very blood inspired the Armenians to almost superhuman deeds of valor on the battlefield. So great was the slaughter of the Persians that a compromise, granting our fathers religious liberty, was effected. The despotic monarchs of Persia kept a figurehead over our doomed country till the year 632, when Mohammedanism, which had begun to be a power in western Asia, was destined to send its first caliphs upon Armenia with fire and sword. For two hundred years emperors of Constantinople and Arab caliphs engaged in a long and fierce struggle for the mastery of our land, and with every rotation of fortune's wheel, as the Cross and the Crescent exchanged the coveted victory, our ill-starred land was bathed in blood. At length, Moslem arms having proved victorious, the caliphate gained control of the entire province and governed it by prefects.

Before entering upon the few events of the next dynasty—so little in autonomy and so brief in duration —let me further make a cursory mention of the existing state of our people in the long interregnum.

In Pers-Armenia, with the advent of Islam's conquests in the East, the Persians were brought to their lowest ebb; notably since the decisive battle of Nehavend in 640-42, having sustained a crushing blow at the hands of Caliph Omar, they could no longer sustain the same extreme antipathy and dread with which our people had long regarded them. Yet such an exchange of oppressors, from Zoroaster to Mohammed, should not be considered in the least an improvement; they were both in origin and environment the natural product of the darkest ages of Asiatic barbarism, malicious, cruel, and savage. For our ancestors such a change of persecutors was of no more significance than that of an ill-fated soul's transfer from the paws of Satan into the clutches of the devil. Internally, I deplore beyond words to say that our people were not yet at liberty from the chronic state of rivalry and dissensions. On one side the turbulent princes with their feudal anarchy, on the other the great mass of the populace in their constant strife and disunion, made confusion worse confounded.

Here I take occasion to say that all through our history our hereditary and fundamental weakness has been, in spite of race tenacity evidenced in our loyalty to our faith, language, and home, a lack of coherence and a mutual jealousy, which, with much regret I say, have proved far more humiliating to Armenians than any external disaster.

Turning to the Byzantine side, we find the fortunes of our people by far in a more encouraging state. Bound with ties of one common religious sentiment, though not always by common doctrinal belief and ceremonies, our fathers united their martial ardor with the Greeks against the mutual enemy of their faith. That the Byzantines were anxious for such a union had been demonstrated almost at the start of the Saracen power in western Asia. When, in 638, the first Mohammedan invasion had threatened the Daron province, our people, in their weakened condition, of course could ill afford to make a stand against these fierce warriors of the desert, and so they were about to make a compromise with the Saracens, by the terms of which they were to enjoy the Christian religion unmolested. The Greek coreligionists, however, greatly agitated, threatened arms against our people, as the penalty for affiliation with Islam on any terms. War was averted only by most solemn pledges of fidelity to and co-operation with the Greeks. In the

Byzantine Empire our ancestors were not only an indispensable factor in civil and military service, but they were truly for over two hundred years the foundation of the empire. During this long period the throne of Byzantine was not Hellenic but Armenian. It was Armenians who wielded the scepter and Armenians who led the army; the princes, statesmen, generals, the very backbone of the Byzantine Empire, were Armenians.

My assertions are corroborated by George Finlay, the famous author of " Greece under Foreign Dominations," who says:

> At the accession of Leo III. (717), the Hellenic race occupied a very subordinate position in the empire. The predominant influence in the political administration was in the hands of Asiatics, and particularly of Armenians, who filled the highest military commands. Of the numerous rebels who assumed the title of emperor, the greater part were Armenians. Artabasdos, who rebelled against his brother, Constantine V., was an Armenian. Alexios Mousel, strangled by order of Constantine VI., in the year 790; Bardan, called the Turk, who rebelled against Nicephorus I.; Arsaber (Arshavir), the father-in-law of Leo V., convicted of treason in 808; and Thomas, who revolted against Michael II., were all Asiatics and most of them Armenians. Many of the Armenians in the Byzantine Empire belong to the oldest and most illustrious families in the Christian world; and their connection with the remains of Roman society at Constantinople, in which the pride of birth was cherished, was a proof that Asiatic influence had eclipsed Roman and Greek in the government of the empire.

It is needless to point out herewith that even some of the houses of the Byzantine Empire were founded and ruled over in almost unbroken line by our ancestors.

We must now turn to the fortunes of the third Armenian dynasty.

PAGRADID DYNASTY.   743-1079.

In 743 A. D., a hundred years after the famous battle of Nehavend, in the midst of ephemeral dynasties, raging wars, and dissensions in Armenia, we find a prince of an old and powerful family of Pagrad, by the name of Ashod, who, having gathered sufficient strength, had exercised controlling influence over central and northern Armenia. As to the origin and extent of his power we cannot speak with any degree of accuracy. We know, however, from the evidence of history, that he founded the basis of a sufficiently strong dynasty, the independence of which was properly recognized in 885 by the caliphs under the brave championship of Ashod I.

In the regular line of succession: Ashod II., the "Iron"; his brother and successor, Appas; and Ashod III., the Merciful, were all competent and brave leaders, whose prowess drove the invaders of Armenia to a respectable distance and whose sagacity filled the land with fortified places. Opulence and martial glory and brighter days of former prosperity seemed to have returned under such exploits, which were above the level of their contemporaries, yet the chain of powerful rulers seems to break somewhere in the line of succession, for royal fathers seldom breed royal sons. Such was the case of Simpad, the son of Ashod III., who possessed none of the brilliant qualities of his fathers; in fact, he had a temper and disposition directly opposite to that of his fathers. He was incompetent, cruel, and corrupt

COAT OF ARMS AND FLAGS OF ANCIENT ARMENIA.

in the extreme; yet if exquisite taste of regal pomp and beauty should be considered a redeeming feature in such a depraved character, he did possess it in a most extravagant measure. His royal capitol on the north of Mt. Ararat; the city of Ani, with its palaces, castles, towers, and 1001 churches, whose ruins cope to-day with the antiquities of Babylon in their grandeur, bear adequate testimony to this trait of his character.

Without attempting a detailed account of events of the short line of the Pagradids, we deem it sufficient to state that Byzantine folly and weakness, aided by internal disruption of nobles, caused the eventual ruin of the dynasty.

The name of Emperor Constantine Monomachos stands black in the history of the Eastern Empire. His utter worthlessness as a statesman and as a man of sense of responsibility, his debauched indulgence in selfish and short-sighted gratifications, did not simply cause Armenia's destruction, but opened Asia Minor to the Turks, which was the first step to Islam's subsequent supremacy over the Christians of the East, and to the final overthrow of the Byzantine Empire in 1453. This is the sum and substance of the criminal imprudence of his folly. The frontiers of Iberian, Armenian, and Syrian provinces were exempted from tributary taxation in consideration of maintaining forces in defense of the internal territories and in protection of the central government itself. Monomachos, discarding the wise policy in vogue, ordered the military operations to cease, and that taxes be collected. Such an imbecile act at once threw the southeastern frontier wide open to the torrents of Moslem invaders. Nor is this the whole account of his folly. With unquenchable greed of more taxes, he demanded from Cakig the surrender of his kingdom, and upon his refusal the emperor without scruple entered into an alliance with the Saracens, and, aided by some native traitors too, easily managed the surrender of Ani. The surrender of Ani, the last bulwark of our people, was Armenia's grave, the deadly Waterloo, and resulted in the subsequent overthrow of our dynasty. For such an act, our ancestors justly looked upon the Greeks as oppressors, and in consequence of such a feeling the natural ties of religion which united them against the enemies of their common faith were dissolved, and our people would no longer co-operate with them or fight their battles. The Turks were ready. The frontier provinces, now unprotected, offered an easy entrance to Seljuk inroads, which in the course of time resulted in the final destruction of the Byzantine Empire itself. In the year 1079, amid overwhelming tragedies, the control of the territory passed to Constantinople.

THE RHUPENIAN DYNASTY. 1080–1393.

The Byzantine Empire, under the sway of weak and unstable monarchs, was on the road to rapid decline before the conquering arms of the Moslem. Seljuks poured into Asia Minor like a mighty deluge, and reached as far as to Nicæa, only fifty miles from Constantinople. Meanwhile, Armenian settlements, in the form of semi-independent principalities, were scattered broadcast like isles in the midst of the tempest-tossed ocean of Mohammedanism. The dwindling successors of imperial Trajan could no longer exert any extended controlling influence upon the affairs of the Armenian people. Under such surroundings and circumstances, Rhupen, a relative of Cakig, the last king of the Pagradid house, with sufficient strength raised the standard of independence in the mountains of northeastern Cilicia, and under the shadow of Taurus builded up a petty kingdom, known as Lesser Armenia, whose dominions duly extended over Cilicia and Cappadocia. This little kingdom, for close on three centuries of its existence, was for the most part in a state of comparative prosperity; yet its tranquillity was not perpetuated, for when the Mameluke of Egypt passed through our country with fire and sword, the people, in the hope of protection, allied themselves with the Mongol hordes of Genghiz Khan. Such an alliance, however, proved of no moment to the terrible fury of the conquering hosts of the Egyptian Sultan Schaban, who, with boundless vengeance, made an end once for all to the last ill-fated dynasty of our fathers (1375 A. D.).

Rhupenians are conspicuous for their connection with the crusaders. It was through the aid of Constantine, Rhupen's son, that the Christians captured Antioch; and again in later years we find Levon, who allied himself with Emperor Frederick Barbarossa in the third crusade and aided him in the capture of Iconium (1190). Thus Rhupenians, with the kings of Cyprus, formed the last bulwark of Christianity in the East.

Levon VI. (Ghevond VI.), the last of the line, was captured in 1375, in spite of a vigorous defense at Gafar, and banished into Egypt, where, after six years of captivity, he was set free. Upon his liberation, having spent years of extensive travel through Europe, he settled in Paris, until the time of his death in 1393, where he was buried by the high altar in the Chapel of St. Denis. The following inscription still exists upon his monument :

Here Lies

LEVON VI.

The Noble Louisinian Prince

THE KING OF ARMENIA

Who died 1393 A. D., Nov. 23d, in Paris.

The author counts it his good fortune when in Paris to have visited his tomb. What thoughts filled the mind, what feelings moved the heart of an Armenian youth, as he stood in a strange land by the grave of the last king of his country! Time and distance cannot affect the profound impression of that scene. It is said that his body, clad in robes of white, with a golden scepter placed within his hand and an opal crown upon his head, was carried to the tomb in regal pomp. Thus sadly does the unseemly show of death's procession mock at life's stern realities.

With the disappearance of this last shadow of Armenian independence, our country has remained to this very day a land of many sorrows. Of all the alien dominations in the history of Armenia, none has been so unbearable to our unhappy people as the domination of the Mohammedan power, which still continues to curse homes and fatherland. We find about the year 1300 Tamerlane, the Napoleon of Asia, entered into Armenia and brought upon its people horrors of unspeakable carnage. Indeed, wherever Tamerlane set his foot his conquests were marked with the wholesale massacre of the inhabitants and the utter desolation of their cities and villages. In the city of Van he threw the inhabitants from the walls of the castle, until the corpses almost reached to the height of the walls. At Sivas, ancient Sebaste, he buried over four hundred Armenians alive. These graves are known to this day as "black graves," which places of melancholy interest I have often visited.

In 1604 about forty thousand of the Armenians were forcibly transplanted into Persia, by Shah Abbas, who, after his contest with Ahmed I., had laid waste our unhappy country.

No nation better illustrates the vicissitudes of history than does the Armenian. Her fortunes, like her country's boundary, have varied with every changing generation. Assyrian, Persian, Macedonian, Roman, Byzantine, Arab, Seljuk, Tartar, and Ottoman have all swept across our fair land with fire and sword, with a regularity of the motion of the heavenly bodies in their courses; and yet what a marvelous vitality and strength Armenians must have possessed to have withstood the clash and combat of twenty centuries; while contemporary nations have long since vanished and passed away. As we look upon Armenia's past misfortunes, and her culminating tragedies of to-day, shall we attribute such mutilation wholly to inherent weakness? True, insubordination and jealousy have ever been our people's national sin,—indeed, our national curse,—for which we have paid very dearly. Yet it cannot be said of us that we are craven in spirit or utterly supine. Our people have existed from the deathless and forgotten past to this very day, and this fact alone, when compared with the decline of our contemporaries, is ample proof that had it not been for the characteristic vitality, courage, and heroism of its people, our race would have ceased to exist long centuries ago. Here it will be most fitting to briefly touch on Armenians of to-day and on their characteristics. The recent massacres, their development and causes, we have recorded at length in another chapter of this volume.

Prior to these widespread Armenian massacres, the great mass of Americans, in their almost total ignorance of Armenians, confused us with the Turks, in a manner not unlike to some of our ignorant people, who presumed the Americans were civilized sons of once uncivilized North American Indians. Quite frequently have I myself been introduced in my lectures to American audiences as "the young Christian Turk with an unpronounceable name." What an undeserved encomium to the Turk; who, ever loyal to the Saracen Prophet, never embraces Christian morals and ethics, and what an unwarranted disparagement to the "young man with an unpronounceable name," whose fathers have been Christians ever since there was Christianity. Nor is religion the only gulf that separates the Armenian from the Turk, but in race, in nationality, in language, in character, and aspect there is equally as wide and irreconcilable a separation, and as truly marked, as the separation of the American from the "Red Man in the West." Let us then briefly consider the distinguishing characteristics of these two antagonistic peoples. Let us first take the race.

Ethnologists treat of Aryans and Turanians among the primitive human families, as to either their complexion or intelligence. Armenians, known as the "Anglo-Saxons of the East," are of pure Caucasian blood and belong to the progressive nations of the Western civilization, to the great Aryan family of races, while the Turks, with a mighty host of Asiatics, belong to the Turanian race and are of Mongolian blood. Thus they do not belong even to the next best of races, the Semitic, but are at the bottom of the race ladder. There is no social intercourse, nor is there any intermarriage between these unlike races; for it has been the ruling trait in the Armenian national character throughout all ages to remain as much isolated as possible from the Turanian and other elements of lower order; and, to be sure, it is largely due to this centuries-rooted separation that our conquered race has not been lost in the alien blood of the conqueror. In nationality, as has been indicated in the first pages of this chapter, the Armenians are the sons of Haig, and we are the aborigines of the region that lies under the shadow of Ararat, the birthplace of civilization, where we have lived for centuries immemorial, amid the hallowed recollections of Eden, and to-day, notwithstanding the wrecks of time, we still cry:

"Might I choose from the world where my dwelling should be,
  I would say, Still thy ruins are Eden to me,
    My beloved Armenia!"

There is nothing in common, in the national memories of the Turk, with the Armenian, except the fact that, as a member of one of the most widely scattered nomadic tribes of central Asia, he has encamped in the land of our fathers, as an alien tyrant holding our people in bondage; and, after the lapse of five centuries, he is to-day every inch the same alien tyrant, hostile, intolerant, and destructive. Among other nations, when a conquest has continued as long a time as Turkish conquests have in Armenia, both the conquerors and the conquered have managed to affiliate in a peaceful fellowship, and in most cases have become one people, with a common interest and government, but this has not been the case with the Turk. Turk he is, Turk he has remained, and Turk he will remain to the end. His religious and political interests are not the interests of the Armenian, any more than the interests of the Turk have been the interests of the Greek, the Bulgarian, and many other races whom he has conquered in their own lands. In the strictest sense, the Turkish Sultan is not the national sovereign of the Armenians, or even of Turkey itself; for Turkey is made up of different peoples of diverse interests and aspirations. So let us clearly bear in mind that while we speak of the Armenian as being a Turkish subject, we should not associate ideas of national affiliation and fellowship, which we are usually accustomed to associate with other countries.

That there is a great contrast in the character and aspect of these two peoples, so diverse in their characteristics of religion, race, and nationality, can easily be understood. To Turkish dullness, depravity, and worthlessness, as a government and as an individual, we have, in the pages of this book, frequently referred on good authority, and from personal observation and well-authenticated facts.

Consider a moment as you reflect upon the career of the Turks, and you will scarcely find a people on the face of the earth so hateful to all civilizing influences of the age as the Turks. They have come in contact with Europe, but have not been influenced by its civilization. Whatever the evolution of the times has done for other people, it has done nothing for the Turks. Branded with the stagnation of primitive times, they have contrived to abstain from the blessings of civilization. Science and philosophy are alien to the minds of even their high governmental and religious functionaries. Rev. J. F. Riggs, one of the American missionaries in Turkey, relates that the late Sir Henry Austin Layard, the English diplomatist and archæologist, toiled along with one of the Turkish pashas to interest him in astronomy. He gave glowing accounts of the sun, moon, and stars, and especially he described the comets, with their strange mystery. When he paused at last, the pasha said, "Well, you say that the comet comes near and then goes away again?" "Yes, I said that," replied the veteran Englishman. "Very well," retorted the pasha, "let it go." Such a response from a Turkish governor, who represents the highest culture of his people, might well illustrate the scope of Turkish intelligence.

As to Armenians, we have our own civilization and culture. If our civilization and culture are not as high

JOHN AYVAZOVSK, THE ARMENIAN PAINTER.

as those of Western nations, we are a progressive people, at least, which is a marvelous quality to possess in a land like Turkey, where stagnation reigns supreme.

One need only become acquainted with the Armenian race to convince himself in regard to the superior place which our people occupy in the advance march of civilization. We have our own literature, rich with poets, historians, critics, translators, and scholars. Nor are the Armenians less conspicuous in the field of commercial and political activity. Indeed, in spite of the most gigantic obstacles thrown on the path of the progress and development of our race, the Armenians have, as a people, always occupied an advanced position in everything that requires energy, capacity, and intelligence. This is true not only of the Armenians in the Ottoman Empire, but in Russia and in India, and, indeed, wherever they may be found. Should my reader be disposed to think that the encomium I have paid to my race is overdrawn or too loud, let him read the following abstracts from men of the greatest authority, who know our people, and whose names alone are sufficient guaranty for the disinterestedness and sincerity of their motives. While there is a host of them, I shall quote only from a few men.

The historian Professor James Bryce says:

> They are a strong race, not only with vigorous nerves and sinews, physically active and energetic, but also with *conspicuous brain power*. Thus they have held a very important place among the inhabitants of western Asia ever since the sixth century. If you look into the annals of the East Roman, or Byzantine, Empire, you will find that most of the men who rose to eminence in its

service as generals or statesmen during the early Middle Ages were of Armenian stock. So was it also after the establishment of the Turkish dominion in Europe. Many of the ablest men in the Turkish service have been Armenian by birth or extraction. The same is true with regard to the Russian service. Among all those who dwell in western Asia, they stand first, with a capacity for intellectual and moral progress, as well as with a natural tenacity of will and purpose, beyond that of all their neighbors, not merely of Turks, Tartars, Kurds, and Persians, but also of Russians.

The famous author Émile De Laveleye says, in "The Balkan Peninsula":

> The Armenians are intelligent, laborious, economical, and excellent business men. They occupy official appointments in the administration of the Ottoman Empire, and in Constantinople they are the chief promoters of economical activity. Their civilization is among the oldest in Asia. Their annals date from the earliest historic times.

The late Rev. H. G. O. Dwight, D. D., one of the pioneer missionaries of the American Board among our people, reflects the observations of many years in these words:

> They [Armenians] have shown themselves to be superior to any other race in commercial tact and in mechanical skill. The principal merchants are Armenians, and nearly all the great bankers of the government; and, whatever arts there are that require peculiar ingenuity and skill, they are almost sure to be in the hands of the Armenians. . . In one word, they are the Anglo-Saxons of the East.

Armenian progress has, owing to the unfortunate condition of the country, made itself more felt abroad than at home. I might draw up a very long catalogue of Armenians who have highly distinguished themselves in various branches of arts and sciences, but a few only need here be mentioned: The painter John Ayvazovsk of the Council of the St. Petersburg Academy of Fine Arts, whose works adorn the imperial palaces of the Czar, the Sultan of Turkey, and other royal dignitaries; Nubar Pasha, the ex-prime minister of the Egyptian government; while Dikran and Boghos Pashas are equally great in African statesmanship. Among expert physicians in Turkey are Doctors Mateosian, Khorassanjian, Dobrashian, Vartanian, etc., while among the greatest lawyers are Mosditchian and Tingnerian. Among musicians are Chonkhajian, Devletian, Surenian, and a young lady named Nartoss, who frequently presides at the piano before the Sultan. The Sultan's treasurer, Portukalian Pasha. The chief counselor in the foreign office at Constantinople, Harontiune Dadian Pasha. The Sultan's photographers, Abdullah brothers and Sebah. The Sultan's personal jeweler, Chiboukjian. H. E. Daud Pasha was the first "Christian" governor, who became, after the massacre of the Christians of Mt. Lebanon in 1860, the governor-general of that region. The magnificent hospital at Smyrna is a monument to Startalian's benevolence. Many steamers which ply on the Mediterranian are owned by Balyivzian. The chess player Adamian, the Berlin mineralogist Azruni, the London archæologist Hormuzd Rassam, the Zurich chemist Abelianz, and bankers and financiers in almost every country prove that Armenia is more nearly abreast of the Western World than is perhaps generally suspected. The splendid Lazareff Institute at Moscow, with its twenty professors of

H. E. DAUD PASHA, LATE ARMENIAN GOVERNOR OF MOUNT LEBANON.

Oriental languages, is an imperishable monument to the enlightened generosity of an Armenian millionaire of the last century.

In Russia there are quite a number of Armenian generals, some of whom have been the greatest in the Czar's army. Let me mention the names of a few of them: Count Yoris Melikoff; Generals Lazareff, Tergukasoff, Lucasoff; Kishmishian, the commander of Caucasus; Hagop Alkhazian, Alexander Lalayian, Demedr Der Asadurian, Ishkhan Mannelian, Alexander Gorganian, Ishkhan Gochaminassian, Aeakel Khantamirian, and others.

In all the great cities of Russia the Armenians are conspicuous. University and college professors, judges, mayors, and high civil functionaries are to be found on every hand. Let me recall the names of a few only: Minister of Education, Count Hovhaunes Telyanian; the Minister of Foreign Affairs in Asia, Gamazian; Counselor of Education, Mugerditch Emin; professor in the Royal University at Moscow, Nerses Nersesian, and De Shilantz in the medical college at Kharcof; A. Madanian, mayor of Tiflis; V. Keghamian, mayor of Erevan, and many others. Nor are the Armenians in Persia and India less conspicuous. Chahanguir Khan, the Minister of Arts and superintendent of the Arsenal; Nirza Melkoum Khan, the ex-ambassador of Persia at London; Nazar Agha, the ambassador of Persia at Paris; General Sharl Bezirganian, the general superintendent of the telegraph service. Go where you will,—Turkey, Russia, India, Persia, Egypt, Poland, Transylvania, Roumania, and throughout central Asia,—and you will find the

Armenian holding a high, if not always a leading, position in trade and arts. In commercial affairs our people are large producers as well as middlemen and financiers. In Asia Minor and Persia the manufacture of carpets and rugs, so renowned throughout the world, is almost entirely in the hands of the Armenians; and, in addition, in Constantinople and every town of Asiatic Turkey our people form the professional class *par excellence.*

I cannot close this chapter on the fortunes of my people without an appeal to that great cosmopolitan nation, the secret of whose marvelous unity is freedom and intelligence, to aid in the enlightenment, encouragement, and consequent liberation of a people, kindred though remote, who, through the thick fogs of tyranny and gloom of oppression, have kept intact the love of liberty, the very font of manhood, together with those qualities that make good citizenship—strength and sobriety.

ARMENIAN LITERATURE.

"The Armenian literature is rich and continuous, uninterrupted through all the Middle Ages. It has furnished philosophers, historians, theologians, and poets."—PROFESSOR ÉMILE DE LAVELEYE.

FOLK-LORE, the mother of literature, with its legends and simple rural songs, forms the fountain-head of every nation's purest thought and noblest sentiment. Long, long ere letters were invented, the enraptured heart of the poet broke forth in song, the rhythm so complete that not a word could be changed without destroying the sense. Was it not so with blind Homer? Armenia's heritage of song is her richest treasure, bequeathed by misty figures of the prehistoric past. So ancient are her melodies that they seem the breath of her body and the light of her soul.

A country's scenery, its lofty mountains, green hills, and fertile valleys exert an influence upon the physical conditions and intellectual standards of its people that cannot be overestimated. Switzerland, with its grand uplifting heights, is famed for the inborn love of liberty cherished by its people. Burns, living close to nature's heart, sang sweetly and truly Scotland's charm; and to-day his songs the world over with magic touch raise fond uplifting memories in many an exiled Scottish heart. Armenia, too, has her bards, whose songs are enriched by the natural scenery which first echoed their refrain. The native poet's passion for birds and flowers inspires his every line, while the varied perfumes of the fields breathe from many a stanza. From the sunny vales and hills, with memories around and the moldering generations beneath, the shepherd's strain floats out and fills the solitary places with the old tuneful names of Armenia's heroic race. How their sweet and mournful melodies lulled my boyhood, and how the memory still thrills my exile heart!

There is a paucity of Armenian written literature prior to the Christian era. This is due in a large measure to St. Gregory's religious zeal, which really amounted to fanaticism; for, in order to give the incipient Christianity a clear headway, he caused a wholesale destruction of everything pagan,—literature, monuments, and temples,—apparently without a moment's consideration of their inestimable worth to posterity. Thus the great illuminator of religion became the eliminator of Armenian literature. However, we have proof that the national enthusiasm for knowledge is not of modern inspiration. So proud a people will not willingly let their deeds of valor on hard-fought fields die unrecorded, and we find that the names of heroes and sages were household words at every family altar and fireside, and that cherished names and historical events, garnered in national song and story, were handed from generation to generation as sacred traditions for centuries, until the art of writing became common.

Modern archæologists have discovered and deciphered ancient cuneiform records which form a valuable acquisition to traditionary lore. Assyrian, Greek, and Hebrew records help to fill in the missing links in an almost unbroken chain, so that Armenian tradition may be said to more nearly approach historical literature in nature and value than that of any other nation of the earth. The unwritten history of the masses is confirmed in most essential points by the modern reading of the records of the few who were able to engrave the facts of history on the rocky face of the everlasting hills. Time has dealt kindly with these precious records, and the curious student may find a full account of their discovery in the annals of archæology. Like the tombs of Egypt, the cradle of the human race is slowly but surely giving up the secrets of thousands of years. The earliest and most valued of our historical sources is the work of Agathangaegos, the private secretary of King Tiridates of Armenia, who flourished in the third century of the Christian era.

The rarest manuscripts I have seen are found in the alcoves of Armenian monastic libraries. About two thousand of them are preserved at Etchmiazin, and twelve hundred in the convent of San Lazaro at Venice. The Royal Library at Paris, through the emissaries of Louis XIV., procured about two hundred, and there are several in the Bodleian Library and the British Museum. Many of these are the work of inferior or obscure writers, but all of them have a great value because of their antiquity and the painstaking care with which the laborious work of copying was done.

In the fifth century, a period of marked intellectual activity, lived Moses of Chorene, known among his countrymen as Movses Khorentzi, by far the best-known and the most important source of Armenian history. Indeed he may be the called the Herodotus of the Armenian people. He treasured in his works the traditional history, stories, and ballads of his time, parts of which were handed down orally with an accuracy unusual in tradition.

Western readers are familiar with the work of Bishop Ulfilas, who first gave literary form to the Gothic by devising an alphabet and translating the Bible. In this same fifth century St. Mesrob, an illustrious prelate of an Armenian monastery, rendered similar service to Armenia by modifying the alphabet to its present form, and then translating the Bible into our language. St. Mesrob is sometimes called the inventor of the Armenian letters, but this is a greater honor than is his due. Prior to his introduction of the Armenian characters the Greek alphabet was used by our nation. It appears that our patriarch Isaac the Great first undertook the translation of the Bible, but, inasmuch as the Persians had destroyed all the Greek manuscripts, he was obliged, with the aid of Mesrob, to make a translation from the Peshito, or Syriac version, and they actually completed their translation from this version. But Jonnes Ecceleusis and Josephus Palnensis, pupils of St. Mesrob, returning from the Ecclesiastical Council of Ephesus to which they were delegated, brought with them an accurate copy of the Greek Bible, the authentic text of which led Mesrob to abandon his translation from the Peshito and to commence anew from the Greek. Hampered by his imperfect knowledge of Greek, he found it necessary to send his pupils to centers of Greek scholarship to acquire a thorough knowledge of that tongue. Upon their return the translation was accomplished, after almost a half century of persevering toil. So remarkable is this translation in its accuracy and beauty of diction, so perfect in its classic style, that to this very day it is known as the "Queen of Versions." In the Old Testament this version closely adheres to the Septuagint, with the exception of the book of Daniel, which follows the version of Theodotion; while the version of the New Testament is faithful to the original Greek.

In the sixth century, upon the occasion of an organic union between the Armenian and the Syrian churches, this version was revised and adapted to the Peshito; yet the original has suffered much interpolated alteration, notably in the thirteenth century, when King Hethom of Armenia, an ardent Roman Catholic who afterward became a Franciscan monk, adapted the Armenian version to the Vulgate for the purpose of opening the way for the union of the Armenian and Roman churches.

The translation of the Bible operated powerfully on our language and literature by giving a great impulse to literary and intellectual activity. The Grecian philosophy, which was held in profound admiration by our scholars, was called to the aid of our Christian theology. An eager crowd of Armenian students and writers flocked to the educational centers of the Orient and the Occident, and brought back home with them the best of learning for the cultivation of their own literature. To their translations we are indebted for the preservation of many valuable works partially or wholly lost in the original. Among these are: The Chronicle of Eusebius; the Discourses of Philo; homilies by St. Chrysostom, Severianus, Basil the Great, and Ephraim Syrus; the epistles of Ignatius, translated from the Syrian version; the Catechesis of Cyril of Jerusalem; several homilies by Chrysostom, etc. Of this period, the late Professor Philip Schaff of Union Theological Seminary says:

> In spite of the unfavorable state of political and social affairs in Armenia during this epoch, more than six hundred Greek and Syrian works were translated within the first forty years after the translation of the Bible; and as in many cases the original works have perished, while the translations have been preserved, the great importance of this whole literary activity is apparent. . . The period, however, was not characterized by translations only. Several of the disciples of Mesrob and Sahak left original works. Esnik wrote four books against heretics, printed at Venice in 1826, and translated into French by Le Vailliant de Florival, Paris, 1853. A biography of Mesrob by Korium, homilies by Mambres, and various writings by the Philosopher David have been published; and the works of Moses of Chorene, published in Venice in 1842, and again in 1864, have acquired a wide celebrity; his history of Armenia has been translated into Latin, French, Italian, and Russian.

From the seventh to the tenth century is the period of Armenia's most flourishing literature; while the sixth century, which marked the separation of the Armenian from the Greek Church after the Council of Chalcedon, may well be called the dormant era of the Armenian literature, in view of the fact that all intercourse with Greek centers of learning was cut off by the Persians.

From the seventh to the twelfth century many historical, theological, and biographical writers and writers of hymns flourished. The twelfth and the thirteenth centuries, in which Syriac influence predominated, was a period of great literary activity. In the twelfth, among leading writers Nerses Shinorhali stands foremost as a poet, whose hymns of deep spiritual intensity are still chanted in the Armenian churches. Nerses Lambronensis was also famous as a biblical scholar and orator. Michael Syrus the historian, whose work has been edited with a French translation by Langlois (Paris, 1864), was not less famous. The leading authors of the thirteenth century were Krikor Sgnevratzi, Kevork Sgnevratzi, Mukhitar Anetzi; and Bishops Vanayan and Vartan, who wrote commentaries and historical works.

Later the Armenians of the West gave to literature such names as Rivola (1633), Villote, La Croze, Osgan, and others, who were all eclipsed by St. Martin. In Russia and France the Armenians ranked among the best writers; while Justi, Neumann, and Pertermann in Germany have made enviable reputations. For my readers the names of Armenian literary lights would be only a tedious catalogue of unpronounceable words; to write something of their lives and activities would require volumes. It is sufficient, however, to note that, in spite of the political disasters which have signalized our history, the Armenians have always maintained a national literature of the highest order, and our language has at the same time been perfected by modifications and changes in orthography, syntax, and style. As to its relation to other languages, there are conflicting opinions among scholars. By some it it held to be an original tongue, so distinct from the rest in its fundamental character that it cannot be classed with any of the great families of languages; while by others it is classed with the Medo-

Persian family. To this latter classification, however, we cannot subscribe; for the apparent similarity, we believe, is simply due to the adoption of a few words resulting from our country's conquest, while no fundamental likeness can be shown. The prevalent belief now is that the Armenian belongs to the independent branch of the Indo-European family of languages. It is an inflected language with four conjugations and twelve declensions. In syntax, particularly in the use of the participle, the classical Armenian bears a close resemblance to the ancient Greek, but it has no grammatical gender or dual form, and its definite articles are suffixes of a single letter. As to accent the language is deficient, there being no stated rules; but it generally falls on the last syllable.

The modern Armenian literature commences in the sixteenth century, as all other modern literature commences. Just as in religion the Reformation was the greatest movement in the sixteenth century, so was the Renaissance in the revival of letters. The action of European literature on Armenia commences in the first quarter of the present century. Distinction of the ancient and modern literature consists in that ancient Armenian is almost entirely composed of religious writings, both in verse and prose, while the modern Armenian deals with secular themes, political, social, scientific, patriotic. Classical Armenian flourished in the Church, while the modern Armenian flourished outside of the Church as well as in the Church. In the mediæval ages monasteries were the repositories of learning as well as the bulwarks of religion. The monks were the only scholars down to the time of the modern era, while in the modern Armenian literature it is the scholar who is the teacher as well as the priest who writes. Instead of monasteries schools of learning have sprung up, and when these schools do not give sufficient scope to the intellectual activities of the Armenians they are attracted by the Occidental colleges and universities.

Geographic locality has also influenced the Armenian language. All the climates under which the Armenians flourished have placed a peculiar stamp upon the language as well as the life, and thus the language of the Armenians in Turkey, in Russia, in Persia, in India, in France, and in the United States has its distinctively local characteristics. And the local governments in these countries have affected the Armenian thought to the degree of latitude and margin they have given to the expansion of human thought; and thus in Russia, despotic as the government is, the Armenian intellect has found a greater scope of activity than in Turkey. In Russia novelists such as Raffi, and patriotic poets such as Batkanian and Nalbantian, and journalists such as Arzrooni, have flourished. In Turkey the Armenian language has not found as large a scope as in Russia, but even in the prevailing vexatious restrictions of the Turkish censorship of the press, the Armenian language has flourished to a marvelous degree. The Armenian language in India comes next to that of Russia and Turkey in importance; but it will find its best expression, and Armenian intellect its greatest scope of activity, in France, England, and in the United States, owing to the kindly, genial, friendly, and liberal atmosphere that prevails.

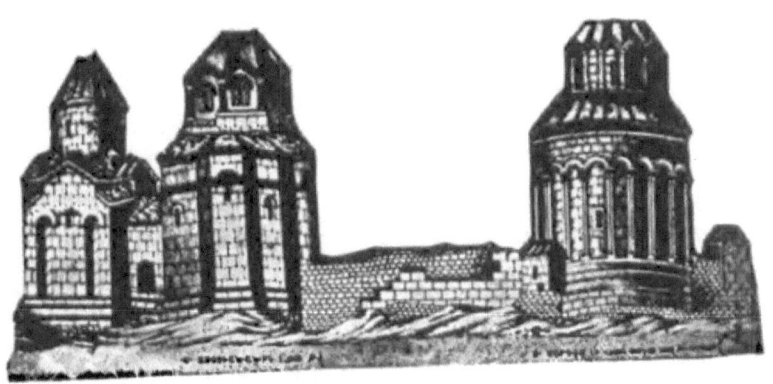
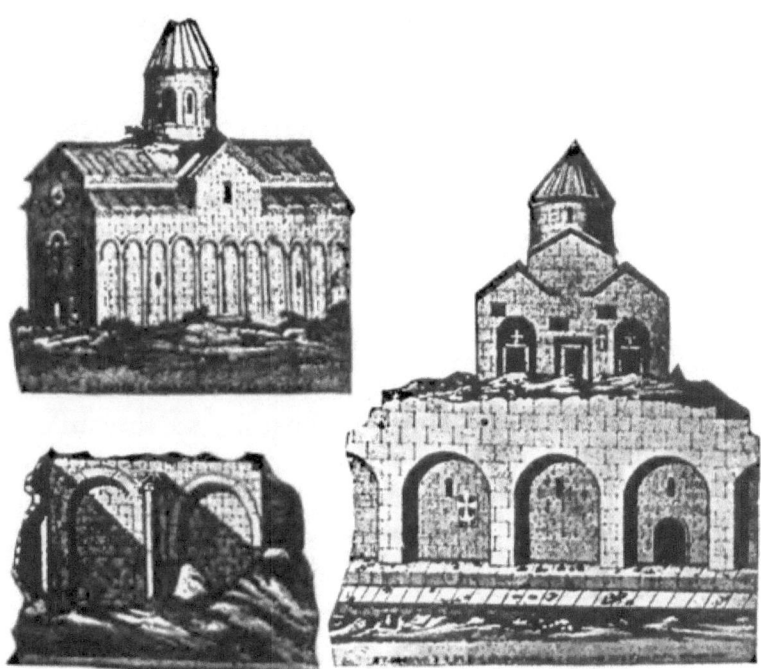

EARLY ARMENIAN MONASTERIES—REPOSITORIES OF LEARNING.

In the present century, the work of Armenian Romish monks of the convent of San Lazaro, Venice, may rank first, as it has given a great impetus to the development of the literature. This convent is a relic of mediævalism modified by modern influence. From it have come original works and periodicals, many translations of standard books from European languages, particularly from Italian, French, English, and German, together with valuable dictionaries and volumes of reference. This most renowned of monastic organizations was founded in 1701 by Mechitar de Petro, D. D., a former priest and a secretary of Archbishop Michael of the Armenian Church, who, while in the service of his mother Church, was in secret a proselyte to Rome and a Jesuit. In 1700, while he was a pastor at Constantinople, strife arose between two rival patriarchs of the national church, and the community was divided into two parties. To Mechitar this was a signal opportunity to advocate submission to the Romish Church. Such an advocacy, however, brought upon him the fiery indignation of the Armenian Church. Indeed the storm of hostility so threatened to overwhelm him that the French ambassador's protection was sought and readily afforded, whereupon Mechitar removed his mask and openly professed the Roman Catholic faith. The increasing animosity of the Armenians, however, drove him to Smyrna and from thence to Modon in Morea. In 1701 he had founded in Constantinople a new religious movement with eleven members. At Modon the Venetian government granted him an estate upon which to build a convent of the new order, and he took possession of it in 1703. War between the Turks and Venetians necessitated removal, and Mechitar, coming to Venice in 1715, petitioned the Venetian senate for a safer site. In 1717 they generously gave him the Island of San Lazaro, where a convent bearing Mechitar's name was duly erected and opened September 8, the birthday of the Virgin Mary.

Mechitar, ever alert and ardent, never abandoned or lost sight of his inspiring aim, the education of his countrymen. Himself a born scholar, he did not lay aside his pen until death in 1749 took it from his hand. His works are largely theological and philosophical; but popular hymns, written while he was yet in the fold of the mother Church, are still sung and bear witness to his poetic skill and spiritual fervor. Establishing printing presses in the convent, he labored with untiring zeal to revive the high literary standard of Armenia's bygone days.

After a lapse of almost two centuries, the Mechitarists still bear the indelible impress of their founder's devotion to letters; for, in accordance with its original aim and mission, the place became not only a convent of monotonous ecclesiasticism, but an academy not unlike that of the French Immortals, venerable with years and rich in imperishable memories; for many rare spirits have imparted something of themselves to these sacred buildings, where they have dreamed and worked and waited, where they have endured and lost or won. Here, indeed, are places associated with poets and statesmanlike scholars, whose story is the best heritage of the intellect and literature of Armenia, for in them all the ethical and spiritual instincts of the nation found representation. The convent is particularly interesting to modern students and tourists, because it was there that Byron sojourned for a time, deeply interesting himself in Armenian literature and in the learned monks who were its expounders. The room, table, and chair where he studied the Armenian language are shown to visitors at the convent. Aside from Byron, Victor Hugo, Lamartine, Henry W. Longfellow, and other conspicuous lights in the world of letters have been ardent admirers of our literature. Some of the "Oriental poems" of Victor Hugo are adaptations from Mugarditch Beshiktashlian's poems. Longfellow, too, has rendered a few Armenian poems into English verse. This remarkable establishment has been so distinguished for its eminent services in the cause of morality and learning that, in 1810, when a general order for the suppression of all monastic institutions in Venice was issued, San Lazaro alone was exempted from its sweeping effects. Another proof of the high estimation in which the monastery stands is in the fact that the Pope made it his custom to confer upon each new abbot of San Lazaro the title and dignity of archbishop, although the prelate thus honored had neither province nor subordinate clergy.

We must not forget the Armenian missionaries, who have furnished scientific text-books and are increasing the number from time to time. An Armenian who can afford them may have as good a practical library in his native language as the artisan or merchant could desire. Concerning this work I have spoken in the chapter on evangelical missions.

From these facts some interesting conclusions can be drawn. Through four-fifths of the Christian era Armenian literature has enjoyed a more perfect continuity than that of any other Christian nation. When Europe was passing through the Dark Ages the Christian Armenians of the Orient were enjoying a season of unparalleled intellectual activity and creating a literature of no little value; and the day may yet come when their purest songs and highest thoughts may be ranked among those classics which are not the possession of any one tongue or people, but have in them so much of man's heart and life that they are the legacy of the race. This may be seen in the poems quoted in this chapter. They are the productions of various writers and of different centuries, but their truth and beauty belong to no one age or clime; for the catholicity of true song is theirs. Armenia's mountains, hills, and valleys, her birds and flowers, her kings and battles, her thwarted yearning for freedom, even the broken heartstrings of her stricken mothers, are woven into a bitter-sweet burst of song, amid whose gladsome strains sounds of woe are mingled, sunbeams and shadows, joy and pain.

POEMS ON NATURE.

Nature poetry finds in spring a strong incentive. Grim, slothful Winter lingers long, holding gentle Spring in his icy grasp. Then she rises suddenly in her youthful strength, and snowflakes change to flowers with a suddenness that surprises the stranger. This quick transition, this annual resurrection, is the theme of many a bard. Spring poetry is addressed to the stork, as harbinger of the season, who, when he comes to stay, brings summer with him.

The ancients declare that spring was under the special care of the goddess Amahid. All the people joined in the feast of *Varthavar*, or "Rose Blossoms." In Christian times this has been supplanted by the three days' festival of the Transfiguration. The ancient name, the Feast of Rose Blossoms, indicates the love of the beautiful, which leads to the true and can have its origin only in the good. There is a religious halo about the very names of the Armenian flowers. The "Fountain's Blood" is a floral wonder. Was it the blood of righteous Abel that sprang from the ground as this crimson flower on a leafless stalk, calling to God in its blood-red simplicity for vengeance on the murderer? These beauties of the field and glen have called forth exquisite gems of thought which are treasured to this day.

Summer—the short, sweet, seductive summer of Armenia—does not last long enough to produce *ennui*. This brief, bright pageantry of blooming, fragrant flowers and ripening fruit comes quickly, does its work in haste; and a chill, gloomy winter succeeds, suppressing autumn before it fairly has a chance to exist.

How much these long winters, coupled with the utter seclusion of the Armenian homes far away from the centers of population, have had to do in developing the poetic instinct, we can well surmise. These patriarchal abodes are snow-bound from October until May; and from such retreats, chiefly, has come the ancient and modern literature of Armenia. With what poetic fancy the return of spring is greeted may be seen in this little poem:

> Scarce are the clouds' black shadows
>   Pierced by a gleam of light,
> Scarce have our fields grown dark again,
>   Freed from the snowdrifts white,
> When you, with smiles all twinkling,
>   Bud forth o'er hill and vale.
> O firstborn leaves of springtime,
>   Hail to your beauty, hail!
>
> Not yet to our cold meadows
>   Had come Spring's guest the swallow,
> Not yet the nightingale's sweet voice
>   Had echoed from the hollow,
> When you, like Joy's bright angels,
>   Came swift to hill and dale.
> Fresh-budded leaves of springtime,
>   Hail to your beauty, hail!
>
> Your tender, verdant color,
>   Thin stems, and graceful guise,
> How sweetly do they quench the thirst
>   Of eager, longing eyes!
> Afflicted souls at sight of you
>   Take comfort and grow gay.
> New-budded leaves of springtime,
>   All hail to you to-day!
>
> Come, in the dark breast of our dales,
>   To shine the hills between!
> Come, o'er our bare and shivering trees
>   To cast a veil of green!
> Come, to give sad-faced Nature
>   An aspect blithe and new!
> O earliest leaves of springtime,
>   All hail, all hail to you!

Come, to call up for newborn spring
    A dawn of roses fair!
Come, and invite the breezes light
    To play with your soft hair!
Say to the fragrant blossoms,
    "Oh, haste! Men long for you!"
Hail, earliest leaves of springtime,
    Young leaves so fresh and new!

Come, come, O leaves, and with sweet wings
    Of hope from yonder sky
Cover the sad earth of the graves
    Wherein our dear ones lie!
Weave o'er the bones so dear to us
    A garland wet with dew,
Ye wings of Hope's bright angels,
    Young leaves so fresh and new.*

The life of Archbishop Khorene Nar-bey, author of the above, occupies a conspicuous place in the literary and clerical circles of our country. A direct descendant of the royal family of Lusignan, of the last dynasty of Armenian kings; educated at the convent of the Mechitarists in Venice, yet early leaving the Roman for the Armenian Church; a pupil of Lamartine and a friend of Victor Hugo; he was poet, theologian, author, orator, linguist, and also a diplomat of rare skill. Endowed with so many attainments, he consecrated his powers to the welfare of his countrymen by carrying to a successful issue many a delicate diplomatic mission, notably during the Berlin Congress in 1878. His ardent patriotism roused the Turkish government against him, and he died at Constantinople, poisoned, it is commonly believed, by the Sultan.

* Most of the poems that appear in this chapter are rendered into English verse by Miss Alice Stone Blackwell.

The birds of Armenia, like the flowers, are countless in number and variety. Her poets seldom write without embellishing their lines with reference to some of their fragrant or feathered friends of the field. The lament of the wandering Armenian in Totochian's song to the swallow will touch the heart of many a homesick exile :

> O swallow, gentle swallow,
>   Thou lovely bird of spring!
> Say, whither art thou flying
>   So swift on gleaming wing?
>
> Fly to my birthplace, Ashdarag,
>   The spot I love the best;
> Beneath my father's roof-tree,
>   O swallow, build thy nest.
>
> There dwells afar my father,
>   A mournful man and gray,
> Who for his only son's return
>   Waits vainly, day by day.
>
> If thou shouldst chance to see him,
>   Greet him with love from me ;
> Bid him sit down and mourn with tears
>   His son's sad destiny. .
>
> In poverty and loneliness,
>   Tell him my days are passed;
> My life is only half a life,
>   My tears are falling fast.
>
> To me, amid bright daylight,
>   The sun is dark at noon;
> To my wet eyes at midnight
>   Sleep comes not, late or soon.

> Tell him that, like a beauteous flower
>   Smit by a cruel doom,
> Uprooted from my native soil,
>   I wither ere my bloom.
>
> Fly on swift wing, dear swallow,
>   Across the quickening earth,
> And seek in fair Armenia
>   The village of my birth!

In the following stanzas, rendered into English verse by the author, it appears that the partridge is a special favorite:

> With flowers of every hue
> Thy nest is covered over,
> Thy place is full of dew,
> Thou lovest the sweet odor.
>   Little partridge, how
>   Pretty, pretty thou!
>
> When the partridge leaves the tree,
> And chirps its happy song,
> The world sings merrily,
> The heart forgets its wrong.
>   Little partridge, how
>   Pretty, pretty thou!
>
> By all the birds thou'rt blessed,
> And all thy feathered tribe
> To thee who art the best
> Their songs of love ascribe.
>   Little partridge, how
>   Beautiful art thou!

The crane is the harbinger of summer as the stork is of spring, and has received his share of poetic tribute. To the Armenian under foreign skies the flight of the crane is always suggestive of home. His thoughts will recall the poets of his Oriental fatherland. "Crane, whence comest thou? Hast thou no news of my country?" Thanks to modern scientific research, news flies faster than the crane, and the Armenian in America is abreast with the times on the Armenian question, and has the news before the Armenian resident on the foothills of Ararat can possibly get it.

The tender regard of Armenians for the birds of the air has its origin in the ancient superstition of the transmigration of souls. Among the ignorant it is still believed that the spirits of the departed visit the scenes of their youth in the form of birds. For this reason the denizens of the air are seldom disturbed by the Armenian peasants. Many of the poetical fancies in regard to them are born of the idea that they are the custodians of the spirits of departed friends.

The limpid, laughing waters of Armenia's swift-descending streams, as they babble through the rocky channels or bound from shelving precipices in a musical cascade, have shared the poet's fancy with the star-reflecting blue of the crystal lake. A delicate expression of the poetic charms of a mountain torrent watering fields and gardens in the lower valley is the following:

> Down from yon distant mountain
> The streamlet finds its way,
> And through the quiet village
> It flows in eddying play.

THE TURK AND THE LAND OF HAIG.

A dark youth left his doorway,
    And sought the water-side,
And, laving there his hands and brow,
    "O streamlet sweet!" he cried,

"Say from what mountain com'st thou?"
    "From yonder mountain cold
Where snow on snow lies sleeping,
    The new snow on the old."

"Unto what river, tell me,
    Fair streamlet, dost thou flow?"
"I flow unto that river
    Where clustering violets grow."

"Sweet streamlet, to what vineyard,
    Say, dost thou take thy way?"
"The vineyard where the vine-dresser
    Is at his work to-day."

"What plant there wilt thou water?"
    "The plant upon whose roots
The lambs feed, where the wind-flower blooms,
    And orchards bear sweet fruits."

"What garden wilt thou visit,
    O water cool and fleet?"
"The garden where the nightingale
    Sings tenderly and sweet."

"Into what fountain flowest thou?"
    "The fountain to whose brink
Thy love comes down at morn and eve,
    And bends her face to drink.

"There shall I meet the maiden
    Who is to be thy bride,
And kiss her chin, and with her love
    My soul be satisfied."

THE SCENE OF ARMENIAN POETS' FANCY.

BALLAD POETRY.

To ballad poetry the Armenian singer frequently turns. Many examples of this branch of the art are connected with the famous Lake Van, around which countless traditions have gathered. An excellent example of this class of poetry is given below:

> We sailed in the ship from Aghthamar.
> We directed our ship toward Avan;
> When we arrived before Vosdan
> We saw the dark sun of the dark day.
>
> Dull clouds covered the sky,
> Obscuring at once stars and moon;
> The winds blew fiercely,
> And took from my eyes land and home.
>
> Thundered the heaven, thundered the earth,
> The waters of the blue sea arose;
> On every side the heavens shot forth fire;
> Black terror invaded my heart.
>
> There is the sky, but the earth is not seen,
> There is the earth, but the sun is not seen,
> The waves come like mountains
> And open before me a deep abyss.
>
> O see, if thou lovest thy God,
> Have pity on me, forlorn and wretched;
> Take not from me my sweet sun,
> And betray me not to flinty-hearted Death.
>
> Pity, O sea, O terrible sea!
> Give me not up to the cold winds:
> My tears implore thee
> And the thousand sorrows of my heart. . .

The savage sea has no pity!
It hears not the plaintive voice of my broken heart;
The blood freezes in my veins,
Black night descends upon my eyes. . .

Go tell to my mother
To sit and weep for her darkened son;
That Hovhannes was the prey of the sea,
The sun of the young man is set!

RELIGIOUS POEMS.

This little poem of the Christ-child comes to us from St. Gregory of Narek, who lived in the tenth century :

"The lips of the Christ-child are like two twin leaves;
They let roses fall when he smiles tenderly.
The tears of the Christ-child are pearls when he grieves;
The eyes of the Christ-child are deep as the sea.
Like pomegranate grains are the dimples he hath,
And clustering lilies spring up in his path."

There is a sad Armenian elegy on Adam's expulsion from Paradise, in theme not unlike portions of Milton's "Paradise Lost." But our poets have seldom wandered in this direction. Their themes are of the heart, varying, with the fortunes of the people, from a tone of joyful victory to that of subdued melancholy.

Armenian literature is imbued with a profound faith in the final justice of God, which finds no parallel except in the literature of the Hebrew race. A literal translation of the following stanza, though sadly marring its artistic effect, does not destroy the poetic thought and religious hope which save from despair a bereaved mother grieving for her child:

> "I gaze and weep, mother of my boy,
>   I say alas! and woe is me!
> What will become of wretched me:
>   I have seen my golden son dead!
> They seized that fragrant rose
>   Of my breast, and my soul fainted away;
> They let that beautiful golden dove
>   Fly away, and my heart was wounded.
> The falcon Death seized
>   My dear and sweet-voiced turtle dove and wounded me.
> They took my sweet-toned little lark
>   And flew away through the skies!
> Before my eyes they sent the hail
>   On my flowering green pomegranate,
> My rosy apple on the tree,
>   Which gives fragrance among the leaves.
> They shook my flourishing beautiful almond tree
>   And left me without fruit;
> Beating it, they threw it on the ground
>   And trod it under foot into the earth of the grave.
> What will become of wretched me!
>   Many sorrows surrounded me.
> O my God, receive the soul of my little one
>   And place him at rest in Thy bright heaven."

The simple pathos and exquisite conception of bird-and-flower analogies by the rural bards are touchingly illustrated in the above selection.

LOVE POEMS.

The Eastern nations are noted for the delicate sentiment and profuse imagery of their love poems, and in this Armenia is not lacking. Some of her poets are worthy to be ranked with the singers of any nation.

One of these, Bedros Turian, resembles Robert Burns in some respects. Yet there are no contradictory traits in the character of the Armenian poet. Earth's vile passions never marred his pure love and noble aspirations after a higher life. He was the son of a blacksmith in Constantinople, and died of consumption in 1871, at the early age of thirty-one. He left a number of dramas and poems that enjoy a great popularity among my countrymen, though his fame came only after his death, when it was too late to give him the recognition he so vainly desired in life. Indeed, his life was full of adversity and sadness, and it appears that the very hardships which hastened his death gave power to his poetic genius in fathoming the depths of the tempest-tossed ocean of human tragedy. Poverty-stricken beyond endurance, helpless, friendless, and hopeless, sick and alone, disappointed in love, he touched the silvery strings of his lyre, bringing out soft, floating melodies full of sweet melancholy, misty sadness, and fainting loneliness. A few days before his death, amid the soft rustle of trees so like the gentle whispering of lovers, as his wandering steps lingered beside a little lake, his impassioned heart burst forth in this poetic strain :

> Why dost thou lie in hushed surprise,
>   Thou little lonely mere?
> Did some fair woman wistfully
>   Gaze in thy mirror clear?
>
> Or are thy waters calm and still
>   Admiring the blue sky,
> Where shining cloudlets, like thy foam,
>   Are drifting softly by?

Sad little lake, let us be friends!
  I, too, am desolate;
I, too, would fain, beneath the sky,
  In silence meditate.

As many thoughts are in my mind
  As wavelets o'er thee roam;
As many wounds are in my heart
  As thou hast flakes of foam.

THE LITTLE LAKE.

But if heaven's constellations all
  Should drop into thy breast,
Thou still wouldst not be like my soul—
  A flame-sea without rest.

There, when the air and thou are calm,
  The clouds let fall no showers;
The stars that rise there do not set,
  And fadeless are the flowers.

Thou art my queen, O little lake!
   For e'en when ripples thrill
Thy surface, in thy quivering depths
   Thou hold'st me, trembling, still.

Full many have rejected me:
   "What has he but his lyre?
"He trembles, and his face is pale;
   His life must soon expire!"

None said, 'Poor child, why pines he thus?
   If he beloved should be,
Haply he might not die, but live,
   Live and grow fair to see.'

None sought the boy's sad heart to read,
   Nor in its depths to look.
They would have found it was a fire,
   And not a printed book!

Nay, ashes now! a memory!
   Grow stormy, little mere,
For a despairing man has gazed
   Into thy waters clear!

The following lament over his early death serves to bring out his intense patriotism:

To thirst with sacred longings,
   And find the springs all dry,
And in my flower to fade—not this
   The grief for which I sigh.

Ere yet my cold, pale brow has been
   Warmed by an ardent kiss,
To rest it on a couch of earth—
   My sorrow is not this.

Ere I embrace a live bouquet
  Of beauty, smiles, and fire,
The cold grave to embrace—not this
  Can bitter grief inspire.

Ere a sweet, dreamless sleep has lulled
  My tempest-beaten brain,
To slumber in a earthy bed—
  Ah, this is not my pain.

My country is forlorn, a branch
  Withered on life's great tree;
To die unknown, ere succoring her—
  This only grieveth me.

The two following, by the same author, embody the thoughts of lovers the world over:

Were not the rose's hue like that which glows
On her soft cheek, who would esteem the rose?

Were not the tints of heaven like those that lie
In her blue eyes, whose gaze would seek the sky?

Were not the maiden innocent and fair,
How would men learn to turn to God in prayer?

" She was alone. I brought a gift—
  A rose, surpassing fair;
And when she took it from my hand
  She blushed with pleasure there.

" Compared with her, how poor and pale
  The red rose seemed to be!
My gift was nothing to the kiss
  My lady gave to me."

But the dearest and most frequent theme of the Armenian poet is his country—her beauty and her woes, the bravery of her sons and their ceaseless struggle for freedom from tyranny. These ideas are found in all classes of poems, from the lullaby the mother sings soft and sweet to hush the babe, to the most stirring songs of liberty and the fiercest notes of war. These ideas are illustrated in the following poems. The first, entitled "We Are Brothers," is the work of Professor Mugurditch Beshiktashlian, a Roman Catholic Armenian who was born in 1829 and was educated at the famous Convent Mechitarist. He died in 1868, and on his gravestone were carved the last lines of this, his song:

> From glorious Nature's myriad tongues,
>   Though songs be breathed by lips of love,
> And though the maiden's fingers fair
>   Across the thrilling harp-strings rove,
> Of all earth's sounds, there is no other
> So lovely as the name of brother.
>
> Clasp hands, for we are brothers dear,
>   Of old by tempest rent apart;
> The dark designs of cruel Fate
>   Shall fail, when heart is joined to heart.
> What sound, beneath the stars aflame,
> So lovely as a brother's name?
>
> And when our ancient Mother-land
>   Beholds her children side by side,
> The dews of joyful tears shall heal
>   Her heart's sad wounds, so deep and wide.
> What sound, beneath the stars aflame,
> So lovely as a brother's name?

We wept together in the past;
Let us unite in harmony
And blend again our tears, our joys;
  So shall our efforts fruitful be.
What sound, beneath the stars aflame,
So lovely as a brother's name?

Together let us work and strive,
  Together sow, with toil and pain,
The seed that shall, with harvest blest,
  Make bright Armenia's fields again.
What sound, beneath the stars aflame,
So lovely as a brother's name?

Another of the most brilliant lights in our modern literature is Raphael Patkanian. He is a poet beloved by the muses, and is known and admired by Armenians everywhere. His work is peculiar yet refined, melodious and tender; and, again, loud and stormy, sparkling with artful rhymes and measures, and ever throwing a magical enchantment and melancholy sadness over existence. Many of his poems were written during the Turco-Russian war, when the Armenians in Russia cherished bright hopes for the deliverance of Armenia from the Turkish yoke. This poet was born in 1830 in southern Russia. While at the University of Moscow he assembled his Armenian fellow-students and organized a literary club among them. Patkanian died in 1892, after forty-two years of continuous activity as an educator, journalist, and author. The following poem, entitled "Cradle Song," is a specimen of his work:

  Nightingale, oh, leave our garden,
    Where soft dews the blossoms steep;
  With thy litanies melodious
    Come and sing my son to sleep!

RAPHAEL PATKANIAN.

> Nay, he sleeps not for thy chanting,
>   And his weeping hath not ceased.
> Come not, nightingale! My darling
>   Does not wish to be a priest.
>
> O thou thievish, clever jackdaw,
>   That in coin findest thy joy,
> With thy tales of gold and profit
>   Come and soothe my wailing boy!
> Nay, thy chatter does not lull him,
>   And his crying is not stayed.
> Come not, jackdaw! for my darling
>   Will not choose the merchant's trade.
>
> Wild dove, leave the fields and pastures
>   Where thou grievest all day long;
> Come and bring my boy sweet slumber
>   With thy melancholy song!
> Still he weeps. Nay, come not hither,
>   Plaintive songster, for I see
> That he loves not lamentations,
>   And no mourner will he be.
>
> Leave thy chase, brave-hearted falcon!
>   Haply he thy song would hear.
> And the boy lay hushed and slumbered,
>   With the war-notes in his ear.

We cannot more fittingly close this chapter than by quoting the jewel of our songs of liberty. Its author, Professor Michael Ghazarian Nalbandian, was born in Russian Armenia in 1830. After graduating from the University of St. Petersburg he led an active life as an educator, author, and editor. Being suspected by the Russian government, on account of his political opinions, he was imprisoned for three years and then exiled to the province of Sarakov, where he died, in

1866, of lung disease brought on by the rigors of prison life.

In Russia it is forbidden to possess Nalbandian's portrait, yet pictures of him, with his poem on "Liberty," are circulated secretly among his countrymen.

> When God, who is forever free,
>   Breathed life into my earthly frame,—
> From that first day, by His free will
>   When I a living soul became,—
> A babe upon my mother's breast,
>   Ere power of speech was given to me,
> Even then I stretched my feeble arms
>   Forth to embrace thee, Liberty!
>
> Wrapped round with many swaddling bands,
>   All night I did not cease to weep,
> And in the cradle, restless still,
>   My cries disturbed my mother's sleep.
> "O mother!' in my heart I prayed,
>   "Unbind my arms and leave me free!"
> And even from that hour I vowed
>   To love thee ever, Liberty!
>
> When first my faltering tongue was freed,
>   And when my parents' hearts were stirred
> With thrilling joy, to hear their son
>   Pronounce his first clear-spoken word,
> "Papa, Mamma," as children use,
>   Were not the names first said by me;
> The first word on my childish lips
>   Was thy great name, O Liberty!
>
> "Liberty!" answered from on high
>   The sovereign voice of Destiny;
> "Wilt thou enroll thyself henceforth
>   A soldier true of Liberty?

The path is thorny all the way,
　　And many trials wait for thee;
Too strait and narrow is this world
　　For him who loveth Liberty."

"Freedom!" I answered; "on my head
　　Let fire descend and thunder burst;
Let foes against my life conspire,
　　Let all who hate thee do their worst:
I will be true to thee till death;
　　Yea, even upon the gallows tree
The last breath of a death of shame
　　Shall shout thy name, O Liberty!"

THE ARMENIAN CHURCH.

"The Armenians may justly claim to be the oldest Christian nation in the world."—H. B. TRISTRAM, D. D., LL. D., F. R. S., Canon of Durham, England.

PREHISTORIC RELIGION IN ARMENIA.

ACCORDING to the testimony of the Scriptures, after the resting of the ark "upon the mountains of Ararat," Noah offered burnt offerings upon the altar. Since these mountains are in our central province, Armenia may be said to be the earliest home of divine worship, and from here the patriarchal monotheism was transmitted to Noah's descendants. In the patriarchal observance of religion the father was the high priest of the family, officiating daily at the rude family altar. He was regarded with a peculiar reverence which we might well wish to see restored in many a modern home.

The traditions of Asia Minor would seem to indicate that pure monotheism was the prehistoric religion of the Armenians, as it was the primitive religion of all other Aryans. We cannot, however, positively determine the duration of that pure religion in Armenia. By degrees, through the influence of idolatrous neighbors, the people embraced polytheism of the Assyro-Babylonian type. Our cuneiform inscriptions give us many details of the names of the deities and the regulations for daily sacrifice.

With the supremacy of the Medo-Persian Empire, there arose in western Asia the dualistic religion of Zoroaster, teaching that there are two supernatural beings—Ormazd,* the creator and preserver of all things good, and Ahriman, the source of evil and mischief. These rival gods, having in command good and evil spirits, were in perpetual strife. Fire, which was the personification of Ormazd's son, became the supreme object of worship. This was the religion of the Armenians from the latter part of the seventh century B. C. until the introduction of Christianity.

INTRODUCTION OF CHRISTIANITY.

The Armenian Church should be of interest to every Christian of every country, because of its associations with early Christianity. It should be a delight to trace down the centuries the fortunes and misfortunes of a church founded by the first disciples of our Saviour.

Cast a glance at the condition of the Eastern World at the time of Christ's advent. When Zoroastrianism was multiplying its gods and at the same time multiplying vice and immorality, when the ancient Babylonians were in eager endeavor to keep their old, dying Sabaism alive, when many branches of heathenism were contemplating the manufacture of some new and better gods, when even the sacred religion of the Jews had fallen into formalism; in a word, when the dark and threatening clouds of strife and controversy had overcast the Oriental sky, and the people were blundering in the darkness of superstition and igno-

---

* Ormazd of the Persians is the same as Armazt of the Armenians and Jupiter of the Greeks.

rance, then rose the Sun of Righteousness to illumine the whole world, bearing in its radiance that angelic benediction, " Peace on earth, good will toward men."

The cherished tradition of the Armenian people is that during the reign of our King Abgar of Edessa, Bartholomew, one of the Twelve, and Thaddeus, one of the Seventy, went about preaching the gospel in Armenia. As a result of their faithful labors and the power of the new gospel they proclaimed, the king and the royal family were converted and baptized in the river Euphrates, and, following their example, the whole nation turned from idolatry to the true God. The conversion, however, proved transient, and a short time after the death of Abgar the nation relapsed into its former religion.

It was reserved for St. Gregory, a prince of the Arshagoonian dynasty, a man mighty in the Lord, to turn the erring people back to Christian faith and worship. And with his life and work the history of the Armenian Church emerges from the mists of tradition and comes out into the clear light of history. This learned man was sent by Tiridates (Durtad) to the Greek bishop Leontius of Cæsarea for ordination ; and under the influence of his preaching the king himself embraced Christianity, and the people began once more to worship God, in spirit and in truth (302 A. D.). From this period to the present day the faith of Jesus Christ has been the faith of the Armenian people.

Tiridates bestowed on his people the imperishable honor of being the first nation to have a Christian ruler. The baptism of this Armenian king and his court into the Christian Church antedates that of Constantine ten years. Commonly the latter is referred to as the first Christian emperor, through paucity of information on Armenian history in the libraries of Europe and America.

With Christianity came a quickening of the intellectual life of the people, and the century following was the golden age of Armenian literature. Schools were established in every part of the country, and as a crowning triumph the Bible was translated into the Armenian language in 410 A. D. Our bishops sat in all early councils of the one common Christian Church, catholic in spirit, liberal in doctrine and government.

THE STRUGGLE IN THE FIFTH CENTURY.

It was not without one final struggle that Zoroastrianism gave place to the incipient Church. In the fifth century the time came once more when the Persian conquerors offered as an alternative religious submission or annihilation by the sword. It was a most critical moment. They must wade through a carnage of death to religious freedom, or desert the pure religion of their fathers. "Christian homes, or Christian graves," was the unanimous watchword that echoed from the Armenian ranks.

> "Her head was crowned with flowers,
> Her feet were bathed with spray.
> Hers were the lands of Eden,
> The cradle of our race.
>
> "But then upon her borders,
> Shouted the Persian horde:
> 'Fall down and worship fire,
> Or perish by the sword.'

> "Then up sprang Armenia
>   And raised her voice on high,
>   And back to haughty Persia
>   Rang loud the warlike cry:
>
> "'I will not be a heathen,
>   I will not be a slave;
>   If I cannot have a Christian's home
>   I'll find a Christian's grave.'"

Men, women, children, all stood on the battleground in defense of their faith. One universal resolution prevailed: "From this belief no one can move us, neither angels nor men, neither fire nor sword, nor water, nor any tortures." In that vast throng of clergy and laity Prince Vartan Mamigonian, the valiant commander-in-chief of the Christian host, lifted his eloquent voice in a thrilling exhortation. "I entreat you, my brave companions," said he, "fear not the number of the heathen, withdraw not your necks from the terrible sword of a mortal man. That the Lord may give the victory into our hands, that we may annihilate their power and lift on high the standard of truth."

In the morning, with the clash of arms, the army of the Persians was advancing. No time could be lost; the decisive battle was soon on! After partaking of the Holy Communion, the Armenians marched on with brave hearts and with these words on their lips: "May our death be like the death of the just, and may the shedding of our blood resemble the blood-shedding of the prophets! May God look in mercy on our voluntary self-offering, and may he not deliver the Church into the hands of the heathen!" The battle raged furiously. Never fought men with greater

LEGENDARY PORTRAIT OF VARTAN MAMIGONIAN.

heroism. Though few in number, and though their noble commander was first among the slain, the courage of the determined heroes of the Cross increased until they shook the Persian throne to its foundation; and the Persian monarch, retreating in confusion, sought compromise, granting religious liberty. This was the last of Zoroastrianism, and from this blow it never recovered.

SEPARATION FROM THE CATHOLIC CHURCH.

It was these persecutions which we have just described that prevented Armenia's representation in the fourth Ecumenical Council of Chalcedon, at which Eutyches was condemned for his heresy relating to the person of Christ. Our Church reserved its decision, and was generally supposed to have indorsed the heresy; but this was by no means the case. Owing to the poverty of our languages in theological terms, we had at that time but one word for "nature" and "person"; consequently the declaration of the council that Christ possessed two natures in one person was unintelligible to the Armenian Church. They had no language in which to express it. In 451, therefore, this doctrine was formally annulled by our patriarch in full synod, an act which resulted in the separation of the Armenian from the Greek and Roman churches, Documentary evidence is not wanting to show that the Armenian Church was essentially orthodox at that time and has ever been so. Her indifference to theological discussion and her traditional reverence for antiquity, coupled with a rooted aversion to rationalism and skepticism, have preserved this Church from the confusion in which theological controversy has involved all the Eastern churches. These facts are not generally recognized by European and American historians, who have too often relied on bigoted Latin and Greek sources for their information. It was the attitude of the Armenian Church in standing aloof from the indorsement of the Council of Chalcedon which secured its independence and prevented it from being absorbed into the Greek and Roman hierarchies.

RELATIONS TO ROME.

For many centuries the Church suffered the meddlesome interference of the Pope at Rome, who tried to place it in subordination to the papal power. Many apostatized to Rome (notably since the Council of Florence, 1439 A. D.), perhaps in the hope of better protection from a stronger and more dominant organization. The superior schools of the Jesuits also undoubtedly attracted a large number from the national Church. Nor is this all. Much of the superstition of the Greek Church has crept in and has exerted a pernicious influence on the national religion, robbing it of its pristine purity and simplicity. In the twelfth century Merses Lambronasses, a celebrated Armenian orator, in a masterly speech, advocated the union of the two churches. The laity and clergy, however, unanimously rejected the idea, feeling that it threatened their independence. Moreover, the doctrines and usages of the two churches differ widely in many particulars. In particular it should be observed that, while the Armenian Church claims to be orthodox, it does

MONASTERY OF ETCHMIADZIN

not claim to be the only orthodox church, and does not deny communion to the members of the Greek and Roman churches. The Armenian Church is liberal, while the Greek is exclusive in the extreme.

Whether owning allegiance to Rome, a convert to the evangelical missions, or yet within the fold of the native Church, the Armenian Christian still esteems Etchmiadzin the most sacred shrine of national adoration. Most ancient of monastic foundations, and the patriarchal throne of Armenia throughout all Christian ages, there is no shrine so interwoven with Armenia's national memories. Here is the first St. Gregory's church, traditionally founded on a spot where Christ descended (as its name implies, *etch* meaning "descent," and *miadzin* "only-begotten"). The Armenians believe that this famous shrine, at the foot of Mt. Ararat, stands on the site of the first Armenian church of Thaddeus the Apostle, which was erected A. D. 40. They also believe that Thaddeus was martyred on a stone near by, and that his bones were subsequently removed and buried in the present building, which was erected in A. D. 650. It is cuneiform in shape and of colossal size, and is made of blocks of hewn stone. Its erection consumed twenty years, and new parts have since been added at different times. Above the entrance are figures of the twelve Apostles and seven deacons in bas-relief, surrounded by angels and cherubim. Its interior is elaborately decorated with the ornaments usual in Armenian places of worship and with inscriptions and many memorial tablets of ancient date.

THE CATHOLICOS.

The organization of the Armenian Church is representative. Of all the clerical officers of the Church the Catholicos ranks highest, the Catholicos at Etchmiadzin being supreme. The present Catholicos is Rt. Rev. Migrditch Khirimian. This great and venerable man of God, who sits to-day upon the patriarchal throne of St. Gregory the Illuminator, is held in the same esteem by the Armenians throughout the world as Gladstone by the English and the Christian world at large. He is universally known among our people as *Hairig*—dear little father. Born at Van in 1820, and educated at the monasteries of Lim and Gdootz upon the islands of Lake Van, his early life was devoted to educational and literary pursuits. In 1854, having taken holy orders, he was appointed superior of Varak Monastery near Van, where he founded a school and set up a printing press—the first, and indeed the last, in that extensive domain. He established a monthly review, a library, and a museum. In 1860, after having traveled in Caucasus two years, he was made a superior in the historic monastery of St. Garabed of Moush. There, too, his extraordinary talents found ample scope in making the sadly neglected and darkened interior of Armenia a center of light and culture. In 1868 he was consecrated bishop, and the following year he was elected Patriarch of Constantinople, to the enthusiastic satisfaction of the Armenians.

From the very beginning of his activities, his stanch patriotism had made him *persona non grata* to the Turkish government. Soon after his installation, upon the first audience with the Sultan, he so ardently and boldly championed the cause of his oppressed flock that he had to resign his office in 1873. Although retiring from the patriarchate, he did not relinquish his patriotism. In 1878, at the head of the Armenian deputation, he pleaded the cause of his oppressed fellow-Christians at the Berlin Congress; and, as a result, the 61st article, a clause looking to the amelioration of the existing condition, was inserted. In the following year we find this saintly man in the district of Van, saving people of all creeds and races from a destructive famine. In 1885, while he was engaged in Armenia in educational work and other enterprises tending to the general welfare of his beloved countrymen, the Sultan became greatly alarmed at his influence and summoned him to Constantinople. While there repeated attempts upon his life were made by the Turkish government, and he was finally banished to Jerusalem, where he was shadowed by the government detectives. On May 17, 1892, to the entire satisfaction of the Armenians everywhere, the noble *Hairig* was unanimously elected as the Supreme Patriarch and Catholicos of all the Armenians; and upon Czar Alexander's sanction of the election he was taken from his exile to Etchmiadzin, and there in the cathedral, with all the pomp and ritual of this ancient Church, he was invested with the mantle of St. Gregory the Illuminator and Nerses the Great.

The author, when in Constantinople in 1889, had the rare privilege of an extended interview with this highest dignitary of the Armenian church and people. He was conducted by the attending clergy of His

RIGHT REV. MIGRDITCH KHIRIMIAN, THE ARMENIAN CATHOLICOS.

Grace into the presence of a man bowed with years and honors, clothed in the usual black gown, with a strong and resolute face, a flowing beard, and a forehead indicative of clear and spontaneous thought. This personage was none other than Khirimian Hairig, by whom the author was cordially received; and the memory of his paternal advice and apostolic blessing will ever linger in his mind as a rare inspiration. When about to depart, the venerable man presented his young countryman with "The Pearl of the Kingdom of Heaven," "The Discourse on the Cross," "Sirac and Samuel," and "The Family of Paradise," original autograph volumes of fervent Christian sentiments which are held as priceless additions to his library.

The executive authority of the Catholicos may be compared to that of the Pope, as he has entire supervision of the general interests and work of the Church throughout the world. His authority, however, is burdened with no dogma of infallibility. After being elected by all the archbishops, he must be confirmed by the Czar of Russia, who guarantees his protection and enforces his decrees. This custom had its origin in 1750, when in the face of persecution our Patriarch appealed to the Czar, and since then our Church has been in a partial sense sheltered by the Russian Church, though not in communion with it. This custom was re-enforced in 1828, when a large portion of Armenia was ceded to Russia, the site of Etchmiadzin itself becoming a part of the Czar's dominions.

ECCLESIASTICAL ORGANIZATION.

There is also a Catholicos at Sis, in the ancient province of Cicilia, and one at Akhtamar, upon the island of Lake Van; and two Patriarchs, one at Constantinople and one at Jerusalem. The Armenian Patriarchate at Constantinople was first established in 1461 by Sultan Mohammed II., who, having captured the city, invited Bishop Hovagnem of Brusa to the office. The function of the Patriarch at Constantinople is more of a political nature, representing the Armenian nation and Church to the authorities. Ecclesiastically, he holds the rank of a bishop, being chosen from a body of one hundred and forty members of the National Assembly, which sits at Constantinople; but his election must be confirmed by the Sultan of Turkey. Next in order are the archbishops and bishops, who are elected to their office by the entire nation and ordained by the Catholicos at Etchmiadzin. Formerly it was the custom to ordain these officers at Cæsarea or Sis, but in the patriarchate of Nerses the Great, who lived 363 A. D., the present practice was inaugurated.

After his ordination a bishop retires to a room in the church for a season of fasting and prayer. During this time he studies the ritual and forms of the Church, and at its conclusion is invested with the power of absolution. The bishops are more highly educated than the priests, being elected from an order known as Vartabets, or doctors of theology. Indeed the Vartabets represent the highest culture of the nation, and to them it is indebted for most of its literature.

The priest, or *derder*, is chosen by the people from

among themselves. As a rule he is a venerable man with a long beard. Celibacy is not compulsory, but a priest cannot rise higher than his order while his wife is living. He performs the marriage ceremony, administers baptism, officiates at funerals, takes charge of the morning services, and looks after the general spiritual welfare of the local church. He receives no salary, but depends on contributions for his support. The Armenian monks are of the order of St. Basil, and live after a much severer rule than those of the Greek Church.

The Armenian Church is apostolic in its teachings, orthodox in its form, episcopal and liberal in its nature. In theology it is Augustinian, adopting the Apostolic, the Nicene and the Athanasian creeds. Both in its doctrinal and ceremonial aspects it has more affinity now to the high Anglican Church than to any other branch of Christianity. It embraces the doctrine of the Trinity, and believes in the incarnated divinity of Christ, separated but blended in perfect harmony in an unapproachable life. It declares that the Holy Spirit is an essence emanating from God, and that it is the source of union between man and God. It believes in the adoration and mediation of saints, but not in the purgatorial penance, though prayer and entreaties are offered for the pardon of departed souls, Contrary to the Greek and Roman churches, it places the Bible in the hands of the people, believing in the potency of the inspired Word for the conviction and salvation of souls. The worship of the Church is liturgical; its liturgy, though ancient and extensive, is yet most beautiful in style and devout in religious sentiment. Every morning at sunrise, and every evening at sunset, the people assemble in the churches, at which time the Scriptures are chanted or read, the sermon being usually preached on Sundays. The ceremonies are always performed in the ancient or classical Armenian, and it is not uncommon for the people to go home before or even during the preaching, because of the lengthy liturgy. The sign of the cross is used at all services. The adoration of pictures of saints and of the cross is believed to be of special efficacy.

There are seven sacraments—baptism, confirmation, the eucharist, penance, ordination, marriage, and extreme unction. The Armenian Church practices a triple immersion of infants, and teaches that by it original sin is washed away, while actual sin requires auricular confession and penance. Confirmation is administered immediately after baptism, the child being anointed with holy oil. The doctrine of transubstantiation is regarded as extremely important, unleavened bread dipped in wine being used in the sacrament. Penance consists in fasting, which occurs every Wednesday and Friday, and also in abstaining from eggs and meat of all kinds. Confession constitutes a necessary preparation for participation in the sacrament of the Lord's Supper. Extreme unction is administered only to the ecclesiastics. There are also many sacred holidays, among which is Christmas, celebrated on the 18th of January; Epiphany on the 6th.

Persecuted by the relentless Saracen, and by the still more murderous Mongol, Tartar, and Turk, Armenians have always held their ground patiently and heroically, and songs of hallelujah they have sung above all strife and conflict. Not with internal controversies, but with the red blood of martyrdom, have they maintained their religion. The historian Gibbon has well said: "Under the rod of oppression the zeal of the Armenians is fervent and intrepid. They have often preferred the crown of martyrdom to the white turban of Mahomet." During the wild storm of massacres that swept over the Armenians from the valley of the Euphrates to the city of Byzantium, many of them had the choice of death or a denial of Christ; and, infused with a fortitude from Heaven, they unhesitatingly chose death. "We cannot deny our Jesus," they said, and the Moslem bayonets pierced them to the heart. Indeed, the countless hosts that thus died the death of hero-martyrs, with the name of the Saviour on their lips, bear an eloquent testimony to the truth that even in this age of materialism and skepticism there are those who "have kept the faith."

Tangible good has resulted from these long centuries of persecution; and particularly has the present crisis drawn our people more closely together, and developed in the faithful an ironclad Christian character which successfully withstands the sensual allurements of Islamism. Thus the Armenian Church has served a double mission, not only teaching religion to the people, but acting as the conservator of the national spirit and unity. Patriotism and a common religion are two important uniting forces of a nation, and of the two religion has proved far more potent in its preserving power, for it is largely due to its influence that the Armenians, even under the Turkish yoke, still preserve

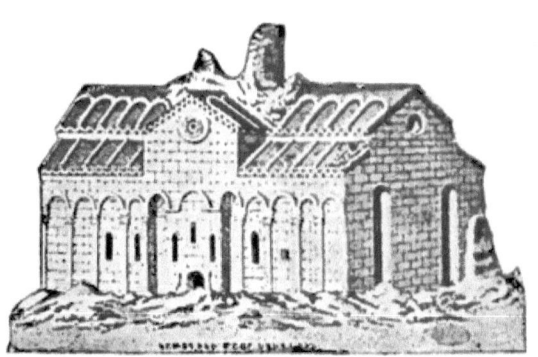

EARLY MONASTERIES AND CHURCHES OF ARMENIA.

their national peculiarities, and are independent in spirit, if not in fact.

That Church has for its corner-stone Christ Jesus, and rests on the firm foundation of the inspired revelation. Indeed, to the truth has been added some superstition, and the religion once so full of spirit and devotion has somewhat lapsed into formalism; and yet one cannot but admire the heroism with which our people have contended for their religion and Church. Armenia ever upholds her torch, which emits its gracious light. The voice of the Apostles, here heard so long ago, has never ceased to inspire our people, and the fire kindled in our souls has never sunk to ashes.

In Armenia the Bible is and always has been in the hands of the people, and our customs and life are permeated with its leavening principles. Thus the obstacles with which foreign missionaries usually have had to contend are not found here. Armenia is destined to a great awakening. Christian missions have flourished and increased here as in no other land.

In conclusion we may well ask: Has the Western World at any time equaled Armenia in its religious loyalty? Does not Occidental Christendom, which to-day enjoys the peace, love, and cordial fellowship of Christianity, owe something to the Oriental pioneer who "fought to win the prize, and sailed through bloody seas"? Let hands be clasped across the wide ocean that separates us; and let Christendom hearken once more to the cry that comes in the night: "Come over and help us."

THE EVANGELICAL CHURCH.

"Nearly everything which has been done for these ancient seats of Christianity by modern Christian nations has been done by American missionaries, whose schools and colleges, planted in various parts of western Asia, have rekindled the flame of knowledge, and stimulated the native Eastern churches to resume the intellectual activity which once distinguished them."—JAMES BRYCE.

THE labor of evangelization among the Armenians has been in its nature fundamentally different from that of most other mission countries.

No heathen idolatry was here with which to contend. No wooden gods and massive temples built by superstition were to be torn down before Christianity could be introduced and a true God preached. The people already worshiped the God of the Christian; the spiritual kingdom needed not a revolution so much as a reformation, and it is with complacency that Armenia can point to one of her own sons as the instigator and founder of the reform movement. We refer to a native priest living near Constantinople, who in the year 1760 put forth a manuscript copy of a book whose every page breathed the spirit of dissatisfaction with the existing state of religious life. Besides speaking in commendatory terms of the great reformer Martin Luther, it pointed out many errors into which the Church had gradually fallen, and urged that a reform of some sort was eminently necessary.

This book, for some reason never printed, wielded a salutary influence in the minds of the people, especially among the higher clergy, many of whom were inspired by it to more or less effective action.

One of the indications of the spiritual lethargy of the times was the extreme rarity of Bibles; and here we take occasion to say that no true and active Christian life is possible without some communion with that stimulus of the soul's higher existence, the Word of God. It was a most healthful sign when an urgent want began to be expressed for more copies of the sacred Book, and it was also a very encouraging expression of the pulse of Christendom when the British and Russian Bible societies, at about the same time, proffered their help in the field white unto harvest. As an outcome of the self-sacrificing interest of these two organizations, in the years 1813, 1815, 1817, and 1823 about twenty thousand copies of the Scriptures were published in our language. The Armenians will ever gratefully remember this timely service. It was soon perceived, however, that much more good would be accomplished were the translations made in modern Armenian rather than in the ancient tongue. The latter the common people were not able to read, and most of the copies published fell, of necessity, into the hands of priests and monks. The modern Armenian is understood by educated and uneducated alike, and the Bible societies referred to did a very wise thing in putting forth another version adapted to the needs of both clergymen and laity, both poor and rich.

The pioneer work in any mission country is the placing in the hands of its people the Word in their own language. It is the foundation for the future edifice, the sowing for the future harvest; and the distribution of the Scriptures at this time was not without its significant fruit in later years, for it has not only produced a higher morality, not merely been the means of spiritual life, but it has also given impetus to mental activity.

We now come to that which is most interesting to those who probably comprise the majority of the readers of this book—the work of the American Board of Foreign Missions. Missionary Levi Parsons met at Jerusalem, in 1821, several Armenians who, according to a custom still in vogue, were on a pilgrimage thither. Becoming interested in them, he proposed the establishment of a mission. They were all pleased with the idea and declared their countrymen would be glad to have one established.

The movement began in Constantinople, and thence gradually it extended to Smyrna, Brusa, Trebizond, Erzrum, Aintab, Marsovan, and so on throughout the Turkish Empire. Constantinople, a description of which will be found in a chapter devoted exclusively to that subject, has over eight hundred thousand inhabitants. The majority are Turks, but the Armenians are next in number, there being over two hundred thousand of our people. In 1831, when Rev. William Goodell, D. D., was called from Malta, where he engaged in missionary work, to this city, about one hundred thousand Armenians were there, offering a very attractive field for effort. This was in June, 1831; but scarcely had he established himself in Pera, one of the suburbs of the city, when a destructive fire necessitated the removal of the mission to a town some few miles up the Bosphorus. Although thus meeting with adversity, the original purpose of the mission was not allowed to suffer, and in the following year we again find Rev. William Goodell in Constantinople, this time accompanied by two more efficient workers, Revs. G. O. Dwight and William G. Schauffler, both Americans. These three men of God were welcomed very cordially by the Patriarch, and suffered no inconvenience that could be prevented. It indeed seemed as though the mission were blessed of God. We will see later on how the Patriarch maintained his first attitude.

In our chapter on the Armenian Church we have described at length its services and forms of worship. It was the policy of the missionaries, from the inauguration of their work, to leave severely alone the outer bulwarks of the Church, for this would only have instigated intense opposition from all quarters. It was thought best to transform first the spiritual, and that being changed, the outer manifestation in material forms and ceremonies would be done away with as a logical result.

That this method was a success was soon seen, and the first fruits of labor were very encouraging. The first year Rev. Dr. Goodell, during a visit, was the means of converting two priests. It is interesting to note that six years afterward, when visiting the same place, sixteen were found who were believed to be earnest converts. In Brusa, too, where a mission had been established, the work was progressing finely. The first converts meant much for the cause, for they were two young teachers in influential positions, having under their tutorship many young people. But, despite all hopes, this tranquillity was not destined to continue long, and opposition very soon began to molest the workers. At Trebizond and at Erzrum, two mission stations of the American Board, outrages were continually perpetrated.

The Patriarch, heretofore so kindly disposed to all mission enterprises, fearing that the movement meant an encroachment upon the National Church, declared himself in word and deed against it. In the year 1837 patriarchal bulls were issued, threatening anathemas against all who should be found guilty of associating with missionaries or reading literature circulated by them. The Patriarch at Constantinople at that time was almost of papal power and influence. He banished a number of Protestants from the capital, imprisoned many, and threatened to exile the missionaries, when the war between the Sultan and Mohammed Ali intervened, attracting the minds of the people to more serious problems. While we sadly lament this action of the Patriarch, we have no doubt as to his conscientiousness. He was, as he thought, protecting his people; for since the State had fallen, the Church remained as the only bulwark of a distinctive nationality, and, if the past was to be taken into account, his fears were not ill-founded. Years before the Roman Church had materially weakened the Armenian Church by proselyting large numbers of her members. Was the present measure, then, injudicious? We believe not.

Let us consider, too, that conservatism is the distinctive characteristic of all Oriental Christians. Ritualism, in vogue for ages, becomes sacred. It cannot be denied that for centuries the conservative ritualism of the Armenian Church was a bulwark of defense against Roman and Greek heresies. The severe animosity existing between the Eastern and Western churches is an apt illustration of the Armenian Church as well. During the siege of Constantinople by the Turks, the union of all Christians against Mohammed was desirable, and to this end the papal legate was to confirm the reunion of Christendom at St. Sophia. Even at this critical moment the fiery protest rose, in unison with Patriarchal Gennadius, from all Grecian lips, "Give us the Sultan's turban rather than the Cardinal's hat." It is easy to imagine, if this was the feeling between cognate churches, what the feelings against a church which is altogether foreign and strange would be. Yet, aside from these considerations, the greatest cause of the Armenian Church's hostility to the evangelical movement was due to the Russian influence, which was by far the dominant factor of the entire situation; and it was, indeed under the influence of St. Petersburg alone that the Armenian Church became for a time a persecuting church.

The nominally Christian Russia is the uncompromising foe of religious liberty, and as such she used all measures in her power to repress the incipient movement. The Russian minister at Constantinople was acting in a double capacity. When Rev. Dr. Cyrus Hamlin's Armenian teacher was about to be banished to Siberia for his affiliation with the evangelical movement, one of the pioneer American missionaries entered a protest. To this protest the Russian minister gave an emphatic answer in the following words, "I want you to understand that my master the Czar will never allow Protestantism to set foot in the Turkish Empire." In the recent agitation the Turkish crusade against the American missionaries was largely due to the pernicious influence of the despotic Czar.

Things slowly came to a crisis; the methods of persecution were many and diverse. Reports of the most absurd nature were circulated everywhere and believed, until the whole Church, with but few exceptions, changed its front to the offensive. Although in the year 1843 the Sultan, urged by the British minister, Sir Stratford Canning, and others, had ordered that no person in the empire should be persecuted for his religious opinions, anathemas and excommunications were repeatedly issued and produced their dire effect upon the minds of the people. With excommunications came social degradation and disgrace; the accursed one was excluded from home and relatives, the bakers were forbidden to sell to him, and he was often confined in prison. The cruelties practiced upon the Christians in the three years following would take volumes to adequately relate. Many were the heroic souls, who, still inspired with zeal, remained steadfast through the storm of conflict. The culmination of it all was the formation in 1846 of the first Armenian Evangelical Church.

However, before we enter into a detailed account of this movement, we propose to present a short account of a factor which all these years had exercised no little power as an auxiliary to the more strictly religious work. Missionaries soon discovered that if the presenting of Christianity were accompanied by educational work, much more tangible good would be accomplished. Accordingly, from almost the very outset, schools were established at nearly every mission station; thus the education of the intellect kept pace with the higher education of the heart. These are the handmaids of civilization.

The school that probably had the most influence in this formative and unsettled epoch was that established at Constantinople in 1827. Indirectly the school had its origin in a farewell letter written by Jonas King, a manuscript copy of which was sent to some influential Armenians in the capital. From this letter the conviction came that reformation was necessary, and the institution referred to was founded with an eminent and learned man, Peshtimaljian, at its head.

We will not speak at length of the valuable services of this school of the mission; suffice it to say that six years later fifteen of its graduates were ordained as priests, one of them, Der Kevork, being immediately placed at the head of another new school in the same city that had just been founded by the Armenians. Had it not been for the earnest work of the missionaries, it is doubtful whether this school would have ever come into existence.

The educational work increased in power and scope; and in the following year, 1834, a high school was located at Pera. Its principal was a very consecrated young man by the name of Hohannes Sahakian, who a short time before had been a student at Constantinople. While there a New Testament had fallen

REV. CYRUS HAMLIN, D. D., LL. D.

into his hands, and as a result he became an earnest Christian and gave some highly valuable assistance in the work of translation at the mission. His companion Senakerim, a teacher in the palace of the Patriarch, was converted about the same time, and also labored in a school for children at one of the stations.

But even the schools received their share of the general persecution, and as a result of the interference of the vicar of the Armenian Patriarch, the High School at Pera was compelled to stop its work. However, the result was not wholly evil, for another was immediately started at Hasskevy by a rich banker, with Sahakian as superintendent and Der Kevork as one of its teachers. Although this school, with an attendance of over six hundred, was recognized by the Armenian Synod and made a national institution, it was done away with the following year because of certain threatenings made by a number of hostile bankers.

The work at Smyrna was significant of a remarkable advance in a country where women were esteemed of little importance. Here a female seminary was opened and, owing to the urgent appeal of an influential citizen, not only repaid the former aid, but the mission soon became self-supporting. The influence of the school, with an attendance of about forty at the outset, cannot be estimated.

Another important educational institution was the seminary at Bebek, a theological school, in which, besides a critical study of the Bible, were taught Latin, Greek, and Hebrew.

As we mentioned before, it was not the object of the missionaries to attack the outworks of the National

Church, nor to found a separate body. From the first they, along with the converted members, objected very seriously to being known by the designation " Protestants," or any other name that would appear as an indication of disunion. However, as persecution became more and more intense, it was apparent that something must be done; and when in 1846 an anathema was issued, formally excommunicating all who adhered to the new faith, nothing was left for the missionaries but to form a separate organization. Accordingly, in the following year a meeting was called at Constantinople, at which the missionaries were present, and, after the reading of a covenant to which all assented, the first Evangelical Armenian Church became a reality, with a due recognition by the Turkish government as a separate religious community. What was intended to be only missionary work in the efforts of re-establishing a purer Christianity in an historic Christian church thus resulted in the organization of a separate religious institution. To whatever causes we may attribute this division, they will not alter the fact that it was a sad and disadvantageous occurrence. This body, at first numbering forty souls, of which three were women, was presided over by one of the former students of the Peshtimaljian school, a man entirely worthy of the trust. The initiatory thus being taken, other churches were almost immediately organized in other parts of the country. In two years there was a very strong church at Aintab, which soon grew to a membership of two hundred and sixty-eight; and others at Trebizond. Erzrum, and Marsovan, which were among the first missionary stations, and also at

Nicomedia and Adabazar. Although the aggregate membership at this time was not over a thousand, it meant much as a beginning.

We must not neglect to speak here of one of the leading benefactors of the new movement, Sir Stratford Canning, through whose untiring efforts concession after concession was made until the Protestant community enjoyed almost the same measure of tolerance as the National Church.

In the treaty of Paris, with the voluntary assent of the Sultan, these rights were incorporated and religious liberty was thus more fully insured. Free schools were organized to the number of thirty-eight, and the work progressed and widened in territory until it was found necessary to divide the field of labor into the four divisions of the present time—the Western Turkey Mission, embracing territorially as its stations Constantinople, Nicomedia, Brusa, Smyrna, Marsovan, Cæsarea, Sivas, and Trebizond; the Central Turkey Mission, lying to the south of the Taurus Mountains and to the west of the Euphrates valley, with Aintab and Marash as its principal stations; the Eastern Turkey Mission, including what lies between these two fields and the Persian and Russian borders, with its stations at Erzrum, Harput, Mardin, Bitlis, and Van; and, lastly, the latest mission in European Turkey. Originally the Central Mission, which was organized in 1856, was known as the Southern Mission, while the Eastern and Western, organized in 1860, were one, with the name of Northern Mission.

As the work progressed it was a source of great satisfaction to see native preachers gradually taking places

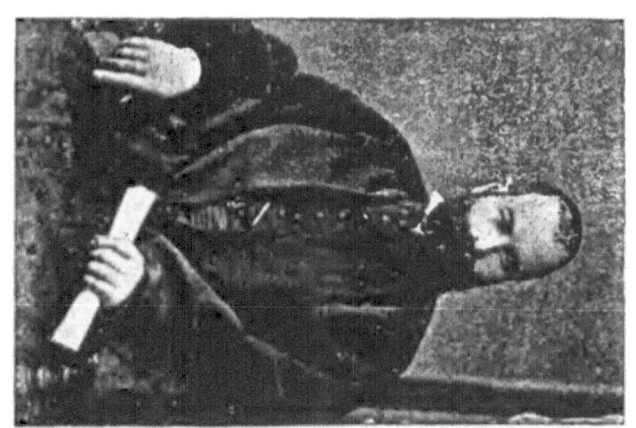

ARMENIAN TEACHERS.

as efficient pastors of the native congregations. They were rarely, if ever, compelled to call on the missionaries for help, as nearly all the churches managed, by sacrifice on the part of both pastor and people, to be self-supporting from the beginning. Revivals became frequent and were the means of the conversion of many. In 1856 occurred a soul-stirring revival in Marsovan, my native city. The theological seminary at Bebek, not far from the capital, experienced a similar awakening, as also did Cæsarea and numbers of smaller cities.

Through the translations of Rev. Messrs. Riggs, Goodell, and Schauffler the work received a new impulse. The former, with the aid of an Armenian, put forth a translation of the Bible in Turko-Armenian, that is, the Turkish language written in Armenian. The latter performed a similar service for the Turks, his translations being in their own language, written in the sacred characters.

Although these translations lent a wonderful impetus to the work, in 1874 it was deemed necessary to appoint a revision committee, who six years later put forth an excellent version, written in both the Armenian and Turkish letters.

It would be useless in a short sketch of this kind to give a detailed account of the individual work of the missionaries, although we fain would do so. We must be satisfied with touching upon the more important events. We cannot pass, however, without some notice of associations and unions that came into being about this time as a result of the constantly increasing number of members of churches.

Organization is necessary to systematic work, and in 1857 the churches at Nicomedia, Adabazar, and Bardizag, formed themselves into what was known as the Bithynian Association.

A much larger and more important organization was the union of the Evangelical Armenian churches of Bithynia, now embracing twelve stations and churches. This was formed in 1864. The next year the Harput Evangelical Union came into existence—a union that did much in the promulgation of the Gospel among the Armenians living in the wild region of the Kurds, some little distance from Diarbekir. Other potent organizations were the Central and Cilician unions, formed at a later date. The results of these various associations were essentially good. Besides putting the churches in closer contact and sympathy with one another they learned to rely more upon themselves, and calls for aid from foreign countries became more and more infrequent.

Nor must it be supposed that the work of evangelization was confined to the Evangelical Church alone, for many members of the old National Church, who were essentially Protestants, effected needed reforms. One of their measures was the publication of a new prayer book, which, though never used to any extent, created much interest and comment. No less encouraging was the fact that in the dissemination of the Scriptures, numbers of copies of the New Testament were disposed of to Mohammedans, which, though undoubtedly bought for mere curiosity, could not fail to have some influence for good.

Within late years, although the growth of the Church

has never been marvelous, its course cannot be said to have been entirely without disturbing influences. Calamity came in the shape of a dire famine, which prevailed in all Asia Minor during the years of 1874 and 1875. At this time thousands wandered about the streets of Marsovan and other cities, begging bread from door to door. A large number died from famine, while some gratefully received aid from the missionaries at Cæsarea and Marsovan. This kindness was not suffered to go unrewarded, for on account of it many opened their hearts to the words of the Gospel. We must especially speak in terms of praise of Rev. Mr. Farnsworth and Rev. C. C. Tracy, who did much to relieve the general suffering.

Among institutions which are instrumental in the missionary work, the Bible House at Constantinople deserves special mention. Thousands of copies of the Scriptures are published here, in modern Armenian as well as in thirty other languages. They are quickly sold and read by people of various nationalities. Besides the Bible, this institution publishes books, tracts, and newspapers of a religious and educational character. While in Constantinople, it always afforded me great pleasure to visit this noble edifice and to enjoy the devotional services conducted there every Lord's Day.

The progress and prosperity of educational work has been, and is, an inspiring fact. We have already alluded to its importance, and have mentioned some of the earliest schools.

The Rev. Dr. Judson Smith, the secretary of the American Board, states that "Education has been a

REV. DR. RIGGS. REV. DR. GOODELL. REV. DR. SCHAUFFLER.
AMERICAN MISSIONARIES TRANSLATING THE BIBLE AT CONSTANTINOPLE.

marked feature of the work in these missions almost from the beginning, and nowhere else in the fields occupied by the board have we to-day so many institutions of a high grade so fully attended." For the great educator Rev. Dr. Cyrus Hamlin my countrymen have a never-dying and the profoundest sense of gratitude. Aside from his educational enterprises, he has been in all his heroic exploits eminently successful.

There are several higher educational institutions at my home, Marsovan, among them being Anatolia College, where I studied. There is also a ladies' seminary and a theological seminary of no little repute. My former teachers, Rev. C. C. Tracy, D. D., and Rev. Geo. F. Herrick, D. D., an eminent Oriental scholar, are the founders and constant inspiration of Anatolia College. We have spoken of the theological school at Bebek; others of a similar nature were founded soon afterward in Marash; there is Central Turkey Female College, and at Scutari the Armenian College for Girls; while Harput is the location of Euphrates College.

Aintab, where missionary work has been exceptionally prosperous, is the site of the College of Central Turkey. But the institution of which Armenians may feel most proud is the well-known Robert College, named after its financial founder, Christopher R. Robert of New York City. This college, located first in Bebek and afterward on the heights of Roumeli Hissar, is one of the best institutions of the kind in the world, being well-equipped with excellent professors and enjoying the patronage of nearly every nationality. It was established in 1863, through the

ANATOLIA COLLEGE.

influence of Rev. Dr. Cyrus Hamlin, an American who has since been its constant inspiration. Though not a missionary institution, yet the prosperity of Christian work among its students has equaled the highest expectations.

Aside from these higher institutions, there are twenty-six high schools for boys; nineteen boarding schools, or seminaries, for girls, with about two thousand students; and three hundred and fifty common schools, containing more than sixteen thousand pupils.

The young men are taking increasing interest in the Church, and a number of Young Men's Christian Associations have been organized. By no means the least blessing is the advancement of woman from her degradation to a plane of culture and refinement, chiefly owing to the liberality of the natives themselves in the cause of female education. What a happy result, that the youth of both sexes share alike the opportunities of culture!

Prospects were never brighter. The number and rolls in the evangelical churches are larger than ever before, and the common-school system is one that promises great results in the advance of civilization.

To this, the largest mission field of the American Board, 700 missionaries have been sent out at a cost exceeding the sum of $6,000,000. Its present property is worth $1,500,000; it has 176 missionaries now in the field, with 878 native trained ministers and assistants. The board has now 125 churches with about 13,000 members and 30,000 adherents, most of which number are Armenians. Indeed, for actual missionary work, our people have been selected as the first fruits of missionary effort because of their ready appreciation of the Bible as the Word of God; and to this very day the work of evangelization in the country has been restricted to Armenians, Greeks, and

PRESIDENT C. C. TRACY AND STUDENTS OF ANATOLIA COLLEGE.

others of ancient Christian churches, while the Turks and all other Mohammedan peoples have ever remained irresponsive and hostile to the light of the gospel. The missionaries from the very start discovered the impossibility of converting them to Christianity.

Encouraged by their success among the Armenians and Greeks, the missionaries were ardently pursuing their work and laying plans for larger usefulness when the storm of Moslem hatred and fanaticism fell upon our land, devastating hamlet and town, city and province. In the afflicted provinces missionary work, as well as all business activity, was at a standstill; and with gloomy apprehension for future labor the missionaries stood at their posts and heroically continued their sacred work, hoping almost against hope for the return of peace and security. These noblest of America's sons and daughters acted in a double capacity: not only did they protect the Word, but at the same time, as a splendid illustration of true Christianity, they reached out to succor the thousands of homeless and destitute Christians of our unhappy land. Herewith let me take occasion to express the everlasting thanks and the heart-felt gratitude of my countrymen for that noble company of Christians in the United States and England, whose hearts being touched by the terrible story of Armenia's woes, sent out material aid in the form of practical sympathy. Such relief has been administered to the best advantage through the American missionaries as well as through the agency of the American Red Cross Association. The Red Cross organization, purely philanthropic in its nature and purport, took the field with its efficient president, Miss Clara Barton, at the head of her corps of trained workers. That such a movement was not in accord with the Sultan's policy of Armenia's extermination was sufficiently apparent at the very outset. The Turkish government hampered and opposed it, and even went so far as to order the missionaries who were dispensing relief out of the country, with a threat that, should they fail to withdraw within three days, serious consequences would follow. Indeed, the European missionaries, in compliance with such demands, abandoned the relief work, while the American missionaries held their ground. Meanwhile this mandate of the Turkish government was so vigorously and firmly opposed by the European powers that the Sultan was obliged promptly to change his attitude upon the subject, and even decided to send troops for the protection of the missionaries. Such an unlooked-for act of the Porte is indeed an entire corroboration of Mr. Gladstone's terse declaration, "The Turk gives heed to nothing but an ultimatum." Nevertheless, in the recent general destruction of life and property, this momentous movement of long prestige, and so largely carried on among the Armenians, has sustained an almost crushing blow at the hands of the Turk. In the whirlwind of butchery and pillage nearly all the mission stations, from the valley of the Euphrates to the Mediterranean, have shared the general calamity of Moslem violence and destruction. True no American missionary has been killed, but many of them have suffered the loss of all their property, have seen their students, converts, and servants slain before their eyes, their flag insulted and trailed in the dust, and they themselves have been compelled to seek a place of shelter. In Harput alone eight of the twelve American buildings within the inclosure were looted and burned, the loss being estimated at one hundred thousand dollars. Many of the occupants were killed, and the missionaries barely escaped with their lives. It must not be supposed that this was simply the attack of a mob; for Turkish mobs are not equipped with artillery. The Harput institution of missionaries was assailed by Turkish soldiers, who trained their field pieces upon the buildings. Such deliberately planned official havoc is more inexcusable when we remember that the Sultan had given specific assurances to the United States that the lives and property of the missionaries should be protected. As yet not a word of apology nor a cent of indemnity has been exacted from the Turkish government. The truth of the matter is that of all the civilized nations the United States has proved the most inactive in protecting the natural rights of its citizens in the Ottoman Empire. On this point Dr. Grace N. Kimball, who has labored for the past few years as a missionary among the Armenian refugees, makes this assertion, "Even the American flag was powerless to shield us; and had it not been for the protection of British consuls, we would have suffered the same fate as the Armenians." That the missionaries have vested rights, property guarantees of protection dating back to 1830, and a generation of work behind the present, no one will deny; yet it is sufficiently evident that American citizens in Turkey have not been protected nor their wrongs redressed.

In the midst of this violence and treachery the late American minister to Constantinople, Mr. Alexander Terrell of Texas, cut a pitiable and shocking figure. His diplomatic incompetence and ignorance of the Eastern situation on the one hand, and his

AMERICAN MISSIONARIES AT MARSOVAN.

weak, faltering, and pusillanimous policy toward the Sultan on the other, made him a most unfit man for such a responsible post at such a critical time. Brave and true as I hold America to be, she should make her "Stars and Stripes" a protection to her people, her best people—the benefactors of my race and, indeed, of humanity. In such a crisis both principle and prudence demand a bold and unflinching course of action. That the Sultan has ever proved a persistent and cruel violator of all his treaty obligations should satisfy common sense that further promises would not be worth the breath that uttered them. He will not yield to reason or entreaty, but he has yielded and will yield to the argument of force. The only sort of argument for which the grim tyrant of the Bosphorus has any respect is that of ironclads and cannon. After the massacres of Syrian Christians by the Turks in 1860, the French citizens having suffered, the French government dispatched a corps of ten thousand men to Syria; and as a result redress was obtained at once. Sixty of the ringleaders were put to death, and the memory of such intervention has given security to Syria and to French citizens ever since. Unless the United States rises above its present lukewarmness and inefficiency in defending its citizens and their interests at the cannon's mouth, as the French did after the massacre in 1860, further and worse outrages will be the result.

For many years Algerian pirates preyed on the commerce of Christian nations in the Mediterranean Sea, and the powers of Europe dared not to raise their arms against them, when in 1815 this young America arose and dealt them such a blow that no more robbers could be seen on the Mediterranean. Would that the old fire of heroism were rekindled to-day in the American breast! I doubt not that, should the United States rise against the Turk, there would not be a nation in Europe but would welcome its intervention as the least dangerous solution of the Turkish question; for this country has no territory to acquire, no balance of power in Europe to break, no prestige to win.

SOCIAL AND HOME LIFE.

> "Home of my childhood! how affection clings
> And hovers round thee with her seraph wings!
> Dearer thy hills, though clad in autumn brown,
> Than fairest summits which the cedars crown."
> —OLIVER WENDELL HOLMES.

AS I turn to this chapter the remembrances of my Oriental home rise before me, hallowed and strengthened by time and absence. Over its shadows and sunshine are thrown gleams of mellow light that bear my lonely soul on the wings of emotion to the far-away land that rocked my cradle. What days of sparkling mirth! what days of saddening gloom! Yet to my longing heart the sunshine and shadows of home are merged in a heavenly radiance.

To you, my reader, I now extend an invitation to walk with me among the scenes of my boyhood. Our people are deeply interested in your bright country and people, and I am sure in turn you would find much to interest you in the manners and customs of our old and romantic land. Our culture and manners, perhaps not always of the highest, are always clean and respectable; our heroism, true; our beliefs, sincere; and our faults are not crimes, but delusions. Were our country and people free from the iron grasp of Turkish aliens, brighter homes and more speedy progress would be ours. And yet, strange as it may seem, the power of

AN ARMENIAN FAMILY—RELATIVES OF THE AUTHOR.

ARMENIAN CHILDREN.

tyranny, with all its stagnation and blight, has practically exerted no influence in marring the holiness of family ties. It is certainly a lasting tribute to the character of the Armenians that, after five centuries of subjection, no social intercourse or intermarriage has been effected with the Turk.

Let us journey, then, through the land of Asia Minor, where the homes of these two peoples, though standing side by side, nevertheless present the widest contrasts in their inner life.

As the morning light first touches the mountain tops, so our glimpses of home life begin with the higher classes. But whether high or low, all have to pass through the same filthy, zigzag streets that run from everywhere to nowhere. So thronged are they with dogs, horses, donkeys, and sometimes with long trains of supercilious camels and buffalo arabas, that you have to challenge everything and elbow every being for the right of way. Above all, a lively time is expected with the famous Turkish dogs when they are contending for a bone. Fortunately, in the portions of the country where the Armenians and Europeans dwell they have somewhat disappeared from the streets. Those you meet are quite respectful to Mohammedan and Christian alike; while the old breed would howl at a Christian, but remain quiet when a Turk passed by. Even the dogs are getting civilized, which is more than can be said of the bipeds of the slums.

Of the defunct dogs we may say the redcoats were their assassins, and loaded walking-sticks, used in the night, the weapons. One English sea-rover vowed he

A CHARACTERISTIC STREET SCENE.

would kill a dog every night when returning to ship from his games. He kept his word and more, for when unlucky at cards he would dispatch two or three curs in ambling down the hill. Dogs became rapidly scarce on his route. At length he took to the narrow side streets, and one night a fellow friendly to dogs—of course a Turk—waylaid the Briton, and with some assistance sent him to his berth a battered specimen of humanity.

Besides the dogs, it is characteristic of Turkish streets to be peopled here and there by a careless, lazy-looking set of vagabonds sunning themselves on the street corners. Next to tramps they are the most absolutely good-for-nothing nuisances on earth, without an excuse for their wandering existence except the fact that they were born. Their motto seems to be, "Grab and eat as much as you can, and whine." They do nothing but hang around anywhere and everywhere, all day and every day. Lucky for them if they can outdo some wandering dog in securing the most shaded corner where they may stretch their lazy bones in peace. Fruit-sellers, Turkish grinders, and *hammals*, or porters, are also to be seen on every hand.

It gives a strange effect to the street scene to see the houses and yards, like castles or picturesque fortifications, surrounded by solid black walls, varying in height from ten to twenty-five feet, with a heavy gate before each house and an iron hammer suspended as a knocker from its center. Most of the residences are two-story houses, built of sun-dried brick around an open courtyard, and plastered within and without. There are few stone buildings and still fewer of wood. Most of the houses have a balcony overlooking a tangled garden, with window ledges abloom with flowers. The roofs are tiled, and the numerous small windows are closely latticed on the outside with a network of iron bars arranged in pairs. As a rule, the residences are very close together, with a space between them of not more than six feet, so that a distant view of the dwellings makes them appear as though erected in a block.

Entering the gate, and passing through the yard, we come to the house. In the courtyard, and in the rear of the building, there are generally gardens, with lofty trees surrounding the house and overshadowing it with their green branches. Sparkling fountains play in the rich sunshine amid flower beds, exquisite in variety and hue; while the air is perfumed with roses and made melodious by the song of the nightingale. These garden spots are found in profusion in my birthplace, the city of Marsovan, and may be seen with no less frequency in most of the cities and villages. Indeed, the whole land is one of bloom and blossom.

As we enter the house we meet with a most cordial reception from the household, for hospitality and kindness to strangers are the first law in the Orient, and are a most pleasing and characteristic feature of Armenian society. The kind words and the eager display of hospitality, each vying with the other in supplying your wants, form a striking scene to an American. Indeed, our people are the most friendly of friends; they enjoy life because they make other people enjoy it. Home is a philanthropic institution with them—so much so that some regret the introduction of Western ideas in the founding of hospitals and orphanages, since custom will not allow a stranger within the gates of an Armenian home to suffer from lack of food or shelter. He is given a seat at the table, and to sup with the master of the house means to lodge with him and to be furnished with slippers and nightrobes. The guest is expected to entertain all callers with some account of himself, his country, its laws, religion, manners, and customs.

Interchange of visits among neighbors and friends is the rule, for the people love to congregate and greatly enjoy meeting together to smoke and talk over their affairs. In Christian homes men and women meet in the reception room; but generally ladies, gentlemen, and children form separate groups and chat on general topics, which vary according to the social position and intelligence of the company. In a Turkish house there are two apartments, the *haremlik* and *selamlik*—the former the ladies' reception room and the latter for gentlemen.

Holidays and long winter evenings are usually devoted to a pleasant and ancient pastime, which is indeed one of the happiest features of Oriental life. The master of the house opens the door of the house and welcomes the guest with numerous expressive gestures of whole-hearted hospitality. In the immediate entrance of the house there is a place where the etiquette of the country requires you to remove your shoes and put on slippers before entering the inner apartments; but hats, like the bonnets of American ladies, are not necessarily taken off. After exchanging graceful salutations, formal civilities, and inquiries after each other's health, the guest is ushered into a cheery court and

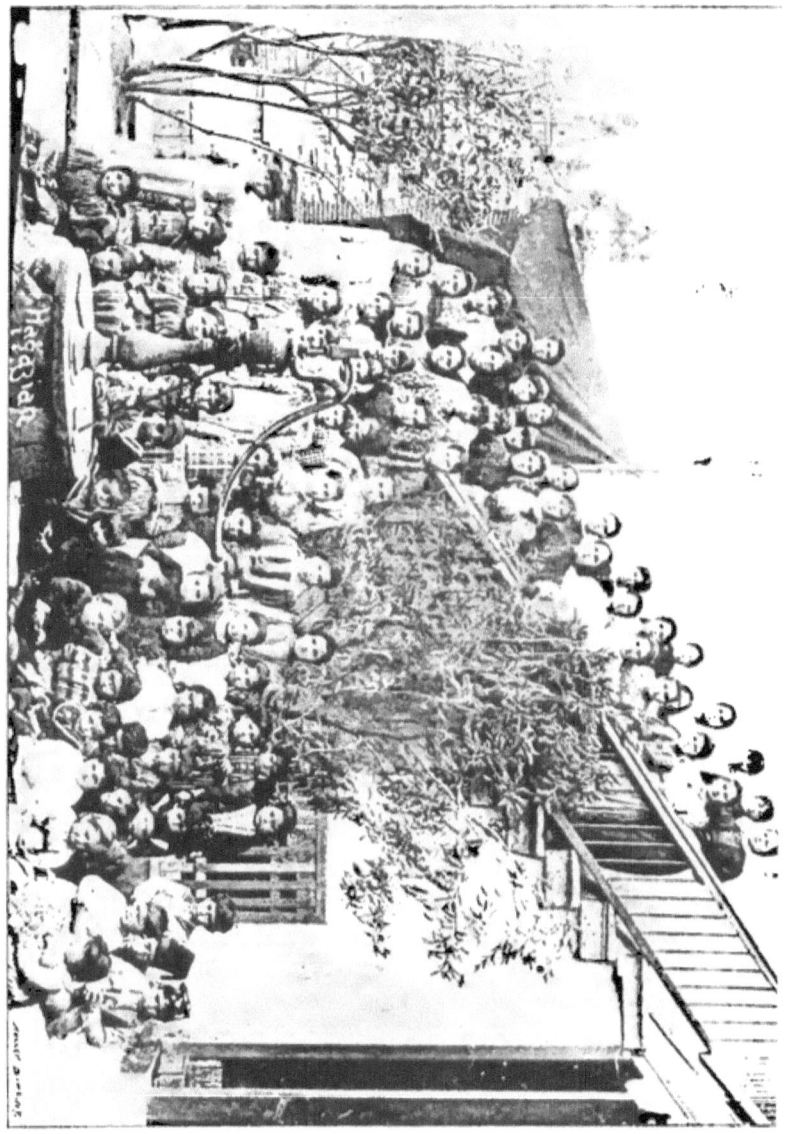

SCHOOLGIRLS IN ARMENIA.

thence into a reception room, where coffee, the universal beverage of the Levant, is served on a silver tray in tiny goblets like egg-cups. The square room which the company occupies is comfortably fitted and arranged with a profusion of divans, embroidered cushions, and mattresses for sitting and reclining, and perhaps a few chairs. The floor is covered with rich Oriental rugs, while curtains and shawls of fine texture hang about the sides and across the ceiling. In the center of the room is placed a stove or a charcoal brazier. The room is lighted with bright lamps, the old-fashioned tallow candle or olive-oil wick having been long abandoned. The lady callers all cluster about the genial hostess, who sits by her babe singing, soft and low, the sweet, simple cradle song; while the men may be engaged in a discussion of current events, though they often exchange remarks with the ladies. The little folks have a lively time by themselves in much the same kind of merry, innocent frolic that is the delight of American boys and girls. Oriental children, too, have their marbles, their skipping-rope, and little toy plows, into which cats and kittens are harnessed in play. Little girls with rosy faces are clustered with their dolls and kittens around the good old grandmother, who tells them riddles and amusing stories, while the white-bearded patriarch, bowed with years, begins to recount anecdotes of his bygone days. The remarks of the venerable man are always interesting, yet they reveal no progress in the lapse of time; for the Oriental life and customs have been preserved with little change from a remote antiquity. The house servant is busied with such functions as arranging the shoes in pairs, that the guests may easily find them when departing. After games and conversation, the company indulge in cigarettes, coffee, sweetmeats, and the bubbling *narghileh*, or flexible rosewater pipe, a smoking apparatus very similar to the *hookah* of Hindostan, which is always filled with Shiraz tobacco. Time wears pleasantly on, and the guests are sure to depart late, nearly always with the satisfaction of having had an enjoyable time.

A gathering like the one described is a great time for story-telling. Many capital anecdotes are current among the people, and nearly all have a moral. Nasr-ed-din-Hodja, a teacher and notorious wag, who is the ideal hero or victim of many Munchausen-like tales, is supposed to live in Bagdad. Several stories concerning him are worth recording in English. For the translation of the following I am indebted to Hon. Samuel S. Cox, the late American Minister to Turkey:

A belated beggar knocked at the Hodja's door.

"What do you want?" he called down from an upper window.

"Come down, good Hodja, and I will tell you," replied the mendicant.

Having descended and opened the front door, the beggar asked for alms.

"Come upstairs," said the Hodja, and the mendicant was taken to the top floor.

"I am sorry, poor man," said the Hodja, "but I have no alms for you."

"Why did you not tell me so at the door?" inquired the beggar angrily.

"Why did you not tell me what you wanted before I came down?" retorted the Hodja.

One day the Hodja was too lazy to preach his usual sermon at the mosque. He simply addressed himself to the congregation, saying:

"Of course you know, O faithful Mussulmans, what I am going to say?"

The congregation cried out with one voice:

"No, Hodja, we do not know."

"Then, if you do not know, I have nothing to say to you," replied the Hodja, and left the pulpit.

Next time he again addressed his congregation, saying:

"Know ye, O faithful Mussulmans, what I am going to say to you?"

Fearing that if, as on the previous time, they said "No," the Hodja would leave them again without a sermon, all cried:

"Yes, Hodja, we do know."

"Then, if you know what I am going to say," quietly remarked the Hodja, "of course, there is no need of my saying it," and he again stepped down from the pulpit, to the consternation of the congregation.

A third time, the Hodja again put his question:

"Know ye, O faithful Mussulmans, what I am going to preach to you?"

The congregation, determined not to be disappointed again, took counsel on the question. Accordingly some of them replied, "No, Hodja, we do not know," while others cried, "Yes, Hodja, we do know."

"Very well, then," said the Hodja, "as there are

TEACHERS AND PUPILS OF AN ARMENIAN SCHOOL.

some of you who do know, and others who do not know what I am going to say, let those who do know tell it to those who do not know," and quickly left the pulpit.

"O Hodja! when will the end of the world come?"

"Ask me something difficult; that is quite easy to answer," is the calm reply. "When my wife dies it will be the end of half the world; when I die it will be the end of the whole world."

The Hodja borrows from a friend a large copper vessel in which to do his washing. A few days afterward the vessel is returned clean, washed and polished. Inside of it is another, but much smaller, copper vessel.

"What is this, Hodja?" asks his friend. "I lend you one vessel and you bring me back two!"

"It is very curious," says the Hodja. "It appears that your vessel, while in my possession, must have given birth to a baby vessel. Of course both belong equally to you."

"Oh, thank you, good Hodja," says the man, laughing, and without more parley agrees to take back both vessels.

Some time after this the Hodja again applies for the loan of the large vessel—"the mother vessel," as he describes it. The demand is readily granted. Before leaving, the Hodja inquires for the health of the "baby vessel." He expresses pleasure at hearing that it is doing extremely well.

A week, then a month, elapses, but no Hodja appears to return the borrowed vessel. The proprietor, at length losing patience, goes himself to obtain it.

"Very sorry," says Hodja, "but your copper vessel is dead."

"Dead, Hodja!" cries the other in surprise; "what do you mean?"

"Just what I say," replies the Hodja, "your vessel is dead."

"Nonsense, Hodja!" says the man—irritated at the Hodja's quiet manner; "how can a copper vessel die?"

"Read up your natural history, my good friend," answers the imperturbable, puffing quietly at his long pipe, "and you will see that everything that gives birth to a child must inevitably succumb in due course to the fate of all mortals. You were willing enough to believe that your vessel had given birth to a 'baby vessel.' I do not see, therefore, why you should now doubt my word as to its being dead."

One night, before retiring, the Hodja said to his wife: "If it rain to-morrow, I shall go to my field; if it does not rain, I shall go to my vineyard."

"Say 'If it please God,' Hodja," suggested his wife.

"Whether it please God or not," replied the Hodja; "I shall go to one or the other."

"Hodja," said his wife, "say 'If it please God.'"

"Nothing of the kind," said the Hodja; "I shall go."

Next day it was not raining, and the Hodja started to go to his vineyard. He did not go far, however, before he was stopped by the king's troopers, who compelled him to work all day in repairing the roads, and it was quite late at night when he was set free. By the time he had arrived at his house everyone was fast asleep. His wife, putting her head out of the window, asked who it was.

"Wife," replied the Hodja, "if it please God, it is I."

A friend calls on the Hodja to borrow his donkey.

"Very sorry," says the Hodja, who does not want to lend the animal, "but the donkey is not here; I have let him out for the day."

Unfortunately, just at that moment the donkey begins to bray loudly, thus giving the direct lie to the Hodja.

"How is this, Hodja?" says his friend. "You say the donkey is away, and here he is braying in the stable."

The Hodja, nothing daunted, replies in a grave manner:

"My dear sir, please do not demean yourself so low as to believe the donkey rather than myself—a fellow-man and a venerable Hodja with a long gray beard."

The Hodja used to teach in the parish school. He had taught his pupils that whenever he happened to sneeze they should all stand up and, clapping their hands together, cry out, "God grant you long life, Hodja!"

This the pupils regularly did whenever the Hodja sneezed.

One day the bucket gets loose and falls into the well of the schoolhouse. As the pupils are afraid to go down into the well to fetch up the bucket, the Hodja undertakes the task. He accordingly strips, and tying a rope to his waist, asks his pupils to lower him

SOCIAL AND HOME LIFE. 171

carefully into the well and pull him up again when he gives the signal. The Hodja goes down, and having caught the bucket, shouts to his pupils to pull him up again, but when they have drawn him nearly out of the well he suddenly sneezes. At this the pupils immediately let go the rope, begin to clap their hands together, and shout down the well, " God grant you long life, Hodja !"

In many Armenian homes pianos and organs are coming into use, but they are not as yet common. Our young men play the flute with exquisite expression. The old-fashioned bagpipe of the Orient is a peculiar instrument, the bag being of sheepskin, with a small mouthpiece, and the instrument being a combination of cowhorn and three reeds with holes in them. The dulcimer is of Oriental origin, and has to some extent taken the place occupied by the pianoforte in an American home. The music of the Orient is characterized by a plaintivenesss quite charming to the ear, which is due to the frequent use of the minor keys.

Now comes our dinner time! Will you not come with us, my reader, for it gives us peculiar delight to have Occidentals accompany us to the table. I assure you our Armenian cuisine is suited to Western palates, and our people well understand that a man's stomach is an easy avenue to his heart. First hands are washed, and then all are seated around the table, with brightly polished brazen plates, neatly folded napkins, and spoons of boxwood and tortoise shell by the side of each. Soup comes first; then *pilav*, a dish resembling porridge; then meat, cooked in various Oriental styles, similar in general to those of France, but lambs are roasted whole in Homeric fashion; then olives, cheese, and fruit. Lastly come *halawah*, or sweetmeats from Smyrna and Scio. After coffee-sipping and chibouk-puffing the ceremony of eating comes to a close. Wines of the rarest vintage are to be found on the table during all the courses.

SUPERSTITIONS.

Among the low and ignorant, where popular education is of a meager sort, superstition has full sway—especially among the Turks. Many of their beliefs are amusing to strangers, though Orientals believe in these absurdities as firmly as they do in religion. For instance, they deem it a serious matter to be the victim of an evil eye, though fortunately a remedy has been invented for every emergency. Garlic and a word from the Koran are antidotes for the evil eye. Dog bread is used as a charm, and blue beads on horses, donkeys, and buffaloes are charms against the malice of the envious and evil-eyed. That nothing must be wasted that can be used as food by dog or fish is a superstition tending to promote economy. You bring bad luck by entering a house with the right foot. The darkness is peopled by creatures of dim, unspeakable shapes from the regions of hell. For astrological calculations some days are unlucky, and even the Sultan himself will postpone an interview if it falls on an unlucky day. Sometimes a long-forgotten and lost grave of a saint suddenly becomes a reputed center of miracles. Someone will tell his neighbors that while crossing the grave of a certain saint his disease at once departed from him; and although no one knew before whether the grave was that of a saint or a devil, or whether the originator of the report is worthy of confidence or not, the story goes with lightning speed, bringing throngs of the sick and infirm from the remotest parts to the magic mound.

When at home I scorned and laughed at such odd spectacles, with a sense of mingled contempt and pity, but since I have seen Americans throng about the fortune-teller, I have had more charity for our Oriental credulity.

EDUCATION.

Compulsory education is unknown in Asia Minor. As a rule, the government renders no assistance to non-Mohammedan schools, so that each nationality has its own schools quite as distinct as its churches. Of the Armenian higher institutions and colleges we have spoken elsewhere.

Mohammedanism teaches that secular education is subordinate to, and dependent upon, religious instruction. Consequently, all the schools of early times were attached to mosques and under the direction of the Ulemas, or religious teachers. Education independent of religious instruction did not begin until 1846. Those who complete the course of study in the higher schools are granted a degree and given a mastership in a primary school, but several years more of training are required of those who wish to be Ulemas and teach in the mosques. The most proficient students are trained

A TURKISH SCHOOL.
(From a painting.)

in the legal profession, for much of Turkish law is founded on the Koran. The revenue for the support of this system of education is derived from the church lands of the empire. National schools are to be found in all the principal cities. In Constantinople, for instance, the Armenians alone have over fifty schools for both sexes, but many of the small villages have none.

The Mohammedan boy's entrance into school, at the age of seven, is a festive occasion. The whole school goes to the home of the lad, who is placed on a richly caparisoned donkey; then, formed in double-file procession, they escort the young student to the schoolhouse, singing songs. This is certainly a beautiful custom, and tends to impress on the minds of the young the importance of this new epoch in life. These Turkish common schools present a very singular scene to a stranger. The pupils are all seated cross-legged on the bare marble pavement in the porch of the mosque, formed in semicircular clusters around the *hodja*, or teacher. The *hodja*, as a rule, is an old man with a white beard, who holds in his hand an extremely long stick, which reaches to all parts of the school. As he is quite old and too lazy to move from his seat in case of mischief among the pupils, he stretches this unmerciful stick over the unruly ones. He is asleep nearly half the time, and, on opening his eyes, he often finds the entire school a playground of wild disorder, but his long stick soon establishes peace and order. I remember many stories of how these young students got even with their patriarchal teacher by anointing his head and whiskers with oil and wax while he was in his usual sleep in the schoolroom, and of what a time he frequently had to find his stolen stick. The strangest feature of these Turkish schools is the manner of studying. All read their lessons aloud in shrill and deafening voices, and recite at the same time in a loud monotone. When I passed by a mosque where these Turkish schools are held I used to cover my ears.

THE BAZAAR.

An Oriental bazaar is a mart of luxury, a vast shop of wonders, a labyrinth of curiosities, which has always been a source of interest and entertainment to those who are strangers to Eastern life; particularly the bazaars of Constantinople, for here all antagonistic races, creeds, and tongues, with every shade of complexion, in an infinite variety of costumes, are mixed and mingled—not as we see them at an international exposition, but in the full swing of real life. The omnipresent Jews are here, with their short stature and long, attenuated countenances. Bronze-colored Arabs, with keen coal-black eyes, in their flowing robes and loose trousers, singularly contrast with the Mongolian negroes, with curly hair and round black faces. The Aryan group is represented by Armenians and by many Europeans of well-bred, dignified carriage and uniformity of dress. Persians in their sheepskin caps; keen-eyed Greeks, cadaverous and proud; with the steady, stalwart sons of America, complete the motley congregation—except, indeed, for its predominant element, the red-faced, indolent Turk. The babel of languages, the rush and crush of carriages, dogs, and busy people do not affect his cool, calm disposition or

AN ADVANCED MOSLEM TEACHER AND HIS PUPILS.

quicken his steps! For Mohammed has said, "To hasten is devilish." His turbaned head is filled with pride that this great *pot-pourri* of commerce and scenic enchantment is, in some sense, his.

Every avenue of the bazaar is appropriated to a particular branch of commerce. There are, for instance, the shoe bazaar; the armory bazaar, where weapons of almost every period and nation are exposed for sale, each occupying a separate avenue or *bezestan*. The avenue of money-changers and bankers, a trade almost entirely monopolized by Armenians, is a glittering scene where jewels, turquoises, pearls, brilliants, and the most costly gems in the world are in store. The embroidery and shawl bazaars present a most gay and novel appearance. There hang Broussa silks, Genoa velvets, European satins, hangings of Tyrian tapestry, shawls from the goats of Thibet, Koran-inscribed Damascus sabers, and rich scarfs from the costly looms of Persia and Mecca, vying with each other in beauty of design and richness of color. These, of all the bazaars, have an air the most Oriental. Let us approach this one midway, where the stuffs seem particularly rich. Ah! the aristocratic tradesman has already a customer—an American, certainly, from the particularly frank and natural bearing; a Westerner, I should say, from the attire—perhaps a Chicagoan. Here are the fifteenth and nineteenth centuries face to face. The Oriental who, of all Orientals, has never emerged from the Middle Ages; the Occidental who, of all his brethren, has his foot most firmly planted on the threshold of a new era. But the matter of selling and buying in the Orient is very different from the rapid business transactions of Western nations. Turkey is not a country of fixed prices, and a person must bargain for everything he intends to purchase. Here one must keep a sharp lookout, both upon the quality of the article he would purchase and the price he shall pay, for, with the Mussulman, to get the best of the bargain has no possible moral significance, and is merely an intellectual feat. The storekeeper asks three or four times more than the real worth of an article; and the buyer is never supposed to pay the prices asked him in the first instance, but he must engage in professional jabber for an unconscionable length of time to develop and settle a bargain. To the merchant selling is a stilted, punctilious ceremony. To the customer buying is a necessary act, to perform with the same freedom and naturalness as eating or breathing.

"How much will you take for that shawl?"

"Does his lordship refer to this delicate Persian fabric?"

Often the Turks apply titles of distinction to American purchasers, knowing only too well how susceptible they are to this subtle form of flattery. If they ever "talk shop" at home, however, I have no doubt they confess it works best with the women.

"I mean that reddish, buck-colored thing—here—this," pulling it down rather unceremoniously.

"Your lordship will observe that it is very delicate."

"I don't think it will wear very well, but what do you ask for it?"

"It has lasted already more than a century. It is

still fresh. The gentleman's great-granddaughter should most certainly wear it."

"Not married, my good friend; it's for a sister, you know. What's the price of it? Is it really a hundred years old?"

Again the wily Turk has touched a weak spot, for the newest of nations has proverbially the greatest fondness for old things.

"Oh, your lordship is from a new country! I have carpets here that have been slept on by ten generations of noble blood. Will the gentleman look at this rug of Bokhara?"

"Not now," says the pertinacious Yankee. "How much is this shawl?"

The Oriental sees that the next move is to name a startling price, so he says indifferently, "Five hundred dollars is a small sum, your lordship."

The Turkish trader guesses your nationality at a glance, and is always ready to deal with you in your own coin, and to talk in its figures.

"Five hundred dollars!" exclaims the Westerner. "You might as well say five thousand."

Oriental dignity is offended at this. The turbaned Turk draws himself up proudly, and turns to arrange his wares, saying quietly, "The gentleman may take the shawl; it is his—a free gift."

Then the Yankee tries his game, too. As if tired of dickering for the shawl, he picks up a Damascus blade lying beneath a pile of tumbled silks.

"What's this?"

"A blade of Damascus."

"Is it a good one?"

THE BAZAAR DE DJERKLER-ALTI IN CONSTANTINOPLE.

BY PER. OF THE CHRISTIAN HERALD, NEW YORK.

"Let his lordship bend the tip and hilt together, so; bend it farther, if you choose. It will never break. Swords of this kind are not made to-day."

"This is old, too, I suppose?"

"The Sultan's signature which you will find on the hilt is that of the great Sultan Saladin, with whom the Franks fought for the tomb of the prophet Jesus."

"But it bends so easily; you couldn't kill a man with it."

"The gentleman may try."

"On myself?" laughing.

"On his humble servant."

These extravagant remarks of the Turks are not jests, but the mere forms of politeness, and expected to be taken seriously.

"What are these marks engraved on this blade?"

"Verses from the Koran, promising reward to those who die in battle fighting for Allah." Then, under his breath, and making a slight salute, "There is no God but God, and Mohammed is his prophet."

The Westerner is by this time convinced that his deflection from the main point is of no avail. The Turk will go on forever about the Damascus blade, apparently quite oblivious of the fact that there has been any talk of buying a Persian shawl. If the buyer wants the shawl he must come back to it himself. He does so in his characteristically abrupt way:

"Well, how much have I got to pay you for this shawl?"

"His lordship is a gentleman. He evidently wants the shawl greatly. I will part with my treasure for four hundred dollars."

"I will give you one hundred dollars."

"The gentleman is jesting. Some Persian woman toiled twenty years, perhaps, to complete this wonderful fabric. Such articles are the work of a lifetime."

The American has taken out his money. He counts out one hundred dollars and says nothing.

"His lordship wouldn't have me the loser on his account. It is eight years now that I have kept this shawl in my shop, waiting for a purchaser wealthy enough and worthy to carry it away. I must have three hundred and fifty dollars."

"We are wasting time, my friend," says the foreigner, who seems somewhat experienced. "You know you will sell this article for much less than that, so why not name your price?"

"Camels brought the delicate fabric over many miles of desert, a long and weary journey. I have given the shawl to the gentleman, but he would not accept it. I think he can easily give me three hundred and fifty dollars for it."

"I am a good ways from home, and if I get rid of all my money how shall I get back?" uneasily; but his countenance does not change its expression nor his manner descend to haste.

"By the beard of the Prophet, it has cost me more. I must be in need of my bread before I could part with so rare an article for such a price. I can show you shawls for that figure, but I could not sell this one for less than three hundred dollars."

From this time on the abatement of price is by smaller and smaller sums, until it goes down a dollar at a time.

"His lordship is indeed in a strange land. The Prophet bids us be kind to strangers. I would sell it to the gentleman for two hundred and seventy-five dollars."

"My friend, I have told you how much I will give. You see it here. I cannot give more."

He holds the money under the glittering black eyes of the trader. He, too, knows his antagonist's weak point. The glistening coin is a temptation. The Oriental fingers are working eagerly. Suffice it to say, the Turk will move steadily downward on his figures, but at his own gait. He cannot be hurried by importunity or indifference, by argument or by direct appeal. Moreover, he will never come quite to his antagonist's figure, but if the Yankee is a good waiter, as this one seems to be, he will doubtless get the article, say for one hundred and fifty dollars; and when this bargain is completed, the Oriental will be ready to spend another tranquil hour in selling him a rug from Smyrna or a scarf from Syria.

THE FAIR SEX.

One of the questions most frequently asked me by the young people of this country is concerning the courtship and marriage of our Eastern youth. The frequency of this question has led me to conclude that this is a favorite theme of young Americans.

Oriental harems have been the basis of many a delusive fiction, for the secluded privacy of their indoor life has thrown about them the charm of mystery. Islamism does not allow women to appear in public

A TURKISH LADY OF RANK.

save when they are closely veiled; and even at their homes their apartments are entirely separated from those to which male callers are admitted. For centuries the women of the harem, isolated from society, had no knowledge of the outside world, except what they saw in their limited field of observation or heard from the men of their own household; for in the mosque and in public conveyances, as well as at home, they are kept in special apartments. What a contrast to the American woman, who is a queen in her own land by right of her independent birth—that heritage of every true-born American citizen! Aishe, Mohammed's wife, is said to have originated the custom of seclusion, and the traditions and customs of centuries do not readily yield to innovation. The Arabic word *harem* is synonomous with the English word "home" and means "secret" or "forbidden."

Turkish women sometimes disregard the law and escape in groups to shady nooks and glens, throw aside their veils, and have a right good time. A Swiss traveler relates that in a narrow lane of Constantinople he met a Mohammedan lady so enrobed that he could see nothing of her but the tips of her fingers and her sparkling black eyes. As she was followed by female slaves, she looked about to see that none of the faithful were in sight, then pulled down her veil, exposing a face of rare beauty, and laughed merrily at the surprise she had given a Christian.

Those alone are esteemed the "upper ten" of the Orient, the model wives of the East, who are confined to their own homes, devoted to the care of their children. Happy indeed is she who finds herself the one wife of an affectionate husband! The practice of polygamy among the Turks, though somewhat exaggerated, nevertheless does exist, and its very existence is an evil in itself and a most crying reproach upon social and public decency and morals. Nothing can be more encouraging than the gradual disappearance of the custom, for whoever has reflected on the subject can understand that there can be no home life worthy of the name except where one woman reigns as queen.

Mohammed tolerated, but did not encourage or enjoy, polygamy. The Koran says, "If ye fear that ye shall not act with equity towards orphans of the female sex, take in marriage of such other women as please you, two, or three, or four, and not more." And yet it appears that what was intended as a favor to unfortunate females proved the source of their undoing; though the Prophet unquestionably had respect for women, as he owed his success largely to one of his wives.

The education of the Turkish women is limited to housekeeping of a respectable order, and to the culinary art, while for accomplishments she learns to dance, sing, and play the dulcimer. It would not do to omit that in their fancy needlework, rugs, drapery, etc., there is much to be admired. Silk scarfs with love ballads from Hafiz or sacred verses from the Koran wrought in golden threads upon them, jewel-sprinkled cushions, richly ornamented robes and garments, indicate expert skill and good taste. In fact, a great many of the furnishings of their homes are the products of household industries.

A MOSLEM SLAVE GIRL OF THE HAREM.

In common with all other women, they have a fondness for fine dress, and their costumes conform to the latest Western styles, as fashions are introduced direct from the French capital. The purely indoor dress is simple, yet rich, in silk, velvet, and satin—an undergarment of light gauze material with full and long sleeves; then bright-colored, baggy trousers of the zouave pattern more or less concealed by the gold-embroidered robe or outer garment, which is open in front and has slits at the sides of the wide, flowing sleeves. Such a costume is certainly a good one from a sanitary point of view. The zouave sleeveless vest is worn whenever weather or taste calls for it, and the head-dress is usually a velvet cap decorated with tinsel and jewelry. The neck and arms are literally loaded with silver and gold bracelets and necklaces set with costly stones. The feet are encased in the dainty Oriental slippers with upturned pointed toes.

The Turkish woman suffers from too rigid restraint, and lives a life of almost absolute stagnation. A Turkish husband may lash his wife with tongue and hands before her children and servants to his heart's content; he may be as profane as he pleases, and may apply to her any number of humiliating or obscene epithets; and to all sorts of ill-treatment from him she must submit without a frown; for if her actions in any way displease him she is in imminent danger of missing paradise. Her prime duty is to court and obtain his good will. A wife whose tongue has made trouble for her husband will have that "useful" appendage lengthened to one hundred and fifty feet at the judgment! With such a weapon, what man would dare to marry one of them! The Prophet himself declares that he would not officiate at the funeral of his own daughter if her husband was displeased with her.

The Armenian woman, though so close a neighbor to the Turkish, radically differs from her in many particulars. Circumstances have been more propitious for her advancement; seclusion, polygamy, or divorce do not darken her present or threaten her future. In youth she shares alike with young men the advantages of culture and education. American customs, as well as American furniture, pianos, and sewing machines, bring comfort to her home. She entertains callers of either sex, but takes particular delight in the company of the wives and daughters of European and American residents. She reads, writes, and dresses in Western fashion, and is thus quite responsive to the evolution of the times. It is not to be denied, however, that, with all her modern accomplishments, she is not permitted so much liberty, neither is she esteemed or valued quite so highly, as the women of America.

It is a pleasure to mention in this connection that the rising generation of the best type of the Turkish ladies is also indicating a slight tendency toward Western progressiveness. The old-fashioned *yeshmak*, which once almost completely hid her features, is being gradually superseded by a thin gauze veil, which is indeed so thin that, like a transparent glass, it shows more clearly the beautiful countenance of the *hanoum* within. Thus, even in the changeless East, the "new woman" is evidently asserting herself. The disregard of even the thin veil by some of the Turkish women went so far as to call forth an *irade* from the Sultan

THE FAIR WOMEN OF THE HAREM.

SULTAN'S HAREM ON THE BOSPHORUS.

commanding them to cover their faces. The Turkish woman, too, is seeking the acquaintance of her European sisters, and is endeavoring to acquire their manners and customs as far as her religion will allow; but the general diffusion of knowledge and freedom, like everything Turkish, is very slow. The ignorance, superstition, and bigotry of the nation are largely the result of uneducated mothers. In the absence of the father on affairs of business during the day, the child is under the direct influence of his mother at home, and every characteristic of her conduct has a molding influence on him. If her words be wise and her conduct refined, the child will thus be molded; and, on the contrary, if she be ignorant and rude, her defects will be reproduced in her child. Thus women largely determine the standard of civilization for their country, and it is altogether the exception for an empty-headed mother to bring up clear-headed, intellectual children. With woman's intellectual, ethical, and spiritual elevation the nation rises; while, with her degradation and humiliation, the nation sinks to the lowest level of civilization. If we traverse the ages covered by history, we shall find these statements fully verified. We need not go to past ages for conviction, but need only compare the old stagnant dullness and darkness of some Asian countries of to-day with bright and prosperous America, whose fair daughters share alike with their brothers the highest education of the land. Happily, the Armenians are realizing the seriousness of this problem more and more, and are accepting the education of woman as a vital part of the Christian faith so generally held by our nation.

Is the Turkish woman responsible for the semi-civilized position she occupies in the world? As has been indicated, she is more than anxious to take her true place among her progressive sisters, but the religious institutions under which she is unfortunately placed create all these inhuman customs—seclusion, polygamy, and blind submission to ill-treatment—which she is under moral bonds to obey. The religious institutions, therefore, are directly accountable for her sad position. Did Mohammed live in the present era, I do not believe he would approve of these customs. The improvement or elevation of the condition of Turkish women, then, is to be only through a reformation of the Mohammedan religion.

While it is a great thing to know other people, it is a greater thing to know ourselves. A man does not know or see himself in a true and impartial light. His character, good or bad, is like a basket on his back. He may be conscious of it, but cannot see it as other people do. What is true of individuals is also true of nations. Does the American woman see herself as she is seen in her exalted position, towering in freedom above her sisters of all other climes? And yet she is not satisfied and asks for the enlargement of her sphere. The womanhood of this land is certainly doing well in its own realm; as to whether woman would accomplish more outside of her dearest kingdom, the home, it is not within the bounds of my Oriental ideas to predict, much less to decide. I am, however, a believer in the good doctrine of Confucius that "True virtue consists in avoiding extremes." Suffrage might and might not benefit womankind; yet in either case should woman enter the turmoil of politics, it is my humble opinion that her sacred mission in the home, where she reigns supreme, would be somewhat neglected and suffer accordingly.

While acknowledging the superior intellectual attainments of the American woman, her grace of manner, her social charms, I contend that her Armenian sister, if not a peer, would at least have become a close rival, had she been privileged to enjoy equal advantages. Within recent years a limited number of higher institutions have been opened to the women of Armenia; and their fair occupants have conclusively proven that it is not brains that they are lacking, but a larger environment and freedom from the old stagnation of Oriental tradition.

COURTSHIP AND MARRIAGE.

The matches and courtships of the Turks are beset with more difficulties than in Western countries. Young Turks do not call on their lady friends and prolong the tale—indeed a tale of long hours among some Americans! Most Turkish girls cannot even write, but many generations of practice have developed a unique system of symbols by which they communicate with young men whose friendship they wish to encourage. A *hanoum*, or young lady, sees in the private grounds of a neighbor over the wall a comely youth whom she admires, and then proceeds to communicate with him. She prepares an affectionate surprise, not with paper and ink, for she cannot write, but she makes up an expressive token of regard with a piece of string,

A TURKISH YOUNG LADY.

delicious fruit, fragrant flowers, and pretty bits of stone, each of which has a meaning. When completed it is tossed over the intervening wall, and, lying near his favorite ramble, is soon found and read like an open book. The thoughts expressed are those in vogue the world over under like impulses, and ere long she will find an answer beneath her window similar to her message. This strange correspondence will continue for a varying period. By and by, if the tokens are indicative of unaltering affection, the young man brings the question of his matrimonial scheme to the consideration of his parents, inspiring them with the same zeal and determination that Patrick Henry displayed in the Continental Congress when he exclaimed, "Give me liberty or give me death!" and the marriage of the young lovers is arranged by mutual agreement of the families. This is but the formal sequel to an affair of the heart, romantic in its inception and natural in its results. With such a system of communicating her thoughts, many a Mohammedan girl does not regret her inability to write; she has no conception of any other use which she could make of the pen.

Doubtless she has been quite willing to submit to those forms of marriage ceremony and wedding festivity which make her almost a dummy for the occasion. To be enveloped and thickly blindfolded in a colored sheet, and placed in a corner for hours, mute and motionless, like the corpse at the Irish wake, is the fate of the Turkish bride, and though the marriage *fêtes* are prolonged for several days and are an occasion of great joy, enlivened by music and dancing, she is not allowed to be exposed to the public gaze. It has always been a wonder to me how such an odd custom was ever inaugurated and allowed to dominate for so many generations; how the happiest occasion of life should be spent in such a state of humiliation!

With the Armenians the usages are quite different, although among the more old-fashioned parents contracts for the marriage of their children are made while they are yet infants, and neither the boy nor the girl has any voice in the matter. In many well-ordered Armenian homes, however, courtship and marriage—indeed, social life in general—follow the *régime* of Western civilization. In the matter of choice for future companionship, both the young woman and the young man have their say in a manner not unlike the free expressions of the independent American youth. Betrothed Armenians, too, have their garden walks, afternoon and evening calls, and social receptions, but to elopement or marriage without the formal sanction of parents seldom do they resort, for the influence of tradition and social customs in the "changeless East" is strong and does not yield to this phase of Western civilization.

As the time for an Armenian marriage approaches, the parents of the bride and groom send out a large number of invitations to their respective friends and relatives. Thus the wedding becomes a picturesque concourse of guests gathered from far and near at the homes of the bride and groom, all dressed in gala attire, with profuse gifts for the bride. The presentation of the gifts, known as the bride's toilet, is an interesting ceremony, always witnessed by the coterie of girl friends whom she has invited. On this occasion the bride's hands sparkle with diamonds, while her finger-tips and palms are dyed with *henna*, a sort of powder made of dried leaves of camphor. It is considered proper for the maidens about her to feel sorrowful, and they indeed vie with one another in their profusion of tears and plaintive songs to the sound of tambourines, expressive of regret for the departure of their friend into a new sphere of life. A similar ceremony is being enacted at the home of the groom, except that all is mirth and hilarity with them. But no matter how many tears custom may cause the young maidens to shed, the wedding is made an occasion of the greatest joy and merriment. Everything puts on a most brilliant appearance, with much gaud and glitter, pomp and pride, everywhere. What a display of rich robes! What a vision of flashing jewels! After much music, dancing, and refreshments, the companions of the groom advance in procession to the home of the bride, who, arrayed in wedding gown and veil, awaits the event of her life, the arrival of the bridegroom—near the midnight hour, if the old custom is followed. Then all the guests, accompanied by the bride and groom, march in gay and noisy procession, with beating drums and sounding pipes and brightly flaring torches, to the church, where a simple yet impressive ceremony is performed in the presence of many witnesses. Upon entering the sacred shrine, the bride and groom in rapt devotion make the sign of the cross three times, with a prayer; then moving toward the altar steps, they take their positions there side by side. The service is chanted in the classical Armenian, and portions bearing on marriage are read from both

AN ARMENIAN MERCHANT AND FAMILY IN MARSOVAN, TURKEY.

the Old and New Testaments. Then the priest, from the altar steps, asks the bridegroom and the bride separately whether they are acceptable to each other. At this time should either person object to the union the objection is accepted, and the marriage stops then and there. Such incidents, however, scarcely ever happen. At the conclusion of the formal acceptance, the couple stand with their foreheads touching, while a cross is held between them as a symbol of the Holy Ghost. A golden cross with a silk cord is fastened by the priest on the forehead of each, and these are not removed until the next morning. Upon the conclusion of the marriage ceremony the happy pair walk hand-in-hand to the threshold of the sanctuary, and thence the bride, supported by the bridesmaids, marches homeward with the usual demonstrations.

At home, while husband and wife are seated side by side, the guests follow in a regular line, kiss the crosses on their foreheads, and make each an offering for the benefit of the officiating clergymen. In the evening there is generally a banquet tendered by the newly married pair to their friends ; and all the next day, sometimes the entire week, the young couple are busy with merry feasting and the congratulations of callers. To make the greatest occasion in life the greatest occasion of jubilee is certainly a beautiful custom worthy of imitation.

The conduct expected of a newly married bride is very singular indeed, and bears a remarkable resemblance to the old-fashioned patriarchal manners of the Armenians. She utters never a word except when alone with her husband, until after the birth of her firstborn, and then she talks on, as a young mother can to her own. After a while she will talk to her mother-in-law; still later, her own mother may again hear her voice, and ere long she will speak in whispers to the young girls of the household. She will not leave the house during the first year of her married life except to go to devotions. Practically her discipline as a bride terminates in six years, but she will never in her lifetime open her lips to a man unless he is related to her. Such exacting devotion is unknown elsewhere. Young girls of the household are allowed to conduct themselves in striking contrast to the young married woman. They chatter freely and cheerfully, and their ruddy faces, full of mirth, are the brightest part of the domestic picture.

The marriage ties so sacredly formed are never broken, for an Armenian once married is married forever, unless death should break the tie. Should a poor match be made, it is certainly unfortunate; but they have to put up with each other without resorting to divorce; for divorce, while so common with the Turk, who dismisses his wife with a brutal "Get out!" without even troubling the court-house officials, is, indeed, an unknown luxury to the Armenian. Should he have an uncongenial companion, he has to endure it with the same kind of patience as he would endure a sore head, which, though he may try to cure, he will hardly cut off, for it is a part of his body.

AN ARMENIAN FAMILY.

CARE OF THE SICK—DISPOSAL OF THE DEAD.

Let us turn our steps for a while from these brilliant nuptial gayeties to solemn scenes of sickness and of death.

In cities medical science and treatment of the sick are very much on the same plan and in much the same condition as among Americans, and within the last quarter of a century expert foreign and native doctors have multiplied. In small villages and hamlets inhabited by Turks, however, the care of the sick is very singular indeed, for professional nursing is unknown and quacks are numerous. The invalid wants to be cured at once—in a few hours. This universal desire to get rid of disease in a hurry makes him willing to try anything and everything that promise immediate victory over his malady. The larger and more repulsive the dose, the better he thinks his chance of recovery, and he cannot understand what good a few drops or a sugar-coated pill can do. They do not apply for a doctor until the sick is about to give up the ghost ; in fact, the practice of medicine is not generally recognized as a distinct profession among ignorant villagers, but the neighbor who has traveled and seen much of the world is supposed to know best what should be done in case of sickness. All educated foreigners, therefore, are considered to be doctors, and are constantly importuned day and night to treat the sick. On account of this ignorance and credulity, quacks have their hands full, and play without mercy on the confidence of their patients. For instance, they give the dust of the earth, plain white paper soaked in water and adminstered in teaspoonful doses, or colored water to be applied in various forms—all of which pleads with mute eloquence for the medical missionary to save the bodies as well as the souls of those who have yet to learn that God's natural laws are as imperative as the moral code. Physicians have found that the naturally vigorous constitutions of the people respond readily to scientific treatment when the quacks can be kept away.

When a man is ill, in order to divert the mind of the sufferer, all his relatives and friends gather around his bed, where they keep up a loud conversation, smoking their long pipes and laughing loudly, while in a corner of the room the young boys play, shout, and fight. By such soothing processes the patient is sometimes lulled to slumber, often the slumber of death! No wonder the graveyards are numerous and thickly populated!

Diseases vary according to locality and the occupations of the people. Smallpox makes sad ravages at times, causing great loss of life, though Pasteur's system of inoculation by virus has long been understood and practiced here. Indeed, mothers have long been known to protect their infants from the virus of serpents and scorpions by giving them the diluted poison in infancy, and such children can be seen handling scorpions with impunity. Thus it would seem that Asia Minor is the cradle of modern applied science, as well as of the human race.

When death knocks at any door, that house is the scene of the wildest demonstrations of grief. Frequently the stillness of the night is so disturbed by the zealous mourners that sleep in the neighborhood is almost impossible. They cry aloud, bewailing their loss, and sometimes they tear their hair and embrace the lifeless body, proclaiming the real or imaginary virtues of the deceased. Burial follows quickly upon death. The body is taken out into the yard, washed, wrapped tidily, and placed in an open bier, which is carried upon the shoulders of friends and neighbors, first to a church where the service for the dead is chanted, then to the cemetery where it is placed in a shallow grave. The cemetery is at a distance from human habitations, and is often one huge common grave. Mohammedans, however, do not bury twice in the same place, which makes their cemeteries much larger than those of Christians. Among them, immediately after death, the body is removed to the porch of the mosque. After the usual noonday worship, the congregation come out to the yard of the mosque and stand devoutly in regular order. As the sonorous voice of the holy man comes from the sacred shrine, the entire congregation take off their shoes, throw them on the ground, and stand erect, putting their hands to their ears. At the second call all the hats are removed, and all the heads are bowed down to the ground in devotion; at the third call, the entire congregation, having put on their shoes and fezes, follow the corpse to the cemetery, where it is taken from the coffin and buried without further ceremony. Then the coffin is taken back to the mosque to await another funeral.

Individual graves of the Armenians often have interesting monuments. Designs indicating the occupation or profession of him who reposes beneath are carved upon them. A blacksmith's grave, for instance, is marked by a hammer and anvil. Those who suffered martyrdom have the fact indicated by a cross. In the Armenian provinces of Asia Minor the oldest gravestones are in the form of crouching rams, the inscriptions being cut on the sides.

Mohammedan memorials are free from the desecrations too commonly seen in Christian cemeteries. The headstone is a large block with inscriptions, and at the foot of the grave is another of almost equal size, the space between being built up with marble slabs to resemble a chest or casket.

In large cities forests of cypress trees cast deep shadows of mourning over the resting place of the dead. In his description of these cemeteries, how graphic are the words of Byron:

> "The place of a thousand tombs
> That shine beneath, while dark above
> The sad but living cypress glooms
> And withers not, though branch and leaf
> Are stamp'd with an eternal grief,
> Like early unrequited love."

THE RURAL DISTRICTS.

If you have leisure and a fondness for rural beauty, let us mount on horseback, or on little donkeys, and seek a village where we may cross the threshold of an old-fashioned Turkish dwelling. On our way to the country, as we ride along, enjoying the glories of the summer, giving and returning the salutations of peace and welcome, we shall find much that is interesting both in objects and scenery. We hear the rippling of

A CARAVAN.

the wayside brook, and the notes of the birds as we pass under the arching trees. Our eyes are greeted by lovely hillsides and dales covered with beds of fragrant wild flowers or by waving fields of grain, stretching away to the horizon. Yonder is the mountain side, dotted with log houses and with the slowly moving caravans of Syrian camels, journeying for many weary *saats*.* In the absence of railroads, these animals perform the duties of locomotives, although at a somewhat slower rate. The peculiar feature about this mighty host of camels is that they are led by a little sleepy donkey. This gives origin to one of our proverbs. When a mighty intellect follows the counsel of an insignificant one, it is said "The camel is following the donkey." Here and there we see large droves of horses, buffaloes, sheep,† and oxen pasturing on the great sweeps of grass. Yonder from the high, wooded hills a host of donkeys with loads of wood on their backs and loud, jingling bells suspended from their necks, braying, kicking, and jumping, are on the road to their respective homes; for each donkey knows where he belongs and needs no direction in finding the place. These little creatures are collected from various homes every morning by a donkey-man, and returned in the evening with a burden of wood for the use of the household. As we approach the cottage

---

* Natives reckon distances by hours (*saats*) and never by miles. Camels move at the rate of twenty-five or thirty miles a day with burden of nine or ten hundred pounds.

† The sheep here, unlike those in America, have broad, heavy tails of pure fat from three to six inches in diameter and from thirteen to fifteen inches in length. In fact, the tail is one-half as heavy as the body of the sheep. The fat of the tail is fried and used as lard.

all the dogs in the village are thoroughly roused by our knocking. Our host is the type of a Turkish patriarch, with a brown, weather-beaten countenance and a venerable beard sweeping down his chest. By common consent he bears the title *kehyah*, or "headman," of the village. Like his fellow villagers, he is simple-minded, good-hearted, honest, but unprogressive, unambitious, and ignorant. He cannot read or write, nor does he know any other literature and history than that of his own immediate ancestors, and he passionately cherishes these legends and traditions of his fathers. He never strives to keep up appearances. He wears a pair of balloon-like trousers of very voluminous folds, and his *abba*, or coat, is a long cloak of sheepskin with the woolly side turned in, which he has worn constantly summer and winter for many years. His head is wrapped in a huge turban as large as a pumpkin. Like neighboring peasants, his life is simple and his wants are few. Many generations have wrought little or no change in his modes and manners. He scorns all modern improvements, and regards them with much suspicion and prejudice. His bigotry and ignorance render him an easy victim to superstition; and, consequently, any Western farming machinery, and any advanced movement that is beyond his comprehension, he pronounces-" devilish," and has nothing to do with it.

Rev. Dr. Cyrus Hamlin, ex-President of Robert College, says the Turks ascribe mechanical invention to Satan, the "stoned devil," against whom they pray five times a day. "I have myself," he says, "for some supposed mechanical ability, been seriously introduced by one Ottoman to another as 'the most Satanic man in the empire.'" Our Turk admits no innovation, as he never pretends or attempts any scheme which was not thought of and followed by his fathers; and thus life flows on in the old channels. He is the head of a great family, grouped together on the mountain side, with its green, sloping pastures, and lives with his flocks and numerous children. An ample roof shelters the nearly threescore members of the family for generations under a single roof, without knowledge or care for the world outside their little village! The glories of great cities, the pomp of pashas and royal dignitaries, are to them like a distant tradition. Yet they are comfortable, happy, and contented in their little round of duties and pleasures, and are blessed with an easygoing temperament. The young man rises with the sun in the morning, and with his flocks wanders over green mountains and hills, by shady groves and still waters, singing cheerfully his native ballads through the woods, or playing his sweet-toned flute. He returns home late, as the waning moon feebly lights up the exquisite landscape. He joins the family dance by the blaze of the evening fire, while the old women weave cotton and yarn, or are occupied in making various articles for domestic use.

The house is built in a picturesque locality by the old *kehyah*, who is the architect and carpenter as well as the government agent of the village. Logs are brought down from the near forest. Bricks are made of mud and straw, and are molded in various sizes and shapes, then put into open fields to dry. In a few days they become sufficiently solid for building a substantial house. The earth which is dug out is banked against the sides of the house, and the rear of the structure is entirely imbedded in the hillside. Light enters through the oiled paper windows in the flat roof, or, when windows are altogether discarded, the occupants are content with what light penetrates down from the low chimney, which is not higher than the roof.

The abodes of the Turkish farmers are more like beehives than human dwellings. They are really huts, mainly one-story, barn and house being built under one roof; and the occupants utilize the warmth of cows and horses in the winter to keep themselves warm. A central oven fills the house with smoke, which finally finds its way out through one of the openings in the roof. Such an abode old Diogenes himself would have coveted. In the summer the stork builds her nest on the broad-topped chimney and raises her brood quite undisturbed. At night the room is illuminated by a feeble, flickering olive-oil wick. A brazier of charcoal is placed in the center of the room and, like the flame of the vestal virgins, is seldom allowed to go out. It serves a double purpose, as a heater and as a cook stove. There are no tables, no chairs, no books, no ornamental decorations, but here and there are spread divans and *minders*, or cushions, with drapery of Kurdish stuffs, upon which the occupants stretch themselves in cross-legged carelessness.

One, or perhaps two, large rooms suffice for sleeping, cooking, eating, and lounging. With such rude belongings, the *kehyah* never seems to think anything is lacking. On the wall, if we charitably term it so, or rather on the partial partition, that separates the living apartments from the vast stable, are saddles, bridles, guns, and the entire paraphernalia of the field and chase. The equine favorites are nearest the family; for, as with all Orientals and some Occidentals, the horse ranks highest in esteem as a domestic animal. Farther on are donkeys, buffaloes, cows, and sheep, with chickens scattered between them.

As we step into the house we are received with a profusion of salaams. We at once find ourselves in the midst of a large Turkish family,—grandfathers, fathers, uncles, brothers, cousins, and numerous children,—all assembled in a large room, dressed in gay and odd colors, sitting cross-legged around the bright, blazing fire and warming their lazy bones. But we fail to see in the great gathering any women, except the old grandmother, the senior wife of the *kehyah*, who is curiously dressed, or rather enveloped, in a woolen garment from head to foot, and sits in a dark corner. The young Turks here must surely have some wives; in such a large family, doubtless there must be some young girls, too; but where are they? All out of sight! As their religion does not allow women to appear in the presence of men, no matter how intimately acquainted, they are all driven into seclusion—a very bad custom, indeed! The more religious a Moslem the more rigidly the privacy of women is enforced, and, as a rule, the country people in this neighborhood are the most zealous of religious fanatics. I sometimes think if one of these over-pious Mohammedan Turks should chance to drop into an American city, and should see the young sons and daughters of America walking arm in arm in the

ON THE ROAD IN TURKEY.
(*From a painting.*)

full swing of social liberty, he would be shocked to death.

At the side opposite the darkest chimney corner, where the grandmother is, sits the old *kehyah*, stretching his feet out and smoking, with Mussulman gravity, his pipe, which is so extremely long that it extends from the corner to the center of the room. In the course of our conversation the old man remarks concerning his residence that his great-great-great-great—that "*great*," however, goes about half a mile—grandfather was born and died on the same spot where he now lives; and that he is about seventy-five years of age, but never has been a dozen *saats*' journey from his home. This is the case with many a Turkish peasant; many, indeed, never set foot outside their farms. No progress is ever made in this pastoral life. Through his own inclination, and the policy of his rulers, the Turk has remained isolated through the ages from the blessings of civilization; and neither European influence nor missionaries have managed to make any ingress to speak of.

As we chat with our host our talk is interrupted by the lusty shouting and fighting of the young boys. Then he is obliged to go out and give them a scolding. Before his return he is called to another part of the house to quell a still louder tumult, for ten or fifteen dogs are having a lively concert of howling and barking. On his return let us ask him why he doesn't kill those useless brutes and get rid of them once for all. He will answer, "It is a great sin against Allah, and a violation of our laws." So numerous are dogs, especially in the country, that when a Turk was once asked the population of the village, he replied, "About one hundred and sixty dogs and one hundred and twenty people."

When dinner-time comes, all the males of the house return from the field, wash their hands and faces, and sit cross-legged on the floor in a circle around the *sufra*, or low table. There are spoons, but no knives or forks. In the center is placed an immense bowl of hot soup. When ready for the fray, the *kehyah* gives them the signal to commence, and immediately all the spoons enter the bowl. The soup is followed with a dish of meat. Each rolls up his long, flowing sleeves, and with bare fingers and unbounded appetite separates the flesh from the bones. Then comes the unfailing accompaniment, *yoghurt*, or coagulated buttermilk, a highly prized species of refreshment. After a succession of dishes, the meal is ended with washing hands.

The *kehyah* is the greatest scientific authority in the neighborhood, for the fact that he is the oldest dignitary of the village naturally makes him the authority on all questions of importance. One night the conversation of the family was interrupted by a bright flash of lightning, accompanied by heavy thunder. One of the children of the household asked the "grandfather" the cause of the bright light and the great noise; then the wise old patriarch grasped his sweeping beard and, in a dignified tone, gave this explanation :

"Up in the clouds," said he, "our prophet Mohammed and Christ went into business together, the profits to be divided equally. One night when Christ was deep asleep Mohammed stole all the profits and left the place. In the morning Christ discovered the treachery of Mohammed and pursued him in his golden chariot, and so the noise of the pursuer and the rumble of the chariots are what make the thunder. The lightning is the bullets of fire which Christ shot at his treacherous partner. At length poor Mohammed, finding escape in mid air impossible, suddenly plunged into a deep body of great water, where he was quickly followed by Christ, and the terrible force of their conflict caused the waters to splash and pour down upon the earth, thus causing the rain."

These stories are handed down from generation to generation, and each "remarkable" son inherits the traditional knowledge of his great-great-grandfather. The odd part of it all is that he is absolutely sure of the accuracy of his knowledge, and has no ability to discriminate between reality and fiction, fact and fancy. The idea of the word science does not seem to have entered his head; to talk to him of science is like talking to a blind man of colors. The primary step to any sort of attainment is the consciousness of deficiency and ignorance. He who does not know that he does not know will never know any more than the nothing he does know. How sad to see, in such an age of enlightenment, midnight darkness settled down upon so many people!

Now let us watch how the *kehyah* works in the field. He has no set time to commence his harvest; he takes his time, as there is not much fear of rain during the harvest season. As soon as the stalks of the crops are yellow, or sufficiently matured, they are cut by hand with scythes and are stacked up in piles in the open field. In due season, the piles are all removed from the various quarters to the village threshing-floor in large *arabahs*, or carts, drawn by buffaloes and heifers. The threshing-floor is a hard and smooth circular piece of ground, from fifty to eighty feet in diameter, upon which the stalks are strewn. Then the threshing machine, a sort of sled, with a woman or boy standing on it, is drawn around on the hard earthen floor by oxen. This threshing implement is made of a hard piece of wood, and set on the under side with sharp, flinty stones like Indian arrow-heads. It grinds the straw into fine chaff, and sifts out the grain. At the evening breeze, the threshed grain is thrown into the air with a light shovel, and thus the broken straw is blown on one side, leaving the wheat on the ground for the granaries. The chaff is also gathered and stored away for the purpose of feeding the cattle during the winter.

The farmer's son does not migrate to towns in search of better employment, but stays where he is born, by his father's cattle, possessed only of what the cravings of nature require, and is immovable in his peasant instincts as well as in beliefs, ideas, and usages. For his dull and unenterprising character and his perpetual poverty, the Turkish government is to a large extent responsible. The system of levying a tithe of all produce, and the additional custom dues for the exportation of products from one province to another, leave no inducement to the outraged farmer to grow more than is required to keep soul and body together, and his family is thus reduced to the condition of a stolid and unprogressive peasantry. Governmental exactions, wrung by dishonest officials from the hard-toiling farmers, are another evidence of Turkish degeneration and decay. Indeed, of all nations, the Turkish government is the last to realize the relation of town and farm;

A TURKISH PLOW AND PLOWMAN.

that the physical health, vigor, and, indeed the progressiveness of a people, in no little measure depend on the nutritive quality of its flour, meat, and vegetables, and that the better the farmer the better will be the quality of his produce, and the higher the prices from his customers in the city. When we add to this trait of stupidity the crude and primitive system of agriculture, which we have elsewhere described, we cannot wonder that the name of the Turk has ever been a synonym of decay and poverty.

In rural districts, such as the one described, the old patriarchal administrative system is still in vogue, where, within the crude and primitive log-house, by the hearth, sits the venerable *kehyah*, whose every word is law to those within. He is, as indicated, the agent for his community in all transactions with the government. In the consideration of important affairs of general interest he meets with the elders of neighboring hamlets; and, acting as a committee, they form the commune —a most striking illustration of the essential democracy of Oriental society with the patriarchal system intact. In the high regard for family rights it is superior to the Greek democracy. Under a fostering dominant power, no reason can be given why it should not continue to the end of time as it has continued from the beginning. In times of adversity it is a bulwark against anarchy and confusion. This system is a perpetual monument to the sanctity of God's first human institution—the family. Indeed, all law originates in the family relation. All attempts to supplant it by military despotism, communism, or celibate asceticism have been failures. The patriarchal system was the application of the family idea to the tribal relation. Recognition of the essential independence of tribes, subject to treaty obligations and payment of taxes, is the key to the permanence of Oriental institutions. This system, free from man's abuses, has never been improved upon, and never will be.

THE TURKS.

"Asia Minor is the recruiting ground of the Turk, and is still almost untouched by the invader."—STANLEY LANE-POOLE.

THE early history of the Turks, if the accounts which we have of them can indeed be called history, is a commingling of war, romance, wandering conquests, and the glory of Eastern courts. For the poet, here are themes strange and untried. For the romancer, there is no dearth of fact as rich as fancy. The political economist here finds his theories in the framework of the material; and the historian, for his portion, contrary to the common parlance, comes last and least. The name and race at their birth are in the swaddling of mystery and myth. Near the central part of Asia, twenty-two centuries ago, we find a people spasmodically nomadic, composed of several kindred tribes, indiscriminately known by the general term Turks. They are of the same origin as those nomadic tribes, the Mongols, Tartars, Calmucks, and Kirgheez. The Chinese, dwelling some distance to the eastward, designated them by the name Hiongnu or, more literally, Tu-kin. Whether or no the modern "Turk" is a corruption of the Chinese appellation, we are unable to say. We do know, however, from evidences that exist even at the present day, that this people, warlike and aggressive, overran Asia, even venturing as far north as the Lena and as far west as the Black Sea.

The Chinese, who had long before held them in subjection, proved troublesome neighbors; and for three centuries constant war was waged between the two powers. The natural outcome of this was that the nation was split into a northern and a southern empire. Among the rich mountains of the Altai were the lands of the northern tribes. They were not destined to remain there long, for the southern Turks, uniting with their former enemies, compelled them to move westward. This was the first migration. These southern people, in turn, were forced by the Mongols and Tungusians to disperse.

The second great movement is known as the second westward migration, and its offshoots may still be found in both Asia and Europe.

As is the case with all movements truly great, the people who were destined to rule the Turkish Empire were humble in their beginnings. Looking back over the centuries, a little time after the two migrations mentioned, we find among the golden mountains of Altai a people slaves to the great Khan of the Geougen. This slavery, in the light of other events, must be considered not a misfortune but a blessing, for it proved a most excellent school for future conquest. Slavery is only a part of the early history of the race, but ignorance has ever characterized it. By employing these Turkish people in the manufacturing of arms the masters were achieving their own downfall, for the former became so skillful in their use that they soon severed their bonds, and established an empire under their spirited leader Bertezema.

Much more than the allotted limits of this book would be required to portray, in its true glory, the grandeur of this early empire. We will simply state that this was an age of luxury and barbaric splendor, golden in fact and in figure. From the accounts of that early period, in which legend and history are mingled, we can obtain but a faint conception of prevailing conditions and manners. It is obvious, however, that there were no fixed habitations, but, as has been indicated, men preferred a nomadic life in valleys and mountains; hunting and warlike exercises being their cherished occupations. This wandering life was so strongly developed into a national characteristic that even to-day we find the Turks chiefly engaged in pastoral and agricultural pursuits, while their neighbors, the Armenians, are largely devoted to commerce.

The early home of the Turks,—Turkistan,—or central Asia, was known among the Persians as Turan, the "country of darkness"; and the inhabitants as Turanians, "sons," or "people, of darkness." Their religion, prior to Mohammedanism, was made up of their ancestral traditions and the doctrines of Zoroaster. They had their priests and worshiped fire, earth, and water. The laws and regulations were communicated to the masses by the chiefs of the tribes. In the middle of the seventh century, however, arose a force that was to have much to do in molding the destiny of more than one nation. The religion of Mohammed, coming out from the Arabian deserts, spread, through the zeal of his followers, with lightning rapidity, north, south, east, and west, until many Turkish tribes, converted from Zoroastrianism and kindred religions, accepted the

Islam faith, which proved to be a great unifying power. In following the fortunes of the people we are considering, it is well to notice the influence of this great movement upon their national ideas and policy. One of the immediate effects was that, instead of becoming peaceful, as might have been expected, the Turks coupled zeal for conquest with such religious fanaticism that every war became a crusade.

The Seljuks were the first Turkish tribe to gain a place in history. They emigrated to Khorassan, under the leadership of Seljuk, from whom they take their name. Here, in a Persian province, they founded an independent sovereignty. The able princes Togrul Bey, Alp Arslan, and Malek Shah extended their empire at the expense of the weak Saracen Caliphate and the shrunken Byzantine Empire. Nowhere in Asia was such a succession of able leaders ever known. The heroic age of the Seljukian Turks corresponds with the Norman age in England. Persia, Armenia, Syria, the greater part of Asia Minor, and the region from the Oxus to the Jaxartes were conquered by them. Their greatest prosperity was under Malek Shah (1072-92), who extended his empire from the Caspian to the Mediterranean, from Khorassan to the Bosphorus. Aside from conquest, agriculture was fostered; public works, such as canals, constructed; and learning was patronized. Their astronomers approximated closely to the accuracy of the Gregorian calendar in reckoning time. In religious zeal they were the most intolerant of all the Turks, and provoked the Crusades. Upon the death of Malek Shah, his realm was divided by his sons into three small kingdoms, which division, and the incompetence of the rulers, made easy the advance of the Mongol hordes under Zenghis Khan. This invasion, in turn, gave place to still another incursion by a tribe of Turks who were destined to found the Ottoman dynasty of the present day.

The political career of the Ottoman Turks commences in the thirteenth century, when a band of fifty thousand nomads, driven out from central Asia by the Mongols, under the hereditary leadership of Suleyman Shah, penetrated *via* Persia into Armenia.

One of the chiefs, Erthogrul by name, while wandering upon the plains of Cappadocia, aided Ala-ud-Din, the Seljuk Sultan, in his war against the Mongols. At the end of a successful contest, Erthogrul was rewarded by the grateful Sultan with small tracts of land in Byzantine provinces as a home for his people. This event gave prestige to the present line of sovereigns of the Turkish empire in western Asia, and serves as the connecting link between the legendary and verified history of this notable Turanian family.

Erthogrul was yet alive when his son Othman, or Osman, the founder of the present dynasty, came forth in the annals of Turkish history, in fanciful vision surrounded with miraculous revelations and marvelous circumstances of birth. His sword is still worn by sovereigns at their coronation ; and from him the native surname Osmanli, and the European corruption Ottoman, have been derived. Modern Turks prefer and take pride in the term Osmanli or Ottoman, while the name "Turk" they consider a disparagement and an insult ; yet all Turks are not Ottomans.

During the famous administration of Othman his

SOME OF THE SULTANS OF TURKEY.

followers spread themselves on the Byzantine frontier, occupying the cities of Eski-Shehr and Kara-Hissar. The Seljuks, as fast as they were subdued, fused with the Ottomans. And so did great numbers of Christians, in the conquered states of Europe. As the two essential prerogatives of an Eastern sovereign, Othman coined money and caused public prayers to be read in his own name (1301). He introduced the absolute ownership of land among his people. After a firm establishment of his power, Othman waged war against his old adversaries, the Mongol hordes, and drove them out of Kara-Hissar. It is alleged that he was of such a just and generous character that the subjects of the East Roman emperor fled to his protection; and it is commonly said that this wise and good man ruled after the former's death. Othman died in 1326, having a short time before fixed his capital at Brusa.

Othman's younger son, Orchan, began his reign with such unusual attainments of imperial wisdom and tact that he even surpassed his father's bright achievements. As the first act of his reign he made himself independent of the weak Seljuk Sultan, and then he mastered a considerable portion of Asia Minor; for the mutual jealousies, and the religious and political demoralization of the provinces of the empire, had made them easy victims to conquest. His reign marked the creation of a most vital military organization, that of the standing army. This new system came a century before the reign of Charles VII. of France, who is considered by the European historians of the Middle Ages the originator of that policy.

His celebrated guards were known by the name *yeni-cheri*, or janizaries, "new troops." Corps of *spahis*, or regular cavalry, were also organized. He married the daughter of the Emperor Cantacuzenus. As a potent advocate of science, art, and religion, he promoted the cause of public instruction, endowing the state with various educational and religious institutions, and was greatly esteemed by men of learning, who were admitted to his councils. His capital, Brusa, was made a center of light. Considering the age in which he lived, he should be placed among the most illustrious of Turkish sovereigns, as a competent leader, prompt executor, and wise legislator. During his administration the first invasion and settlement of the Turks in Europe took place, and the Crescent was planted across the Hellespont.

Orchan died in 1359, and his second son, Murad, or Amurath, inherited both the crown and the military genius of his father. He strengthened his military corps, the janizaries, by recruiting it from youthful Christian captives, and dedicated them to the service of the court and army. The number and power of the janizaries were greatly augmented under succeeding sovereigns, and the greatest of Turkish conquests were achieved by them. Thus, the bone and sinew of the Ottoman troops—indeed, very often the greatest men of the Turkish Empire, while at the height of its splendor—were of Christian blood. While such a system of human tribute has served, in subsequent years, as one of the greatest sources of Ottoman strength, it was, on the other hand, an oppression most unbearable for Christian parents, from whose bosoms their infants were wrested and forced into the service of their oppressors. All attempts of unfortunate Christian parents to elude such a domestic desolation were of no avail. This system once in vogue, it was destined to continue for more than three hundred years; and lads thus sundered from the sacred bosom of parental affection reached the colossal number of five hundred thousand, according to Von Hammer's estimate.

Under Murad's administration the Byzantine Empire was so stripped that there was nothing left but a few adjoining lands around Constantinople, and some outlying possessions in Greece and Macedonia. In 1365 he captured Adrianople and made it his European capital. His last famous contest, against the combined forces of Servia, Hungary, Bosnia, Wallachia, and Albania, was the famous battle of Kossova, in which the Sultan gained the victory with the sacrifice of his life.

Bayazid, the Yildirim or "Thunderbolt," the son of Murad, was the first Ottoman ruler to assume the title of Sultan. He extended his conquests east and west. He besieged Constantinople for years, and the emperor was compelled to recognize his authority by paying an annual tribute. While Bayazid was engaged in the East, the King of Hungary, taking advantage of his absence, with a large army of European knights, besieged Nicopolis. The "Thunderbolt," arrived, however, with his characteristic speed, and overwhelmed the besiegers, and, as a result of the contest, Bulgaria became a direct Ottoman province, while Wallachia became tributary. But Bayazid's brilliant

TURKISH SOLDIERS OF THE OLD MILITARY SYSTEM—JANIZARIES.

career of European conquest was not destined to last long, for, while he was under the very walls of Constantinople, he had to hasten back to meet the Mongol Tartars, who, under the leadership of wild Tamerlane, the Napoleon of Asia, after causing serious destruction in Armenia, had penetrated into the Ottoman Empire. Near Angora the two determined hosts stood face to face in a furious battle (1402), in which Bayazid met his fate; his country was conquered; and he himself was carried into captivity, where he died. The frightful defeat of Bayazid, and the consequent eleven years' interregnum, threatened the very existence of the Ottoman Empire; yet, in the middle of the same century, it became more strong and compact than before.

It is needless herein to follow the administration of successive sovereigns. The sword of Othman descended, in the regular line of succession, through many generations, in the grasp of conquering Sultans. The brightest victory of the Turks was the capture of Constantinople, the capital of the Byzantine Empire. This imperial city of New Rome was the jewel that all the Sultans most coveted, yet the honor of its conquest was reserved for Mohammed II., a man of signal bravery, who stormed the city and victoriously entered within its walls, in the year 1453. Early in the sixteenth century, through the conquest of Syria and Egypt, Sultan Selim the Inflexible received from the Sherif of Mecca the keys of the Kaaba, and Mohammed XII., last representative of the Abbasside Caliphs, who reigned a purely spiritual prince at Cairo, had to surrender to Selim the right of succession to the Prophet and the distinctive ensigns of the caliphate—the standard, the sword, and the mantle of Mohammed.

Selim was succeeded by Suleyman the Magnificent. The reign of this great Sultan (from 1520 to 1566), which was the longest of any of the Ottoman sovereigns', was the high-water mark of the Ottoman power. He threatened to subjugate all Christendom. City after city had heard the clash of the Mussulman's arms and had been compelled to bow before his onward march. Having dealt a crushing blow to a greater part of Hungary, to the great alarm of entire Europe, Suleyman had besieged Vienna itself. However, soon after, the planting of the red flag before the walls of the Austrian capital marked the western limit of the Ottoman advance, for the Turk did not take the city, and farther into Europe the Crescent never found its way.

At this time the Turkish Empire was the mightiest power in the world. Its possessions included all the Asiatic, European, and African countries situated on the Mediterranean, except France, Italy, Spain, and Morocco; all the Black Sea coasts and nearly all of the Red Sea; Hungary and all the kingdoms south of the lower Danube. Yet from this zenith of glory the empire began to decline, for here followed a line of weak and irresolute Sultans. The Ottoman navy, which was once the terror of the Mediterranean Sea, sustained a withering blow, in the latter part of the sixteenth century, from an allied fleet under Don John of Austria. In the succession of wars that followed with Austria, Venice, Russia, and Poland, success and defeat were about equally divided on the field; yet gradually the vitality of the nation was drained by continual carnage. Austria no longer lived in continual dread of Turkish invasion, but took the offensive. European Turkey fast began to shrink in extent. Turkish power on the Danube was destroyed; and in 1699, by the treaty of peace of Carlowitz, Sultan Mustapha II. gave over almost all the Hungarian provinces to Austria, Azof to Russia, Moria and Dalmatia to Venice, and Podolia and Ukaraine to Poland. The causes of Turkey's decline are evident to those who are acquainted with the character of its later sovereigns. The Turkish saying that "the fish first stinks at the head" has been every whit true of the crowned heads of the Ottoman Empire since the death of Suleyman. With perhaps two exceptions, all the later Sultans were absolutely lacking in moral fiber. Shut up in the seraglio with their harem and favorites, they gave themselves up to the indulgence of their own follies and the gratification of their vicious appetites, utterly thoughtless concerning the welfare of their people and the prosperity of their country. As a matter of course, they neglected the discipline of the army and gradually abandoned the direct government of their empire.

The Janizaries, the Ottoman right arm in war, lost all respect for their unworthy masters, and became the power behind the throne. They enthroned and dethroned the Sultans at their will. Military insubordination and revolts—moreover, troubles and hostilities with the Christian states and provinces, by virtue of their superior advancement in wealth and civilization—assumed more and more alarming proportions. Once in a long while a wise ruler like Murad IV. arose and somewhat brightened the darkened political horizon of

MOHAMMED II. WITHIN THE WALLS OF CONSTANTINOPLE.
(*From a painting.*)

the empire; but, in the main, under incompetent sovereigns, the Turkish government lapsed into a condition which went from bad to worse. As we have observed, all the Ottoman princes and Sultans down to Suleyman, with the exception of Bajazet II., were great rulers. True, they were most of them cruel and despotic, but they were resolute and brave; they had integrity of purpose and strength of character; they marched at the head of their own armies; they made use of oppression only when it was needed to carry out their plans of conquest; they were stern, but did not altogether disregard common justice. The later Sultans were quite of another kind. They were a degenerate set in whose veins ran no noble blood. Inebriate, imbecile, incapable, slaves of sensuality, and types of cruelty, they turned backward from the course which was set for them by the aggressive Sultans of former days, and set to enjoying the fruit of the earlier conquests. Thus they became consumers rather than producers, living on the conquered countries without bestowing any practical benefit upon them.

THE PRESENT SULTAN, ABDUL-HAMID II.

In the reign of Abdul-Hamid II., the present Sultan, are combined, by nature and environment, the elements of decay which have characterized the later rulers of the Ottoman Empire.

"I may be the last of the Caliphs, but never a second Khedive," declared this accomplished slayer and tyrant of mankind, when warned by the Russian ambassador, M. de Nelidoff, that the Sultan's obdurate course and the condition of the Turkish Empire had placed the throne and the caliphate in imminent peril. Abdul-Hamid is, indeed, the least of the Caliphs, and doubtless would have been the last of them, with the second- or third-rate power of a Khedive, had it not been for the mutual jealousies of the Powers, who had thought better to maintain a "Sick Man," or even a dead man, on the Bosphorus, rather than to allow a live man to take his place whose position might prove too lively for their keenest rivalry.

Born in 1842, Abdul-Hamid II. came to the Ottoman throne August 31, 1876. Tragic were the circumstances under which he was made Sultan. These very tragedies had much to do with shaping his present policy. His uncle, Abdul-Aziz, was deposed and murdered. To add to this complication, some of the ablest ministers of the state were assassinated by Hassan Bey in revenge for their treachery to the late Sultan. War clouds were gathering black and heavy. Servia and Montenegro had gone to war; Russians were flocking to the Servian camp; Constantinople was seething with revolutionary excitement. Sultan Murad, after three months of reign, was deposed and imprisoned. Then came Abdul-Hamid, with fear and trembling, to the perilous dignity of the tottering throne. It was the contention between the Old Turkey Party and the Young Turkey Party for supremacy in the affairs of the state that had sealed the fate of his two predecessors. The progressive Young Turkey Party had stood for a new order of things and for the regeneration of the Ottoman Empire, while the Old Turkey Party, ever hostile to all new ideas, stood for stagnation.

This party held in abhorrence the very name of progressive institutions, as inventions of *giaours*, for whom they had a whole-souled hatred. Abdul-Hamid had to identify himself with one of the two parties. For a while his brain became a sort of political insane asylum without any keeper. Then he asserted the supreme power of Islam, according to the Old Turkey Party, the results of which during his twenty-one years of reign have borne their legitimate fruits. The expectations and hopes of the Young Turkey Party were shattered, and the establishment of a constitutional government and parliament done away with. In one way or another, beginning with able Midhat Pasha, the chief expounder of the constitutional government, the Sultan rid himself of all advisers whose ideas were opposed to the notions of unrelenting bigots and the flattering set of favorites of the Old Turkey party with whom Abdul-Hamid had surrounded himself.

To-day, with all his powers of autocratic and theocratic absolutism, it is not Abdul-Hamid who rules, but his nondescript palace party, made up of chamberlains, private secretaries, *mollahs*, etc., in whose hands Abdul-Hamid is a mere puppet living in a malarious atmosphere of corruption. This palace party, aside from making confusion in the foreign relations of the empire, has increased its influence in internal abuses, and they are responsible for the corruption, in the form of venality and perfidy, which has infected all ranks of official society throughout the empire. Aspirants for political offices and recognition eagerly seek the favor of these gentlemen of the royal household, and, in most cases, they literally sell favors to the highest bidder, ut-

SULTAN ABDUL-HAMID II.

terly regardless of qualification. It is hard to reach the Sultan without their connivance. Under such conditions bribery flourishes, while the insolent hangers-on at Yildiz, whose main object in existence is self-advancement, speedily grow rich at the expense of the empire.

Abdul-Hamid himself, like his father, Abdul-Medjid, is a great royal spendthrift, squandering untold treasures, careless of the needs and interests of an empire so long as his own pleasures are gratified. The number of his domestics is said to be six thousand, and is made up of imperial sword- and cup-bearers, mutes, dwarfs, or court jesters, eunuchs, pashas, beys, slaves, astrologers, sultanas, kadines, Circassian and Georgian odalisques, dancing women, etc. To cover the annual expenses of such a large household and table twelve million dollars is required. That the Turkish Empire is bankrupt is a matter of course, and it simply exists by the mercenary sufferance of powerful creditors and by the perplexed nature of European politics.

I have a very vivid recollection of my first view of the Sultan. It was an unusually cool and pleasant day in midsummer of 1889, when I started to witness the imperial pageant of *Selemlik*—the Sultan's going to prayers. Upon my arrival near the Yildiz Kiosk, I found that almost every available inch of space between the mosque and the palace was filled with Turkish soldiers and with people of every nation. Happily, I chanced to find a base- and ragged-looking Jew, who had come early and secured a high and commanding position above the heads of the soldiers. Nothing but the jingle of coins would induce him to give up his place.

SULTAN ABDUL-AZIZ.

With a few *paras*, and less parley, I succeeded in exchanging places with him. He thought he had the best of the bargain, but I would not have given up the place for five times the amount I paid him. The new Mosque of Hamadieh, in which the present Sultan worships, is some eighty or one hundred yards from the palace, the Yildiz Kiosk. He rides to it, however, every Friday noon, in an elegant barouche, with all the pomp of elaborate ritual and imposing ceremony. From the palace to the mosque the streets are lined on either side, four ranks deep, with brightly uniformed regiments of gorgeous soldiers, representing every part of the dominion in their picturesque and varied uniforms and with their regimental banners. The roadway on which the Sultan is to drive is carpeted a half-inch deep with fine, clean sand. Pashas and beys, foreign ambassadors and diplomats, ministers and high dignitaries of state are all on hand in full regalia, with glittering uniforms and a profusion of gold lace and decorative orders, while magnificently mounted squadrons of lancers and cavalry are marching to position. About 1.30 P. M. all eyes are eagerly directed toward the Yildiz Palace, as it is time for the Sultan to appear. Then, high above the heads of the mighty throng, rings out from the slender minaret of Hamadieh the impressive voice of the green-turbaned *muezzin*. Presently the iron gates of the palace open, and the Sultan emerges from his seclusion in an open carriage drawn by Arabian steeds, and dashes down the little slope that leads from the palace to the mosque. At sight of the Sultan the soldiers "present arms" and with one voice shout aloud three times, like the booming of a cannon: *"Padisha-*

him chok yasha!" which means, "Long live my Sultan!" Then regimental bands burst out in martial music. Before the appearance of the Sultan's carriage, a few veiled women of his harem, young sons, and male relatives proceed to the courtyard of the mosque. In marked contrast to the gorgeous attire of the imperial princes and other high dignitaries, Abdul-Hamid is very plainly dressed in a black suit and a red fez. Nor is the contrast less marked between him and Osman Pasha, the hero of Plevna, a brave figure of hardy and robust manhood, who sits opposite the thin and pale Sultan in the royal carriage. After half an hour at prayer Abdul-Hamid reappears in an open landau. He takes the reins of the horses in his own hands, and drives back up the hill to the palace, while many courtiers follow on foot, to come to his aid if needed. Cheers and music, pomp and show follow him to the gates of his palace.

This is one of the most gorgeous royal events of frequent occurrence in all the world. The Caliph of two hundred million Mohammedans, and the sovereign of thirty million subjects, attended not only by his own household, but by the brightly costumed ambassadors and consuls of all nations, appears to the public. Official horse-tails, which have led the way to victory or defeat on a thousand battle fields; jewel-hilted swords, sashes, turbans, and fezes, worn by the males in line, even to the little boys on Arabian steeds, lend the charm of novelty to a pageant which, for mere magnificence, is seldom equaled under the sun.

Abdul-Hamid is a small man, with a pale face and weak figure. He is aptly called "the Sick Man," for not only is his country "sick," in the sense of ruin

IMPERIAL PALACE OF DOLMA-BAYTCHE ON THE BOSPHORUS.

and decay, but the Sultan is really the most sickly-looking sovereign in Europe. It is said that he is always cross and continually in a rage. No wonder, since he has so many wives to take care of; for the number of his harem runs up into the hundreds. His character may best be judged by his acts, and certainly he has performed no good acts worthy of notice. Mr. Gladstone speaks of him as " God's curse to mankind"; while the Turkish journals of Constantinople, on his last birthday, January 19, with many flourishes of Oriental adulation, made it an occasion of raptured outbursts praising the goodness and beneficence of Allah for making the earth a present of such a sublime being as his Majesty the Sultan Abdul-Hamid II. "To-day the eyes of the good believers are blinded by the effect of this dazzling light of Islam, and their hearts overflow with happiness," says Sabach—regardless of Christian hearts that overflow with bitterness; and, indeed, many Islam hearts, too, who have experienced the effect of their master's unspeakable tyranny.

The Sultan's glittering palace on the Bosphorus is replete with associations of tragical events. From this abode go forth edicts which involve the massacre of many thousand Christians. Nevertheless, this titled criminal, whose career of bloodthirsty atrocity surpasses that of Nero himself, is not without his punishment. Indeed, the life of a bootblack is happier than his. In constant dread of his life, he lives a prisoner within the walls of his palace. His walks and drives never extend beyond the park of the Yildiz, which is vigilantly guarded, even in broad daylight, with more care than any American penitentiary. His sleep-

ARCH IN RUINS IN ASIA MINOR.

THEATER IN RUINS.

ing apartment is watched over at night with more circumspection than the criminal cell of an ill-fated convict. When the Armenian atrocities were at their height, his uneasiness—indeed, his insanity—drove him to such unheard-of precautions as to change his bodyguard every two hours. He would trust no one, even in the palace; and woe to anyone who might fall under his suspicion! One of his grand viziers narrowly escaped, and fled to British protection. The ghosts of one hundred thousand Armenians seem to haunt him, even in his most secluded chambers. I can never forget my first impression of him, when he drove back to the Yildiz Kiosk from the Mosque of Hamadieh. His black character was as indelibly stamped on his countenance as a seal on a governmental document. What a scared and hunted look on his thin face! and what a twinkle of treacherous cunning and cruelty in his deep-set black eyes! He is a "sick man," and his contagious disease has so spread throughout the length and breadth of his unhappy empire that it will not be very long before the European doctors will pronounce her "dead," and proceed to the burial ceremony.

The sluggish Turk, with his iron feet of destruction, treads on ground under which sleep, mute and silent, the Roman and Greek sires and sages of civilization. With a creed of bloody conquest and ruin, he has always marked his incursions by the destruction of everything and the building of nothing. Truly, as we gaze upon the dilapidated desolation of Ambition's airy halls, we find the saying true that "Wherever the Sultan's horses' hoofs tread, there the grass never grows again." The glory of twenty nations, the seats of great military chieftains and empires, thriving commercial cities, palaces of fame and wealth, speak to the traveler in Asia Minor from their voiceless desolation of fiery hearts and gallant spirits that are no more. No longer do the skies of Ionia smile on the brilliant array of poets who sang beneath her azure arch. Over the graves of Homeric heroes roam sheep and oxen. The land of deathless sages has been plunged into thickest night of desolation and woe. The misrule of five centuries has not only erased the vestiges of the former inhabitants, but has also enslaved the existing population in impenetrable superstition and ignorance, and cradled them in a blind and most debasing fanaticism. The brutal tyranny and passion of the Turk have grown more deadly with every year that they have been tolerated, until now, in our own day of boasted civilization, the smoke from his smoldering embers of crime arises in columns, to mar the holiness of God's earth.

Oh, that the trumpet blast of the nineteenth century would awaken the slumbering soul of Christendom, and raise up a champion of freedom! Would that this land of enlightenment might reflect a ray of light across the waters, where superstition and tyranny have for ages cast a gloom over the otherwise bright and peaceful world!

THE RELIGION OF THE TURKS—MOHAMMEDANISM.

"There is no God but God, and Mohammed is His prophet."
—*The Mohammedan Catechism.*

THERE is no other people in the world whose religion forms such an important element in their national life as Mohammedanism forms in the national life of the Turkish people. So closely interwoven are the religion and the state that for a Turk to deny Mohammedanism is to renounce all claims to his nationality, and for a foreigner to become a Moslem is to become a Turk. To understand, therefore, in any degree the Turk and his country, a study of his religion is absolutely essential.

The study of Mohammedanism, moreover, will cast light upon otherwise inexplicable aspects of Oriental government. The standpoint of its principles is the only one from which to survey the peculiar condition of the Turkish and kindred peoples, who are just now arresting the attention of the civilized world.

Moreover, a view of this religion will be found exceedingly salutary in its broadening tendency, and also serve to clarify our ideas, as well as add to our appreciation, of the supreme features of Christianity. For this purpose, a survey of Mohammedanism has many advantages, because it has so much in common with Christianity, and because differences, apparently so slight, have resulted in so great a contrast in the spiritual power of the two religions.

Naturally, a person's religious belief and loyalty are determined by birth, environment, and education. We embrace the religion of our fathers, and with it a certain amount of bigotry, inherited and acquired. When such a truth is put to us in the nature of a specific charge, we, of course, deny it; but a careful examination attests its verity. We are more or less partial, narrow, biased, in our religious ideas, and are quick to condemn another system because it does not readily adapt itself to our accustomed cast of thought.

Let us, then, place ourselves under Oriental skies, and for the time become right loyal Moslems, asking ourselves why these infidels and philosophers brand us heretics, and assign to our religion an inferior place.

There is much misunderstanding among Christians, and the world in general, regarding the Mohammedan faith and worship. Especially among the Christians, ideas of Mohammedanism are inexcusably vague, and are consequently obstacles in the way to a correct understanding of a religious force that has had no little part in the history of the world.

If the follower of Christ will study the Koran earnestly, he will not fail to find many features that strikingly resemble the leading texts of his own faith. Indeed, he will be surprised to find that the religion which he formerly supposed to be the offspring of heathenism, abounding in superstition and folly, is pregnant with truths that have been inculcated into his own heart and life since childhood.

And it is not difficult to discover a reason for the

similarity. That Mohammedanism should resemble Christianity, and that the Koran should compare closely with the Bible, is only a natural outcome of the training of the great Prophet.

From his earliest years he was taught the Old and New Testaments, and regarded them with a love and respect which he did not withdraw in his old age, for to the last he spoke of the Bible as the word of God. Besides the direct influence of the Holy Scriptures, the surroundings of his household were essentially Christian in character. His favorite wife embraced the teachings of Christ; one of his other wives was a Jewess, and most of his highly esteemed counselors were of the Christian persuasion. All this could not fail to exert a powerful influence, and Mohammed manifested it in all his writings, paying homage to Christ to the last, and looking upon Him as the greatest of prophets.

The question naturally arises, "If this is true, why did Mohammed seek to establish a new religion?"

He did not claim to be more than a man. Although his followers ascribe miracles to him, he did not claim to perform them, and even went so far as to denounce them. He fought not against the Bible, not against Christianity in its purity. He did, however, zealously attack Christianity as corruptly practiced by the people of his time. Moreover, he denied the divinity of Jesus Christ, and violently opposed the apotheosis of the Virgin Mary, whom the popular conception really regarded as a goddess. In opposition to this, he advocated the absolute unity of the Deity, considering these other beliefs as impious and unworthy a Supreme Being.

MOSQUES OF THE MOSLEM FOUNDERS, BRUSA.

BY PER. OF THE CHRISTIAN HERALD, NEW YORK.

And, in the light of history, it cannot be doubted that in his position Mohammed manifested an elevated religious nature and a purified vision. This idea of God's unity was an advance upon the crude conception of the time, as it was a reaction from the prevailing polytheistic nations. Had this been all, Mohammed, so far as regards his conception of God, might still be honored as a Christian reformer instead of a prophet of a new order. But this was not all. With this idea of the unity of God was joined that of His supremacy, and that the most absolute. Fatherhood was foreign to any of His attributes. Above all, infinite, omnipotent, He was the very impersonation of Eternal Force. Indeed, some one has aptly described the Moslem religion as "a pantheism of will." In some of his aspects we are reminded of the God of Judaism; but even in Judaism we find a very important attribute which is absent from Islam's Allah, namely, that of justice. Islam's God is not a just God so much as He is an all-powerful God. He is the universal Sovereign, and obedience is the prime duty of his subjects everywhere.

Notwithstanding the oneness and supremacy of the God of Mohammedanism, there are other spirits, or angel-powers, which hold a subordinate place, and yet are essential to an understanding of the religion. Of these Satan, or Eblis, is not the least important, although not occupying a more conspicuous place than the Satan of Christianity. Gabriel and Michael are mentioned often in the Koran: they are the angels of power. Death is personified in the grim Azrael. And Israfel, "whose heart-strings are a lute," whose legend furnished Poe material for the beautiful lyric of that name, is the Angel of Resurrection.

> "In Heaven a spirit doth dwell,
>   Whose heart-strings are a lute;
> None sing so wildly well,
>   As the angel Israfel,
> And the giddy stars (so legends tell),
>   Ceasing their hymns, attend the spell
> Of his voice, all mute."

God brings himself into relation with his subjects in a number of different ways, sometimes through inspired prophets, and sometimes through sacred writings. Mohammed and his followers believed that he himself was to be the legitimate and final successor of Adam, Noah, Moses, Jesus, and other men, who were considered especial ambassadors, chosen by the Almighty. The Pentateuch was not discarded, and the Psalms and Gospels were accepted as sacred books. But taking precedence of all these is the Koran, said to be the personal product of the inspired Mohammed, in which he embodied his creed for his followers.

It would be entirely foreign to the purpose of this sketch to make an exhaustive survey of even the prominent tenets of this, to the Moslem, book of all books. The curious as well as the accurate student we refer to the Koran itself, which, in a number of English translations, is interesting to read and profitable to study.

One of the prominent doctrines of the Koran is that of predestination, which is presented in its most absolute form. God has foreordained some to an eternal happiness in Paradise; others are foredoomed to the everlasting torment of hell, and naught can intervene between the purpose of the Supreme Being and its eternal execution.

The practical morality of the precepts of the Koran will not be questioned. Intoxicating drinks of all kinds are prohibited the true believer, and in the Orient the difference between precept and practice is not so very great. We also find gambling deprecated as a sin and proscribed by punishment.

Mohammedanism, more than any other religion, has gained its proselytes by force of arms. It is only in keeping with the prevailing ideas of that religion that the true believer should hate infidels and discharge the God-like duty of making war upon them, even if connected by ties of consanguinity. To the Moslem, then, warfare is a religious duty and every crusade an aggression on behalf of Him to whom all men owe life and allegiance. To this principle may be ascribed the motives that impelled Mohammedans throughout their long career of bloody conquest. It was a natural outcome of what they conceived as a religious duty.

Travelers in European and Asiatic Turkey have noted with admiration the devotional spirit of the faithful in their ceremonies and in the observance of feasts and religious holidays. Our Friday is the Sabbath of Islam, when sermons are preached and prayers offered in all places of worship. On this day every Mohammedan is compelled to repair to the mosque and take part in the devout worship of Allah. Do not make the mistake of thinking that this is done merely as a stern, sterile duty; rather is it thought a privilege, and, as we have intimated, the humble spirit of devo-

THE MOSQUE OF AHMET IN CONSTANTINOPLE.

tion is striking. A visit to one of these mosques on a quiet Friday noon would be an eloquent homily on the true spirit with which to approach the Almighty—a spirit so often sadly lacking in the Christian people.

I have intimated the importance of the idea of God as influencing and molding a nation's religion. Looking back over history, we cannot but be impressed by the fact that culture and religion have ever exerted a reciprocal influence on each other. The peculiar conception which a people may hold of God determines not only its religion but its civilization. Looking at Mohammedanism from this point of view, what is the character of the civilization we should naturally expect as a result? What is the civilizing potency of Mohammedanism?

We have seen that the Moslem God is an impersonation of arbitrary *will;* that he is synonymous with cold, loveless, authoritative supremacy; that the first, last, and only duty of his subjects is slavish obedience; in a word, that the idea of liberty, in any true sense, is practically excluded. Now, what is the first requisite of high civilization? Is it not a consciousness of personal independence, of liberty? This principle has been at the basis of all great developments of individual genius. Without it, in one form or other, no nation has ever really flourished and come to a high state of culture.

The first point, then, that we observe is the utter absence of the principle of liberty in the Mohammedan religion.

If we look at the Islam conception of God from a moral standpoint, we find its effects just as baneful.

The believer does right because Allah commands it, and because it is his to obey. This is placing moral obligation on a low basis—on no higher ground than the divine will. The doctrine of predestination, also, which is really a corollary of a pantheistic will, does away in a measure with man's free moral agency, and divests him of that attribute which, of all others, contributes to his nobility. Let it be remembered that a correct conception of duty and an appreciation of man's eternal responsibility are necessary to any advancement in morals, and that the character of a nation's morality is ever a reliable index to the worth and permanence of its civilization. And it must be conceded that the Mohammedan conception is not entirely barren of good. The recognition of God's supremacy exercises a salutary constraint on those who perhaps would abstain from wrong from no higher motive. Its influence on the savage mind must not be condemned as evil, although there is surely little room for the development of the moral nature. The idea of the unity of the Godhead also precludes idolatry, and this is no small step toward the higher and truer life.

Again, it will be conceded that a religion approaches perfection in so far as it proves itself adequate to man's complete nature. In its broadest sense, it exists for the elevation of the soul in all its functions, and a religion which suppresses any of these betrays its inadequacy, its weakness, and its imperfection. If it satisfy the reason to the exclusion of the heart; if it minister to the higher emotions, with no deference to rational demands; in short, if it is not as broad as man's nature and as high as man's loftiest aspirations, then that religion is unworthy of humanity. Arraigned before such a tribunal, the unworthiness of Mohammedanism becomes apparent. It does not teach the law of love as the basis of morality; it does not believe in the fatherhood of God or in the brotherhood of man. Love, which is the leaven of all human relations, is practically eliminated; and Mohammedanism, thus failing to call forth so essential a part of man's nature, must be condemned.

Christianity pleads: "God is love; trust Him." Mohammedanism commands: "God is *will;* obey Him." Mohammedanism is sterile, barren, and irksome in its principle; Christianity is fruitful and permeating—a yoke that is easy, a burden that is light. The Christian God is in us and with us, and it is the delight of His children to breathe out their souls in prayer to Him.

And here we are brought face to face with a strange fact. It is difficult to see what place prayer can possibly have in the Mohammedan theology, and yet we have previously spoken of the humble devotion of the faithful. However, we shall understand this perfectly when we remember that even prayer springs from obedience to Allah, and the devotion that has been so extolled, like most of the liturgy, is a mere formalism arising from no love for, or higher yearnings after, an infinite Father.

The effect of all these detrimental influences may, I think, be found manifested in the character of the individual Moslem. The despotic principle, which holds so prominent a position in Islam, seems to have infected society and government as well, for nowhere is tyranny more cruel and arbitrary than in the Mohammedan countries. The religious slave becomes the political slave also.

Mohammedanism was born in the Orient, was the product of Oriental ideas, and has never ventured beyond the Orient in permanent conquest. Yet the part it has played in history cannot but give rise to the double question: "Is Mohammedanism of divine origin? Has its influence, on the whole, been for good or for evil?" These are not idle questions, and upon their answers hang solutions to many more important problems. If not to the supernatural, to what or whom can we ascribe its rapid inception and growth, its miraculous unifying power as exerted over a thousand warring Arab tribes? To what can we ascribe its dominion over two hundred millions of souls? There is no one who will say that its influence has been entirely on the side of evil, or that it has not been a factor in the onward march of the race; but I think it can be just as certainly asserted that its mission for good is at an end. For, while Christianity admits of almost infinite progress, Mohammedanism raises the devotees to a certain stage, and leaves them there, and is impotent to lift them higher. For, this reason, the future of Islam is limited. The race has reached that stage in its development when it can cast aside the useless shell of former growth and build "more stately mansions" for the soul.

It may be interesting to add to these general observations upon the underlying principles of Mohammedanism some description of a few of the peculiar ceremonies, beliefs, and religious practices which characterize the outward aspect of Islam.

Mohammedanism is essentially a religion of form;

hence the disciple of Islam does not thank God for past blessings or implore his protection for the future, though he rehearses his prayers ostentatiously five times a day. Islamism means submission; hence the efficacy of the service is in the number of times the *nemaz*, or prayer, is said. Before worship a preparatory service of *abtest*, or ablution with cold water, is obligatory. If this were not done in strict conformity with the established usage the subsequent prayers would be of no avail.

In the courtyard of every mosque a large basin of water is provided, and the faithful, standing straight, and facing due north or south, advance in order to it, and say *Bismillah*, meaning, "It is in God's name I do this." The hands are washed to the wrist; the mouth and nose three times; then, beginning at the toes, the feet are washed to the ankles, after which the right hand is dipped gently into water and a part of the head is wet. The arms are washed to the elbows, beginning at the finger tips. Then the rest of the head is wet, the water being dipped up by the right hand. The inside of the ears must also be washed with the index finger of either hand, and the back of the ears with the thumb. So extremely exacting is this ritual that the slightest digression or omission necessitates an entire repetition. Practice makes them expert, however, and they learn to do it quickly and correctly according to requirements. The ceremony is repeated three times. Exemption is allowed where no water can be obtained, but the form must be gone through by touching the hands to dry earth, instead of dipping them into water.

THE MOSLEM AT PRAYER IN THE DESERT.
(From a painting.)

The time for prayers is regulated by the sun. Morning prayer is said between dawn and sunrise. It is due to this requirement that Mohammedans are early risers. Noonday prayer is said just as the sun is passing the meridian, and afternoon prayer at any time between four and five o'clock. The fourth prayer comes at sunset, and the last prayer of the day before retiring. The ritual for prayer is not optional but imperative, and its requirements of formality are as rigid as those for ablution.

At almost every quarter of a mile in a Mohammedan city are built the mosques—solid, substantial buildings whose minarets are the most beautiful spires that pierce the Levantine skies, symmetrical, lofty, and majestic. They contain neither pealing chimes nor tolling bells, but five times daily from the top of these are heard the muezzin's *czan*, or call to prayer, in deep, long-drawn tones, in the strange and impressive Arabic tongue :

"God is almighty! Mohammed is his apostle! Prayer is better than sleep! Hasten to worship! Hasten to prosperity!"

The sacred voice rings from every minaret, until the sound goes around the Islam world, girding it with these never-ceasing vibrations, keeping it awake and at worship. The voice resounds in the highest pitch when it chants, with the threefold iteration, *Laha-il-Allah!*—"There is no God but God." At this call all the faithful Moslems leave their engagements at once and hasten to worship, no matter how inclement the weather or how pressing their business. Their regular attendance and punctuality are bewildering to the Christian world. Would that we, who, by the Lord's resurrection from the dead, have the highest incentive to the sacred observance of the First Day of the week, might take example from Mohammedan zeal!

If a Mohammedan is late, he may at any time join with the congregation in the service, but the blessing to be obtained is deemed far inferior to what would have resulted had he been on time. Tradition says that a follower excused himself to the Prophet on the ground of saving his friend from drowning, at the time of devotions, and hoped that he would be blessed for the kindly act as well as those who were early at prayer. The stern Prophet would not accept the apology. "Though you had camels enough to fill the road from Mecca to Medina, all loaded with jewels, and should give the cargo to the poor, the blessings would not equal those of promptness at prayer. Should you commit the whole Koran to memory and repeat it twice every night, the blessings received would not equal those of beginning *nemaz* with the *imam* (priest). Should you kill all the enemies of Islam, the great rewards would not compare with those of him who is prompt at the beginning of prayer. If by a word the heavens and earth could become paper, the sea be turned into ink, and all angels stand as scribes, yet they would be unable to write all the blessings you may enjoy for beginning prayers with the *imam*." The Mohammedans are deeply conscious of all these warnings of their Prophet, and, though not "in spirit and truth," yet they worship according to their forms most faithfully.

The interior of the mosque is considered most holy;

consequently, all the people take off their shoes as they step within the shrine, and go through a series of pious movements. The religion of "the Prophet," keenly hostile to pagan idolatry, forbids pictures, images, or any other representation of the human form in their houses of worship. On the walls, however, are many inscriptions from the Koran, with censers of burning oil suspended from the dome.

The floor is beautified with the richest rugs of Oriental art, upon which the suppliants prostrate themselves in their devotions, with twenty-six postures, each following the movement of the *imam*, rising and bowing simultaneously with almost military precision.

While at prayer, certain acts, such as looking around, striking at a fly to kill it, raising a foot from the floor, scratching more than three times in one place on the body, laughing loud enough to be heard, must be refrained from, as they would destroy the efficacy of the devotions.

The *imam*, who performs the devotional ceremonies, preaches no sermon, but at noon of each day he reads two chapters from the Koran, and then descends to mingle with the many worshipers, placing himself on a level with the common people. On Friday, however, the holy day of the Mohammedans, the devotions are conducted with unusual pomp and ceremony ; the Koran is recited, prayers are said, and generally a sermon preached.

The language of the Mohammedans in Asia Minor is Turkish, but the Koran is written in the Meccan dialect of the Arabic, an unintelligible tongue to the masses, and only understood by a few of the best edu-

COURT OF A MOSQUE.

cated. Yet their tradition teaches that merely to hear the sacred book read has a miraculous effect, beneficial to soul and body; and so they are made content with the empty sound of meaningless words.

Here let me take occasion to add a word as to the origin and extent of the influence of the Koran. The Koran, the groundwork of Islam, is divided into one hundred and fourteen *suras*, or chapters, originally written on "bits of stone, leather, thigh bones," and all sorts of material. After the death of Mohammed these scattered materials were collected, and, supplemented by the Arab's retentive memory, they were put together regardless of time or subject, one chapter following another without even chronological sequence. Thus, while the teachings of the Koran are sufficiently plain, yet this manifest lack of logical order renders it of all books the least intelligible. But the Koran is not the whole of Islamism. There are traditions which are as powerful as, and even more respected than, the Koran itself. When there is nothing in the Koran to meet an issue, the Moslem would draw upon the oral laws of the Prophet on the basis of what Mohammed said, what he did, what he did not say, or what he allowed others to say unrebuked. In the sixteenth century Sultan Suleyman the Magnificent codified the Moslem law in a volume of fifty-five books, which included, together with all the practices of worship, the laws—moral, civil, political, judiciary, military, and agrarian.

The Moslem's belief in a paradise beyond the grave is all that could be desired. The prayers that he has said will light up his grave as a lamp; no sin will remain to be imputed to him at the resurrection; angel wings will bear him aloft, and even should some sin remain through careless praying he still has a chance of escape, though he does not believe in purgatory. If he has children, their innocence will admit him; and their grief at leaving their father behind will take him through the gates, Peter or no Peter! In eternity, the momentary pleasures of time are to be extended a thousand years, and once in Paradise he has but to express his wishes and they are immediately granted. His food is served on a golden plate, and the bones of the bird that has been devoured will again assume full plumage and fly away to sing as of yore in the leafy bowers. Wine, which is denied to the faithful here, will be abundant there, but will not intoxicate. The humblest in rank will have seventy-two virgins of immortal youth and angelic beauty to attend him. In brief, an ideal temporal paradise, based on the pleasures of earth, is to be magnified a thousand-fold beyond the utmost limit of even an Oriental imagination to depict. Such is their Elysium.

If the Mohammedan description of heaven abounds somewhat in sensual imagery, we should remember that it makes no essential difference how we describe the land of the hereafter, if only we make that description conform to our ideas of true and pure happiness, as all conceptions employing the material as symbols of the spiritual must necessarily fall short of the true glory of heaven. Whether we make it a city with walls of jasper and streets of gold, echoing to the joy of happy hearts, or see with tranquil vision an infinite paradise clothed with wonder and peopled with creations of eternal love—neither is heaven: both are faulty metaphors, halting figures, imperfect symbols.

If the rewards of fidelity are ideal according to sensual standards of pleasure, the punishments of the doomed are cruel to the other extreme, surpassing in horror Dante's best description of the Plutonic realm. The graves of this class are beds of hot coals, where the bones are piled one upon the other for want of room, and fused at white heat, without loss of the sense of feeling; while thirst and hunger, with scourgings, will add the spice of variety to this roasting process, until the resurrection, when Satan will assume control and do as he likes with them for evermore.

Here it seems evident that Mohammed's political and religious ideas were not without reciprocal influence. He did not believe even in a hell-democracy; the Jew-hell would not do for the Christian, and so he straightway orders a separate pit for him. Still, it can hardly be doubted that this arrangement is pre-eminently satisfactory to all concerned. Communism would be a failure even in the nether world. When the Koran proceeds in another place to speak of an intermediate state after death and a final resurrection and judgment, we are struck with an apparent, and only an apparent, inconsistency. Gabriel is represented at the soul's judgment holding scales in his hand; on one side bad, and on the other good, actions are balanced against each other, and the incline of this scale becomes the forecast of the soul's destiny.

The following brief description of Mohammed's traditional journey to Paradise may fittingly illustrate some of the singular ideas of Islam:

The angel Gabriel appeared to Mohammed with an *Alborak*, a strange animal, a cross between an ass and a mule. This long-eared brute began to talk, demanding some concession from the new Prophet. Having promised the creature a golden stall in heaven, Mohammed was permitted to mount. In the twinkling of an eye he arrived at Jerusalem, where, after a pleasant interview with the patriarchs and prophets of all ages, he ascended with Gabriel upon a ladder extending from the "City of David" to the "City of God."

As he arrived at the portals of heaven he saw this large inscription on one side, "There is no God but God," and, on the other, "Mohammed is His apostle." The heavenly host being informed that Mohammed had come, at once the pearly gates were thrown wide open; and upon entering he was quickly embraced by Father Adam, who was happy to meet his most illustrious son. From this heaven the stars, which he described as being hollow silver balls, were suspended by golden chains. What would become of faith in Mohammed's visions if modern science were introduced among his followers!

Quickly Mohammed was taken from the first to the second heaven,—a journey of five hundred years,—where he met the Angel of the Cocks, who was so tall as to reach from the first to the second heaven. Nearly every morning this big rooster joins God in singing a song that fills the entire universe with its melodious strains. Every being on earth hears them but man. In this heaven he met Noah, who was the presiding dignitary, and he was tendered a most cordial reception as he passed through the golden streets. In the third heaven he describes the angels as being very large. One of the most gigantic required seventy thousand days' journey between the eyes! Here, too, he found the same inscription as in the first and second heaven. After a short interview with Moses in the fourth, or emerald, heaven, he was taken to the fifth to meet Joseph; then to the sixth heaven, of carbuncle, where he beheld John the Baptist.

Radiant with light and ruled over by Jesus was the seventh heaven, in which he was attended by a vast multitude of joyous inhabitants and innumerable angels of dazzling beauty, each one of whom possessed seventy thousand heads, with seventy thousand mouths to each head, and seventy thousand tongues to each mouth—all singing and singing, day and night, unceasingly. Here the Prophet, with glorious pomp, was presented to God, whose face was concealed by seventy thousand veils. Here, too, on the sides of the divine throne, Mohammed beheld the inscription, "There is no God but God," and, on the other, "Mohammed is His apostle." God, after saluting Mohammed, commissioned him to return to earth with full authority. All this the faithful most firmly believe.

Charity is prescribed by the Koran for the faithful in two forms—voluntary and compulsory. The latter amounts to the fortieth part of his possessions, but it is only imposed when the property aggregates a certain sum. Voluntary charity is usually dispensed at the time of the feast following the annual fast.

The pilgrimage to Mecca, as a pious duty, is believed

THE MOSQUE OF SULEYMAN IN CONSTANTINOPLE.

to secure certain inestimable privileges for all who can possibly make the trip. Nothing could test faith more than this long and tiresome journey. All the world has heard of the vast concourse there annually assembled from all parts of Asia, Africa, and Europe. At that time every highway leading to the sacred *Kaaba* is a field hospital of the sick and dying, and in the general lack of physicians and nurses, when cholera prevails, as it usually does, Mecca becomes the disseminating point for the plague.

Honors are bestowed on the survivors of the hazardous ordeal of this journey, and they are addressed by the title *hadji*. Among the Armenians, the same title is applied to those Christians who have visited Jerusalem. These Christian *hadjis* usually have a small cross tattooed on the hand to indicate the fact that they have made the pilgrimage to the Holy Sepulcher.

Mohammed has declared that he will not intercede in heaven for unmarried men. So marry you must, or take your chances! Remember Mohammed, old bachelors and old maids, or you will be miserable in this world and in the world to come! The Prophet would have them bring up large families, that his followers may outnumber all others in Paradise. The widows actually pray, " Let me be married before I die, that I may not be ashamed when I meet Allah!" Allah will reward the parents of children, those who pay the debts of another, and the soldiers in holy wars.

Like other religious institutions, Mohammedanism has its holidays, feast and fast days. The most important of these is the holy month of *Ramazan*, a month of fast and penitence. The fast cannot begin until the new moon has been seen. In cloudy weather messengers are sent to the peaks of mountains, and, they having ascertained the appearance of the moon, the Sultan telegraphs to all parts of the empire for the fast to begin, and local announcement is made by the firing of cannon at sunrise. From the rising to the setting of the sun, for the entire month, no food or drink may pass the lips, not even tobacco. Indeed, some go to such undue rigor as even to abstain from conversation for fear of taking too much air into their mouths, and thus breaking their fast, in which case they would have to keep the sixty subsequent days.

Even the touch of a Christian is avoided during *Ramazan*. As every physical enjoyment is proscribed but sleep, devotees sleep nearly all day, except when at worship. "God bless the man who first invented sleep." Those wandering in the streets are like madmen, so that Christians do well to keep out of their way. The asking of questions by "infidel dogs" is promptly rebuked. The law is paralyzed, the fact that they have all been fasting being a sufficient excuse for all sorts of wicked performances. Business is at a standstill, and fanaticism has full sway.

At home, on every day of *Ramazan*, toward evening, with food prepared, all await the signal cannon. At sunset the minarets are illuminated, the cannon is fired, and, at the *muezzin's* call from the slender spires, the fasting is suddenly changed into feasting. Night is virtually turned into day. There is a hasty scramble for something to eat, and excessive eating, dancing, and singing continue until late in the night. This fast and feast are held in honor of the time when Mohammed claimed that God revealed the Koran to him by His archangel. Moslems believe that Abraham, Moses, and Jesus also received divine revelations during this month.

Some traditions attribute this celebration to another event. One day when Mohammed was wandering in the desert one of his camels fled. Poor Mohammed pursued all day, without eating or drinking, and captured it about sunset. Mohammedans are not certain which day of the month this occurred, so in order to make sure they celebrate the whole month.

The green-turbaned Turks are the descendants of the prophet Mohammed, through his daughter Fatima, who married Ali, the faithful disciple. They are known as Emirs, and enjoy religious and political preference. Having a chief of their own, who is a sovereign among them, even to the infliction of punishment, they form a religious institution perpetuating the spirit of Islamism, as the janizaries in their day kept up the military spirit of the empire.

Besides these, there are several other peculiar Mohammedan orders. We shall first describe the Dervishes. The Dervish is an historic figure, with many orders, the first one having been founded thirty-seven years after the death of Mohammed. There are different classes, itinerant and local, asceticism being the most distinctive feature of almost all the different orders. As a religious body they are held in great veneration by the Moslem public everywhere, and their influence in stimulating the religious fanaticism of the Islam troops in times of war is considerable.

By far the lowest in the order of Dervishes is the religious beggar. On many occasions, always to the satisfaction of my intense curiosity, I have visited the haunts of these degraded creatures. With the maxim, "Poverty is my glory," they live a hermit life, somewhat after the fashion of their Prophet, or, indeed, more like the Grecian philosopher Diogenes, with no care in life but to find a place to sleep and something to eat. Their abodes, in deserted quarters of the city, or in mountain caves, are destitute of furniture, and those of the most rigid devotees have not even bedding or a cushion. In personal appearance they are the most hideous-looking beings in the world. They wear sheepskins, and have their whiskers and hair hanging down over their faces and shoulders. They almost always carry sharp hatchets in their hands for protection, and go begging in the bazaars, and praying in the streets in Arabic. Cut off from all family associations, their lives are entirely sanctified to their so-called monastic institution.

Mevlevi, or Dancing Dervishes, are very graceful, and entirely different from those above described, in manner, dress, and principles, and are more human in personal appearance, though at times quite frantic in action. They are generally found in octagon-shaped *tekichs*, or chapels, with polished floors, and wear close-fitting suits, with loose petticoats, and conical hats of grey felt. After the Koran is expounded, the usual *nemaz* recited, and kisses exchanged, the graceful spinning begins under the leadership of Semar Zan, director of the performance. Arms are crossed on the breast, with hands on the shoulders. Slowly at first, then faster as they warm up, the arms and skirts are extended, and, to the strange tune of the flute music, they move around and pass one another, but never touch. With brains crazed by the delirious dance, steadily the spell increases until the climax is reached, when it decreases to the finish; about one hour being the time for a single dance.

Not less curiously interesting are the *rifai*, or Howling Dervishes—demons of religious fanaticism, who, in a shell of a building decorated with spikes, chains, daggers, and like implements of torture, excite themselves, and, swinging backward and forward in circles, repeat all the names of God, accompanied with the awful cry of *La-il-la-il! Hoo-yah-Hou!* Beads of perspiration form on the face, which is distorted as if by mental anguish. Foaming at the mouth like madmen, they proceed, with the fearful energy of deep fervor and rapture, to cut themselves with knives, swallow swords and fire, pierce their ears, burn their bodies, until, all the physical powers overcome, they swoon and fall bleeding to the floor. Two elder devotees will calmly approach the *skeik*, with whisperings of sacred words, and have a skewer thrust through the cheek. You may examine and see that there is no legerdemain.

Islam is not lacking in sects. Indeed, they are innumerable, with infinite shades between them. But there are two great divisions, known in the Moslem world as Sunnites and Shiites. Sunnites, by far the greater in numbers, follow the first three Caliphs after Mohammed; while the Shiites, chiefly confined to

A DERVISH BEGGAR.

DANCING DERVISHES.

Persia, regard these as illegitimate, and commence with the caliphate of Ali, Mohammed's nephew. This sect represents the climax of Mohammedan fanaticism.

While in Constantinople in 1889, during the month of Ramazan, I was permitted one night to witness the horrible religious celebration of this sect—an awful night, never to be forgotten! With the purpose of obtaining merit and forgiveness, for admittance to Paradise without examination, the Persian devotees appeared in a procession at night, clothed in robes of white and armed with swords, iron chains, and other weapons of torture. Long before the spectacle was sighted in the distance, the streets were surging with thousands of clamorous men and women of every nationality and type, in eager anticipation of the death-foreboding pageant soon to come. Then, from a huge building, with unearthly tumult, and amid a profusion of lights, the devotees burst out into the streets in the midst of the many spectators, and moved, step by step, in a circle, amid wild, roaring wails of "Hassan! Hussein! Hassan! Hussein-Shah!"

They inflict ferocious wounds upon their bodies, some mutilating themselves with clubs and iron chains, many gashing their heads and throats with knives. It is the most horrible spectacle ever presented by a group of savage mortals, the body losing all semblance of humanity and assuming the aspect of a hideous monster. Hassan and Hussein, murdered twelve centuries ago, arise that night, and claim the active sympathy of their followers, with fresh blood. Ears, eyes, hands, arms, head, throat, and abdomen are not considered too dear to be sacrificed in this demon-like exhibition of religious frenzy. As the blood pours out in streams, sobbing cries of "Hassan!" and "Hussein!" go on in varying tones and inflame the entire assembly.

My very soul shuddered and recoiled with horror as I gazed upon faces bathed with the blood and sweat of extreme torture. Many keep step more and more violently with the wild performance, until, overcome by exhaustion, they lie gasping for breath, some never again to stagger to their feet. Some women, moved by the agony of the scene, fainted away. Who could look on such a scene unmoved?

Before this awful sight we close our eyes, and the hardest heart turns sick and faint, while in anguish of despair the soul cries out, "O God, is Thy light powerless to penetrate the midnight that hangs pall-like over benighted people of Thine own creation?" And, peering through the darkness, Hope sees the glimmering of a star, the morning star, bespeaking a larger light, before whose powerful rays this awful night of ignorance shall flee forever.

Beholding this Mohammedan paroxysm of self-torture, the oft-repeated question echoed in my ear with more emphasis than ever, "Why art thou a Christian?" and my soul answered: "Because God is love. His religion is a religion of love, a religion of peace. No more sacrifice, for Christ suffered for all our transgressions, and we are free from all penalty. We are not required to commemorate His blood with ours, but to follow the path of eternal life and happiness which He has opened for us through His own death. He died for us; we live for Him."

As regards the theoretical and doctrinal aspects of Islam, a cursory observer finds much that is to be commended; yet the careful student of its true spiritual influence, particularly in the light of the present situation in Armenia, finds much that is to be condemned. This may best be seen by a comparison with the Christian doctrines and practices. Of all the religions of the world, Christianity and Mohammedanism are the only two missionary and aggressive faiths, for they both seek to make converts; but their methods are as diverse as the characters and ideas of their founders. The one does it by the cross and love, the other by hatred and the sword; one by assimilation, the other by subjugation. The theme of Christendom is mercy, loving-kindness, and charity; that of Islam, blind submission enforced by tyranny. The article of faith or the official prayer of Islam, which is used throughout Turkey, and daily repeated in the Azhar University, at Cairo, by ten thousand Mohammedan students from all lands, is the following:

> O Lord of all Creatures! O Allah! Destroy the infidels and polytheists, thine enemies, the enemies of the religion! O Allah! Make their children orphans, and defile their abodes! Cause their feet to slip; give them and their families, their households and their women, their children and their relations by marriage, their brothers and their friends, their possessions and their race, their wealth and their lands, as booty to the Moslems, O Lord of all Creatures!

Can a Mussulman, with consistent loyalty to such religious principles, tolerate those of unlike faith? The massacre of Christians or all others of unlike faith is not only an obligation, a patriotic duty, but the only mode of religious revival with him. The memory of devastating wars waged by Mohammed; the atrocious cruelties perpetrated by his followers upon those of unlike faith; the fact that polygamy exists and was sanctioned by the Prophet himself—all conspire to breed an antipathy within us that is not wholly unjustifiable. The commands of the Koran in regard to methods of warfare do not warrant any admonitions deprecating cruelty in any form; in fact, with the watchword, "The sword is the key to heaven and hell," its soldiers have ever been the concrete expression of fiendish brutality.

From the time of Mohammed's triumphant march from Medina to Mecca, at the head of an army ten thousand strong, through the years when the "sand of the desert, converted into explosive powder, blazed heaven-high from Delhi to Granada," to this very day, when his Turkish devotees, with uplifted scimitar, transform the homes of peaceable Christians, from the Euphrates to the Bosphorus, into a wilderness of blood and fire, the career of Islam has been one continuous and desolating tidal wave of bloodshed, outrage, and rapine in the name of Allah and the Prophet.

True, it cannot be said that Christendom has been more humane in her warfare and religious persecutions in the past; but it must be remembered that the Christendom of to-day is not the Christendom of the past, while the Islamism of to-day is the Islamism of the past. The evolution of centuries has widened the religious as well as the intellectual horizon of Christians into clearer and more charitable ideas of the true interpretation of Christ's teachings of peace and universal brotherhood. Christians have reformed, for the principles of their religion ever teach them to reform; while the Moslems have not, and, in truth, they cannot reform, for the principles of their religion forbid reformation.

That the Turks, like all Mussulmans, are sincerely devout in making their religion an essential part of their daily life cannot be refuted, yet it appears that this very-overdevotion to a deluded and tyrannical faith makes them the most relentless of religious persecutors. But one need not go to the Dark Ages of the past to find a parallel for the incorrigible Moslem Turk's astounding inhumanity. I suggest the present deplorable condition of my native land, Armenia, where all the sacred relations of father, mother, wife, and child are trampled beneath his brutal feet, and one hundred thousand of my countrymen have suffered the most agonizing deaths by fire and sword. Nor is the Armenian crisis the only record of the Turk's religious fanaticism in the present century. In 1822 Greek Christians, to the number of fifty thousand, were put to the sword in the island of Scio. In 1850 Nestorians were butchered with such barbarity that the mountains and plains were covered with "the scattered bones, bleached skulls, long locks of hair plucked from the women's heads, and torn portions of the garments they had worn." * In 1860 Syrian Christians were killed, and Lebanon and Damascus "ran with human gore, in which men waded ankle deep"; †

---

* See Layard's "Nineveh."
† See Van Lennep's "Bible Lands; Their Modern Customs and Manners."

and twenty-one years ago fifteen thousand Bulgarians were massacred in cold blood within a few days.

As we pursue the career of such a heartless religion, so infernally atrocious in theory and practice, our pained hearts cannot help but exclaim, "How long, O Lord, how long!" May we not confidently cherish the hope that the shining cross of the humble Nazarene, that has conqueringly risen above the powers of darkness and tyranny, shall sooner or later, as its final achievement, triumph over the blood-red crescent of Mohammed?

THE TURKISH GOVERNMENT.

"The Sultan's Empire is being rapidly brought to destruction; corruption has reached a pitch that it has never before attained. The service of the state is starved while untold millions are being poured into the palaces; and the provinces are being ruined by the uncontrolled exactions of the governors, who purchase their appointments at the palaces; and nothing can save the country but a complete change of system."—MIDHAT PASHA, ex-Prime Minister of the Ottoman Empire.

LIKE most political institutions, the Turkish government of to-day has been the product of a gradual development; arrested and contorted as it may have been at certain eras of its growth. In order that we may gain even a superficial idea of the government of Turkey, it will be wise for us to go back some centuries and imagine the condition of those days when it first exercised its simplest functions. We find the Turks in the midst of a mighty career of conquest. The people of Asia Minor and of eastern Europe are gradually being forced to acknowledge the sovereignty of advancing armies, whose right there is little heart or means to contest. To *attain* such a sovereignty, and to *retain* it, are two different problems, of which the latter is by far the more complex and the less likely to be solved; especially when the conquered are comprised of heterogeneous nationalities, with ideas entirely different in matters pertaining to religion and the state. This problem the great Alexander attempted on a much larger scale, and failed—because he was mortal; and this problem the conquering Turks were compelled to face, and they solved it—in their way.

The government of this time was necessarily nomadic and, therefore, military in its nature. Accordingly, it was imperative to its strength and effectiveness that power should be centralized as much as possible, and this was accomplished by the inception of a sort of feudal system. Under this system the titles of the territory, as fast as it was conquered, were distributed among the most worthy of the soldiers, who, in turn, were placed under obligation to furnish a certain quota of armed men for the service of the state. It is almost needless to add that a grant of this kind was esteemed a prize and was the effective means of stimulating many to noble deeds and valiant sacrifice.

The smallest variety of fief or grant was the *timar*, comprising from three hundred to five hundred acres. In times of war the "cavalier," or owner of a *timar*, was bound to supply one armed horseman for every three thousand *aspres* of its revenue. Grants of five hundred acres and upward were called *ziamets*, and the very largest fief was the *beylik*.

That this system might be the more effectual, these lands were assigned to districts, each containing a certain number of grants. Over such a district was appointed an officer with the dignified insignia of a horse's tail. Yet the office of *Sandjak-Bey* was no mean one, and he had some thousands of cavalry placed at his command. Though unaccompanied by many of the civilized results with which the feudal system was followed in other portions of Europe, this same system was admirably suited to the exigencies of the times. It afforded the head of the nation ample means for quelling insurrections, and, indeed, insured a loyalty such as no other plan we are able to conceive of could.

We have been considering the government simply in its policy, with no regard to its composition and inner principles; and, in approaching this latter phase, we will anticipate, from what has been said, that its functions were largely discharged by men of military ability. Indeed, should we peruse the Institutes of Mohammed II., we should find the government of those days explained in a military metaphor—that of a tent and the four columns which were its support. And I think it best, because of the quaint simplicity of the figure, to adopt it in this short sketch, which is likely enough to suffer for want of perspicuity. This figure may be made to "stand on all fours" without in the least destroying its usefulness.

The first pillar, then, supporting the fabric of the state, was represented by the viziers, or "bearers of burdens." At the time of Mohammed II. these were four in number. The Grand Vizier, who was a sort of minister of state and an executive officer, was, next to the Sultan, the highest personage in the empire. To him was intrusted the imperial seal, and his was the privilege of presiding over the "Divan," or Council of the Realm, in the absence of the Sultan. Perhaps the highest function he enjoyed was the convoking of this council in his own tent whenever he deemed it necessary. The second pillar was represented by two military judges called *cadiaskers*, who, with their subordi-

PUBLIC READING OF THE SULTAN'S FIRMAN REGARDING THE APPOINTMENT OF A PASHA.

nates, constituted the legal order of the empire. The authority of one was confined to Europe, that of the other to Asia. Immediately beneath them in rank were the tutor to the royal princes and officers called *mufte*. The duty of these *mufte* was to expound the sacred law, and their persons were considered so sacred that not even the Sultan was permitted to put them to death. Yet this restriction was of no value, as the Sultan could depose them from their positions at his pleasure, and then execute them as he could any other subject. In this legal order was also included the Judge of Constantinople, whose office was created somewhat later than the others we have mentioned. The third pillar, a golden one, yet strong and indispensable, was the *deftarders*, officers of the exchequer; and last came the secretaries of state, or *nischandyes*, with whom the figure is complete.

The "Sublime Porte," which has long designated to the world the Turkish government, is an expression whose origin is also intimately connected with the idea of the tent from whose lofty gate, or, in Italian, *La Porta Sublima*, the rulers of old gave forth their decrees. Of course, at the head of all the political framework we have delineated, reigned supreme that arbitrary monarch, the Sultan.

We have said that the Turkish government is a growth. Perhaps we should have stated it more accurately had we said that it is a modification, for, with some few changes and complications, the government of to-day is in principle the same as that of three or four centuries ago; so that, understanding the latter, it will be comparatively easy correctly to comprehend the present system. And first, there has been some change in the political divisions of the empire. In the sixteenth century the *sanjaks*, or groups of grants, which we have described, were made into still larger districts, called *ciatels*. The tendency toward centralization, which was before a desirable thing, soon became an obstacle to effective administration, and the central government was not long in discovering that farther division of labor was eminently necessary. Various alterations were made in the system at different times, but with little result until 1864, when these *ciatels* became separate governmental centers, designated by a new name, *vilayet*. The *vilayet* is to-day what might be called the political unit of the empire, and possesses some degree of independence, although directly tributary to the laws of the whole country. The head officers are the *vali* and his assistant *muavin*, both appointed by the Sultan, to whom they are directly responsible. Of course, these dignitaries are aided by their secretaries, who direct the work of the several departments over which they are placed by imperial nomination.

The governors of the *sanjaks*, the subdivisions of the *vilayets*, although appointed by the Sultan, are considered as representatives of the *vali*, from whom they receive their instructions. The next subdivision is the *kaza*, or district, whose governor is in turn accountable to the head officer of the *sanjak*. Again, the *kaza* is divided into *nahichs*, or subdistricts, comprising houses to the number of two hundred. The inhabitants of these *nahichs* have the usual privilege of electing their own *mudir* and *muavin*, subject, however, to the confirmation of the *vali* of the district. The election is not free from religious considerations, and the religious complexion of the majority determines the fate of the nominee. The very last division, the minimum visible, as it might appropriately be called, is that presided over by the head man of single villages, the *codja bashi*, or *kehyah*, as he is variously called. His powers are very limited, and he is almost entirely an instrument of the *mudir*. Yet it is a rule of local self-government that the people must hand their taxes over to a representative from their own number rather than to a collector directly from the Sublime Porte. In all these instances the directing officer is aided in his administration by appropriate aids and by an Administrative Council, a permanent organization. We may the better comprehend the position of all these officers if, on the basis of the feudal system, we conceive of each as holding a "fief of responsibility," for which he is directly accountable to the one next higher in rank.

The *vali* has direct control over sub-governors and all the employees of the *vilayet*. Invested with such a power, should his tendencies be for corruption and evil, as they generally are, he has the best opportunity and the most unlimited power to gratify them, for he has the entire official body of the *vilayet* under his control; and if a sub-governor has the courage to oppose him, it is so much the worse for the sub-governor. Nor is this the entire extent of the *vali's* jurisdiction and influence. He has the general oversight and management of all the taxes and revenues, and is also the commander of the military forces of the *vilayet*. And

A VALI AND SUITE.

with such unlimited authority, he can generally influence the courts of justice as he chooses.

The supreme head of the empire, the Sultan, who moves the machinery of the administration as the vice regent of God upon earth and as the Caliph, or successor of Mohammed, has an authority unknown elsewhere in the world. To recount his powers would be a hopeless task. He is omnipotent, and all things proceed from and revert directly or indirectly to his sovereign will. His word is absolute for life or death. A few restraints have been forced upon him from time to time, but even these are more fictitious than real. The people at large have no choice as to their ruler, for the office is hereditary, and the succession belongs to the oldest male relative, not to the eldest son, as might naturally be presumed. The executive and legislative authority, under the supreme direction of the Sultan, is exercised by two dignitaries, the Grand Vizier, who is the head of the temporal government, and the Sheik-ul-Islam, the head of the church.

The Grand Vizier, one of the oldest pillars of state, has lost none of his power, and is accountable to no one save the Sultan, by whom he is appointed and in whose name he acts. It is still his privilege to preside at the Medjliss-i-Hass, or Privy Council, in the Sultan's absence, and wherever he is there is the Sublime Porte. We shall understand somewhat his significance if we remember that it is he who nominates to almost all the important offices. To this function is added that of commander-in-chief of the army, which, however, he is not obliged to exercise in person. The salary of the Grand Vizier amounts to about fifty thousand dollars a year.

The different departments of Medjliss-i-Hass, constituting what is known as the Sublime Porte, consists of the following ministers : 1, the Grand Vizier ; 2, the Sheik-ul-Islam ; 3, the Minister of the Interior ; 4, the Minister of War ; 5, the Minister of Evkaf, or Worship ; 6, the Minister of Public Instruction ; 7, the Minister of Public Works ; 8, the President of the Council of State ; 9, the Minister of Foreign Affairs ; 10, the Minister of Finance ; 11, the Minister of Marine ; 12, the Minister of Justice ; 13, the Minister of the Civil List. This Medjliss-i-Hass has weekly meetings, when matters of public moment are presented and considered. It also serves as a sort of advisory Cabinet.

It was in 1453 that the unique office of Sheik-ul-Islam was created. No other nation employs a similar functionary, because the laws of no other nation are in such a peculiar manner related to the sacred writings. While not really a spiritual head, it becomes one of his duties to interpret the Koran as applied to matters of a legal character, and to preside over Ulema, a body comprising the clergy and chief functionaries of the law. In rank this dignitary is not below the Grand Vizier, and he likewise is appointed by the Sultan with the nominal concurrence of the Ulema, receiving the same salary as the former officer. The power of the Sheik-ul-Islam is manifold. Besides acting as counsel to the Sultan, he is at the head of all the law courts of the empire, and his sanction, or *fetva*, is necessary to render a verdict valid. Even the Sultan's decrees are subject to his sanction ; yet this is merely a matter of form, for, should a *fetva* be refused him, the Sultan could use—or abuse—his appointing power, and gain the sanction desired from a more docile servant.

So far as my observation has extended, I have found that people in general have very erroneous ideas regarding the administration of justice in Turkey. I think that a personal acquaintance with Turkish courts would clearly show that if anything pertaining to the Turkish government is worthy of sweeping denunciation, it surely is the so-called Department of Justice. There is really no semblance of justice in Turkish courts in general.

The old-time courts of the cadis, like backwoods courts of America, had substituted their own ideas of justice for established law. They would, for instance, render judgment against the defendant and send him to jail for not paying promptly, and send the plaintiff there, too, for making a fuss about so small a matter, while the witness would get a few days behind the bars for not minding his own business. The modern Turkish courts, however, were forced to adopt a system of laws based upon the Code Napoléon. At the time it was thought a decided improvement; but the Moslem system of laws thus coming into a close relation with the European system, as represented by the Code Napoléon, has resulted in nothing more than that the Turk has put on the robes of civilized nations, only to cover his barbaric inner nature.

It is not new laws that are most needed in Turkey. The existing laws, in all the departments of administration, are good enough for the Turks; but what is vitally indispensable to good government is the honest application of the existing laws.

A TURKISH JUDGE.

In every *vilayet*, as well as in every *liva* (or *sanjak*) and *caza*, we find two different courts of justice. One is the Superior Court, or " Court Sheri," whose head—always a Mussulman—is appointed by the Sultan. The Courts Sheri correspond somewhat to American Courts of Equity, and they expound the sacred law of the Koran, appealing to it for a decision in those complexities where the law of the country is inadequate. Cases relating to real property fall rightly under their jurisdiction. The judgments of these courts are examined and amended by a *mollah* residing at the governing centers. The High Court of Appeals is divided into two chambers, one for Asia and one for Europe, and at the heads of these we recognize the *cadiaskers*, or the military judges who constitute the second pillar of state in our figure of the royal tent. While these Courts Sheri are not the only courts in Turkey, yet the Koran is the only law in the legislation of the country, and it is appealed to as absolute authority in all instances. Not only is this true, but there is another set of courts, which, although inferior in rank, are wide enough in their jurisdiction, and vested with enough of power, to be described somewhat in detail. While in theory to the people properly belongs the privilege of electing judges to these common courts, yet none but Mussulmans are held eligible to the office. Besides a jurisdiction over criminal cases, these tribunals try cases between the two great religious sects—between Mussulman and Christian. Like the Sheri, these courts are located at each *vilayet*, *liva*, and *caza*, each considering appeals from the next lower in rank. The tribunal at the *vilayet* tries the higher cases, involving such sentences as capital punishment and exile; but sentences of death are subject to the imperial sanction. At the *vilayet* is also a Court of Appeals, whose members come from the inferior courts, and who are supposed to be elected by the inhabitants, although in practice their choice has little influence.

The lesser courts of the sub-districts—the *livas* and *cazas*—try the less important suits. Lowest, and of least rank of all, are the minor justices of the peace, found at each village, whose jurisdiction is confined to cases the most petty. At the capital is the Supreme Court of Justice, which considers appeals from all over the empire, even including the Tribunal of Commerce, and whose decision is final, except in sentence of death, which can always be appealed to him on whose special will rest the lives of all his subjects. "In acknowledgment," says Creasy, "of his absolute power of life and death, the title of Hunkiar, the 'Manslayer,' is the one most commonly used by the subjects of the Sultan in speaking of their sovereign."

Whatever may be said of the administration of justice in Turkey, it is patent to all that here, at least, is a system good enough in theory, but purely despotic in practice, whether it be the worst conceivable or no. And I think it may be asserted with truth that, in spite of the many so-called reforms, justice is hardly ever meted out with any degree of equity. As has been indicated, the laws of the land are not based strictly upon the Code Napoléon, but upon the Koran, and these institutes are made to conform to it. Under such a legal system a Christian has no rights whatever.

He can obtain no justice, and has no redress against wrongs that are done him, for even his testimony is not available in Turkish courts of law. As has been stated, it is always the Moslem who sits on the bench; and as he, under the precepts of Moslem law, will not accept the evidence of a Christian against a fellow-Moslem, even though accused of the foulest crimes, how can a Christian hope for justice? It is absurd, let me repeat, to point out to the decrees of the Hatti-Humayoum placing the Christian witness on equality with those of the Mohammedans, for these decrees were never fully executed, and, in fact, they will always remain a dead letter as long as the Turk remains a Mohammedan. I can speak from personal and intimate acquaintance with Turkish courts of "justice." There are scarcely any of them that would not adhere to the old Moslem law rather than the Code Napoléon, when the controversy is based on an issue as affecting Mohammedans and Christians. When, however, the contention is of a Moslem against a Moslem, or a Christian against a Christian, then, as a rule, nothing but the largest *bakshish*, or bribe, can give weight to the balance of Turkish justice.

I have dwelt, in the preceding pages of this chapter, on the administrative phases of the Turkish government, and I wish to add a cursory outline of the area, population, and military system of the Ottoman government, and also of agriculture and taxation.

The total area of the immediate possessions of Turkey, not including the States nominally subject, is estimated at 1,147,578 square miles, and its total population at about 27,688,000. Of this number, in Asia it has 687,640 square miles, with a population of 21,608,000; in Africa, 398,738 miles, and a population of 1,300,000; and in Europe, 61,200 miles, and a population of 4,780,000.

Nominal possessions of the Ottoman Empire, including the Balkan States, Egypt, and Samos, have a total area of 461,662 square miles, with a total population of about 11,542,131.

THE ARMY AND NAVY.

The power of the Turkish army is great, by reason of its fanaticism and its being organized by German officers. In its present organization it is divided into three main divisions, namely: 1, the *nizam*, or the regular army; 2, the *rédif*, or the army of reserve; and, 3, the *muntafiz*, or the territorial army. All Mohammedans over twenty years of age are liable to military service, and this liability continues for twenty years—six years in the regular army, eight years in the reserve army, and six years in the territorial army. All the military forces of the Turkish government are distributed in army corps, with seven headquarters in principal centers of the empire. The effective combatant service of the Turkish army, according to the "Statesman's Year Book," is 700,620 men. Of this, the infantry has 648 battalions, with 583,200 men; the cavalry, 202 squadrons, with 53,300 men; the artillery, 1356 guns, with 54,720 men; and the engineers have 39 companies, with 7400 men.

The Turkish navy is in a sadly neglected condition. Only three ships can now be counted of any fighting value, while the rest of the Turkish ships are of no worth whatever. The Ottoman naval organization is practically the same as that of the land forces. The time of service in the navy is twelve years—five in active service, three in the reserve, and four in the *rédif*, or army of reserve.

Any candid, impartial observer of the Turkish Government will find that the official corruption in all the departments of administration has kept out of gear its political machinery. So incurably dishonest is the whole system that nothing can be done without a bribe. It is seldom that men of requisite qualifications are intrusted with high governmental and municipal offices; but the person who secures an appointment is the one who has the skill to acquire influence in the palace at Constantinople. If there is anything in the United States that somewhat resembles the Turkish government it is the New York Tammany Hall at its worst. True, there have been a few honorable and high-minded officials, who conducted the affairs of the state with some measure of efficiency; but the general demoralization, with the basest forms of venality on one hand and cruelty and misgovernment on the other, has become so widely spread that it would be really difficult to overestimate the utter rottenness of many branches of the administration.

As in all other governments, and perhaps to a greater degree, there is to be found much of dross and much that cannot be looked upon with complacency by right-minded men. Much of excellent theory is transformed into most corrupt practice. Good government can come only through good administration. True, a

A MODERN TURKISH GENERAL.

bad law may seriously hamper the best administration, yet a good law is of no value whatever unless well administered. A thorough cleansing of the administration, with many important modifications of abusable privileges, would do much for civilization in Turkey.

AGRICULTURE AND TAXATION.

At the conquest of the country now known as Turkey four main dispositions were made of the land, namely: first, *miri*, or Crown lands; second, *vacouf*, or pious foundations; third, *mulikaneh*, or Crown grants; and, fourth, *muck*, or freehold property. The first portion, the Crown lands, constituted the private property of the empire; the second was set aside as the exclusive property of the Church; the third division of landed property was granted to the old feudal soldiers in recompense for military service; while the last tenure, the freehold property, does not exist to a great extent. By conforming to certain conditions imposed by the government, the unoccupied or waste lands included under the first division may become private property. Anyone may thus obtain a title to a farm by appropriating as many acres as he can well cultivate, providing he pays the specified tax for a period of twenty years. As a result of this opportunity afforded by the government, many villages, composed almost wholly of these minor farmers, have gradually come into being. It was not until the year 1867 that subject peoples were granted the right of holding real property in their own name. To-day numbers of large farms represent investments of foreign capital, and almost all the farms of the empire have non-resident owners.

The transfer of title to land is a simple matter. Both parties to a transfer proceed to the government house of a district, and there, in the presence of witnesses, make the sale valid. The purchaser pays at once the price agreed and receives a certificate which entitles him to private ownership; later he obtains from the capital the title-deed to his property.

But while the transfer of land is apparently so simple, yet many complexities attend its formalities in the execution of property titles, and these very complexities have been deliberately instituted by the Turkish government for the express purpose of plundering the Christian property-owners.

The *vacouf*, or Church lands, are not exempt from being a source of a great deal of trouble. As has been briefly stated, the *vacouf* is a parcel of land with or without buildings on it; its *dominium plenum* does not belong to the occupant, but he simply has the use of it. The fact that this form of tenure insures freedom from many oppressive measures of the government and fraudulent tendencies of grasping officials induces a great many people to make over their property to pious institutions, such as a mosque, with the condition of using the property during their lifetime. In time this method became so firmly established that to-day the whole of Constantinople is *vacouf* property. Reclus estimates that one-third of the total amount of property in European Turkey is *vacouf* property.

As to how laws and regulations have been altogether disregarded by the Turkish government; and people have been driven from their homes, and their property seized by the officials of the state, I will not here attempt to speak. It would, indeed, open a new chapter of endless wrongs.

We will now consider the mode of managing a large cultivated estate. The landed proprietor himself does not usually attend to the farm, but employs an agent, generally a native, to personally superintend the business; and thus the owner is often the victim of dishonesty on the part of his agent, who has not much fear of discovery. Besides the agent there are numerous farm laborers, who are sometimes paid in stipulated wages and sometimes by a share in the year's produce. The superintendent has also his "staff" of cowherds, oxherds, and similar necessary helpers. By this method, in force on the *beylik*, or " home farm," as it is called, the profits above wages and other expenses revert directly to the landed proprietor. But the *beylik* does not include all of the estate, for a large part of it is let out to tenants who usually work on the *métayer* system—a system so universally in vogue that it will be well to explain it.

The tenant is usually a Christian. Besides a small plot for his own private use, he is furnished by his landlord with seed, and sometimes with a house and barn. At the end of the year each receives half of of what produce remains after paying the usual "tithe," or tax. It cannot be said that this system is one of absolute equity, for if there is any loss to be borne, it largely falls upon the landlord. If the crops are poor, it is he who suffers most; and his tenant is usually indebted to him ; for when compelled to borrow, the tenant borrows from his landlord at twelve per cent., rather than from professional money-lenders, whose rate is two or three times higher. On the other hand, the tenant's lot is not so happy as might be thought on considering his absolute freedom from risk. It is just this lack of responsibility which, by thwarting any spirit of enterprise, is his chief curse. He is sure of support at the hands of the proprietor, and is not very eager to over-exert himself for the highest cultivation of the estate. He also suffers the inconvenience of being compelled to give his time to the service of the government in any emergency when it may be called for. As has been said, the tenant is usually a Christian, and, if he be orthodox and observe the excessively numerous days of religious fast and prayer, he will not work nearly all the year. It will be seen that, in the face of these obstacles, method is utterly impossible, and until there is a reform of some kind progress is not to be hoped for.

When properly conducted sheep-farming is a profitable industry, the only drawback being that the art of breeding is not understood so as to insure the best results. Almost every landed proprietor has grazings which he rents out to flock-masters. In the letting out of these sheep lands is found one instance where the owner runs little or no risk, as at least one-half of the rent is always required in advance, and for the other half the flock itself is ample security. Then, too, despite severe competition, the rents are generally high.

In winter the sheep are taken up the mountain slopes to graze, and when the warmer days of summer come they are again led to pasture in the plains. This summer pasturing extends from the beginning of May to October, and is the more profitable kind.

Turkey has sometimes been suggested as a good place for the more scientific cultivation of sheep. It is certainly true that, with more careful breeding, much more could be realized from this source than is the case at the present time. The soil of Asia Minor is so remarkably rich and fertile that everything grows in great luxuriance, even with little cultivation; although it might seem that the fertile qualities of the soil would quickly be exhausted, as it receives no manure save from the summer grazing of the sheep.

In some localities crops are sown every year, and in others during alternate years. Grains, such as wheat, barley, and oats, are raised. The farmers begin to sow in autumn, although some do not finish until January, and the reaping is done in the month of June. Owing to the nature of the climate, spring crops are usually a failure, but about May or April a great staple of the empire, tobacco, together with maize and other like products, is sown. These are harvested during August and September. Tobacco cultivation has attained a high degree of perfection, and the product brings a good price. Of course, there are extensive vineyards scattered almost everywhere in Asia Minor, and from certain localities of it comes some of the best wine in the world. Nor should we fail to mention the making of silk, which is no mean industry of the empire.

Good farming has been greatly retarded by the very crude methods of cultivation everywhere to be

A TURKISH LANDLORD OF THE HIGHEST TYPE.

found; and it is the deliberate policy of the government to continue this state of affairs. Threshing machines are practically unused, and, consequently, this part of harvesting becomes a very laborious as well as wasteful process.

There are several modes of threshing. Sometimes the grain in the ear is scattered on the barn floor and horses are made to gallop over it. In other localities the process is more elaborate, and a sled with a flinted bottom is used, upon which is often placed a young girl, who balances herself as she is drawn by horses round and round the threshing-floor, amid the admiring plaudits of the beholders. The women, too, are compelled to do their share, and in the threshing season usually commence work with the men, at three o'clock in the morning.

There seems to be a decided aversion to farm machinery of every kind. For instance, the plow which is most extensively in use is little more than a stick.

It is true, the earth has only to be tickled to "laugh in a harvest," but the laugh might be a little more hearty were more modern plows introduced and used. When the material civilization of the West shall penetrate Oriental crudeness, bringing its tools and machines and means of transportation; when human ingenuity shall join hands with nature, there will not be found in all the world better farming countries than European and Asiatic Turkey.

The tax on agriculture is very onerous. The tithe system is in vogue, and it has always varied in amount on all produce. The tax is levied by a person known as the *multeyim*, who purchases from the government

FIREMEN AND FIRE ENGINE IN TURKEY.

the privilege of taxing a certain territory. The purchase price constitutes the revenue of the government from this source, and the profits of the collector are measured by the amount he is able to extort from the people in excess of that sum. Thus the motive of the collector is self-interest rather than public service. One redeeming feature, however, which prevents worse corruption, is the fact that the officers of the state are never allowed to bid for tithes.

Some of the measures of this taxation are extremely harsh. For instance, the farmers are obliged to keep their produce until the collector comes to take his portion, and thereby loss is often suffered. But the greatest evil is in the methods of assessment. The collector, by virtue of the government's sanction, resorts to unrestricted acts of violence and oppression, in his greedy efforts to secure excessive profits. At the time of the collection of taxes, accompanied by the *zabtieh*, or police (in spite of the law that collection of taxes is to be wholly separated from the work of the police), in many cases he actually takes the last cent from the poor farmer. I have known years when the crops failed; nevertheless, the assessor was sure to appear with the police and seize the cattle of the unfortunate farmer. At times, in my native city Marsovan, the yield of grapes was so far overestimated, as they hung on the vines, that when the vineyards were put into the tender hands of the tax-buyer twenty-five or thirty per cent. of the actual product was demanded from the producer. Taking into due consideration such execution of laws with actual conditions, we need not wonder at the unenterprising character and the perpetual poverty of the peasantry. It is needless to say that it would improve the condition of things were the government to collect this tax directly, for, however exorbitant its taxation might be, the heaviest burden of legal exaction is light when compared with the extortion practiced by the *multeyims*.

Corresponding somewhat to the *ashr*, or tithe, on arable land, is what is termed the *sayme*, a tax on sheep, goats, and, sometimes, cattle. Before 1858 this was collected in kind, but since that time one-tenth of the money value, according to appraisement, had been taken by the government.

Similar to the property tax in this country is the *verghi*, which to-day assumes two forms, a tax on income and a tax on property. This is systematic and based upon a fixed principle. The assessment of the income tax is made in public meetings, at which all concerned are permitted to be present, and it differs with the professions and trades, and depends also on the reputed wealth of the individual. In general, however, it is three per cent. on all gross income from invested capital or from any other source. There are a few who are exempt, such as parish doctors, religious orders, and schoolmasters.

The tax on real property mentioned above is placed at four dollars a year per one thousand dollars on the estimated value of all lands and houses, whether subject to tithes or not. The value of such property is calculated at five times its produce, or twenty times its assumed rent, and, with the tithe, this is most oppressive. It may be added that those who receive rent from tenants are required to hand over four per cent. per annum, tithe-paying land alone excepted.

Although the Hatti-Sherif of 1839 and the Hatti-Humayoum of 1856 were to admit Christians into the Ottoman army, the law has never been fully enforced. Save a couple of regiments of mixed Cossacks, there are hardly any non-Mussulmans engaged in the service. The exemption from military duty, however, is not to be obtained for nothing, and a tax, commonly termed the *bedel*, is laid upon all non-Mohammedans not in the army. This tax in itself is not unfair, considering that a Mohammedan has to pay more for the exemption than does a Christian, but, in common with other taxes, the method of assessment deserves our condemnation.

I have known poor Armenian neighbors, with large families, who, upon their absolute inability to meet the government's demands, were thrown into prison, after being subjected to the most brutal indignities, thus leaving their families in a state of hunger and despair. They were not to be released until the government's demands were duly met. I vividly recall instances when the philanthropic spirit of my father was so moved by the miseries of unhappy victims of Turkish outrage that he hastened to pay their taxes, and thus secured their deliverance from Turkish dungeons. This most harassing and oppressive form of taxation has long been the cause of infinite trouble, aggravated by the rapacity with which it was enforced.

Although in the regulations of 1876 freedom from taxation was promised to children and old men, yet, like all good promises of the Turk, this too has remained a

A HOT BARGAIN IN THE HORSE MARKET.
(*From a Painting.*)

dead letter, and a full tax has been exacted from males of all ages. The injustice of such a law is unquestioned, yet Armenians would have small cause for complaint were this the only oppressive feature in the system of Turkish taxation.

Some reforms have been instituted of late years which have somewhat enhanced the prosperity of the Turk. For instance, the eight per cent. tax formerly imposed upon goods passing from one Turkish port to another has happily been abolished, and an excise of one per cent. placed in its stead.

The indiscriminate tariff on imports of eight per cent. *ad valorem* is certainly not in accord with any principle of political economy, for it is often the weapon of exaction and of favoritism, in estimating the value of imports. The tax on exports of native produce is placed at one per cent. if sent abroad, but eight per cent. if sent from one part of the empire to another.

A tax of considerable importance is that levied on tobacco, and, as it is collected by the agent of a foreign company, it is, perhaps, the most frequently evaded. Owing to the severe penalty inflicted upon anyone discovered in the smuggling business, many ingenious methods are employed to elude detection. I have known of cases where tobacco, carefully covered with wool, was concealed in a bag and, as usual, carried on the back. Nor is this the only way in which the wool is pulled over the authorities' eyes. As we have previously stated, the tail of the Oriental sheep is quite large, and some persons, diverting this appendage from the purpose by nature designed, use it to hide a tale more wonderful still. I was surprised one midnight to see a man passing stealthily through the town, not on the street but from roof to roof, with what appeared to be a bag upon his back. As it turned out afterward, the bag was filled with tobacco, which he was trying to smuggle to his home in this unusual and perilous manner.

Various attempts have been made to develop the rich natural resources of the empire and establish manufactories, especially in the country, labor being so abundant and cheap. At one time a new era seemed to dawn, and thousands of natives were employed in factories. English and French influence, however, inaugurated the policy of free trade. Their goods were imported at a tariff of six or eight per cent. *ad valorem*. As a natural consequence the Turkish factories were closed, and workingmen and their families were reduced to abject poverty. The famous Bruse towels were imitated, and sold much cheaper, driving out the native goods, which, though costing more, would last five times as long. Combs, cutlery, and silks came from Sheffield, Manchester, and Lyons. The fine silky fleece of the Angora goat is sold much cheaper to the English manufacturer than to the native artisan, and comes back enhanced in value from fifty- to a hundred-fold. It is safe to say that of the wealth produced by a native goat, forty-nine dollars out of every fifty go into the pockets of foreigners. America may well learn a lesson from the Angora goat, and continue to resist a free-trade system that has closed the factories, destroyed the revenue, and produced beggary in the Ottoman Empire.

In spite of its exorbitant tax system the Turkish government has, in the last half century, been accumulating large debts, and its direct borrowings form no little portion of the general budget. In 1889 the revenue was ninety million dollars, while the expenditures were about one hundred and twenty-five million dollars.

The entire system of Turkish finance is sorely in need of scientific readjustment. The antiquated "farming-out" system should be replaced by a system of direct assessment and levy by officials of the government. The rapacity and greed of the tax-farmer being eliminated, the people would cheerfully contribute to the support of the government. And with the growth of a healthy public sentiment, through gradual modifications, there might be evolved from the present disorder and confusion a general scheme of taxation along progressive and scientific lines. In regard to the industrial incidents of the public finance, manufacture seems to require a discriminating protective tariff, and agriculture seems to require larger expenditures in the line of public roads and other facilities for transportation.

A reliable index to the prosperity of any country is to be found in its system of taxation. Whether such taxes are proportionately divided ; whether the poor are oppressed, and the rich escape from their rightful share in the public burden of expense, are questions the answers to which, to a large extent, determine the character of the nation. The proper administration and regulation of public taxation have been a serious and unsolved problem in all ages. A wise administration of taxes has raised empires to the pinnacle of world-wide glory. A too-sweeping tax adjudication has led many a nation to irretrievable downfall. Taxation is the tyrant's mightiest tool. Rightly conducted, it serves as the people's greatest blessing. One thing is certain: no matter how different the ways in which taxes are levied, they are essential to national growth, and even national existence.

THE EASTERN QUESTION.

> "A sick man—a very sick man. It would be a great misfortune if one of these days he should slip away from us before the necessary arrangements have been made."—NICHOLAS I.

IT is a rash claim for any man to make that he has mastered the Eastern Question. So complicated are its issues that it is hard to define, still harder to comprehend, it. In my conversation with a professor of modern history in one of the leading American universities, who is regarded as a specialist on this subject, he asserted with emphasis, "I do not understand the question, and nobody else does." It is a many-sided question, of which the future of Turkey is only a part; and it leads out into such a labyrinth of political entanglements that, unless a person takes a single point of view, to the utter disregard and exclusion of all side issues, he will never find his way out of it.

For centuries the Eastern Question has been the most engrossing problem that European statesmanship has had to solve, and centuries may yet pass before it will be finally settled. While the question has chiefly interested Russia, Turkey, and England, it is closely studied and watched, with the deepest concern, by all nations of the Continent. Back of all the diplomatic maneuvering, the one great aim of the Powers is to have, each and all, an outlet upon the Mediterranean, and, with this ultimate object in view, to join in the division and get the largest possible slice of Turkey. So long as a practical method of accomplishing this end is lacking, by reason of their common greed and mutual jealousies, just so long will the Eastern Question continue to exist. Calm and peaceful as it may sometimes appear on the surface, there are elements beneath that only await the touch of the fuse to evoke an eruption that will cause the political world to tremble.

In the preceding chapter we have pointed out that with the Sultan Suleyman the Magnificent (1520–66), the Turkish Empire had reached the zenith of its power and glory. He had led the nation into the grandest epoch of its history. He was undisputed master of the Mediterranean, and woe betide the ship flying a hostile flag upon its placid bosom! But there came a change. Unlike his brave father, who had marched at the head of the army and died at the age of seventy-six amid smoking ruins and captured cities, Selim shrank from leading his army in person, and gave himself to the excessive indulgence of vicious appetites. His example was followed, with rare exceptions, by the Sultans who succeeded him. Their folly and corruption would have put an end to their rule long ago had it not been for the mutual jealousy of the Powers of Europe. In the reign of Selim II. occurred the first conflict between the Turks and Russians. He decided to connect the Caspian and Black seas by uniting the rivers Don and Volga by a canal, by means of which a Turkish fleet could be sent into the Caspian. This had always been a plan that Russia most desired to carry out herself. When, therefore, Selim dispatched five thousand laborers and eighty thousand soldiers to consummate the cherished plan, he met with opposition from the Russians. The Turkish soldiers attacked the town of Astrakhan, the possession of which was necessary to construct the canal, but were repulsed and driven back. At this time the Russians, while patriotic and aggressive, occupied only a limited portion of southern Europe, and were but little known. Their antipathy to the Turks dates from their heroic defense before the walls of Astrakhan.

For one hundred years the Ottoman Empire had stood alone in power and might. Its armies had penetrated victoriously into the heart of Europe and had advanced to within two score miles of Vienna. From that city the Roman emperor fled before them, and the mighty Cathedral of St. Stephen barely escaped the fate of St. Sophia at Byzantium, in becoming a mosque of Allah and the Prophet. But soon the bright splendor of the Star and Crescent was obscured. In 1571 the ships of the Christian Powers, under the command of Don John of Austria, encountered the Turks outside of the Gulf of Lepanto, and in the furious conflict that ensued the Ottoman fleet was almost annihilated. Such a result proved of great moral value to Christians. They learned that the Ottoman navy was no longer invincible on the seas. Defeat after defeat, instead of the usual victories, followed the Turkish armies in quick succession, and but for the aid of the Poles the result would have been the utter destruction of the Ottoman Power. Turkey, however, continued to decline, and though she made

SANTA SOPHIA, CONSTANTINOPLE.

an occasional re-conquest, it was not of sufficient importance to turn the tide of her ill fortune.

In the year 1664 the Turkish army was completely routed in a war with the Germans, and twenty years later another bloody defeat was suffered at the hands of the Austrians. Turkey was urged into a war with Russia by Charles XII. of Sweden, who had taken refuge in the Sultan's empire after the disaster of Pultowa. The contest nearly resulted in the crushing defeat of the Russians, who were deserted by the Moldavians, upon whose aid they had in a large degree depended. In 1711 the Grand Vizier Baltiji Mohammed marched into Moldavia against the forces of the Czar, and on the right bank of the Pruth he completely blockaded the army of Peter the Great. Here the Vizier had his tireless foe entrapped in a precarious position, and finally compelled him to surrender. But his stupidity, and the adroit tactics of the Czarina, allowed Peter the Great to escape on the easiest terms.

In 1736, with the capture of the fortress of Azof and other important strongholds, the attitude of the Russians changed to the aggressive, and in their subsequent career of ceaseless warfare they proved to be a far more formidable adversary to the Turks than the Austrians. Austria now entered into an alliance with Russia to secure the ruin of Turkey and divide the spoils between them. The discovery of this scheme led the Turks to a war, in which the Austrians were defeated and driven across the Danube, while the Russians victoriously penetrated into the very heart of Moldavia. Again, in 1769, the Russians invaded

Moldavia, captured the fortress of Choozin, and, in the following year, conquered Moldavia and Wallachia, and blockaded and set on fire the Turkish fleet off Chios. The notable treaty of Kutchouk-Kainardji, made in July, 1774, closed the war. It provided for the absolute independence of the Tartar territory on the Crimea, with Kuban and the surrounding districts, and it further stipulated that under no pretext should either country meddle in their affairs.

Scarcely had the treaty been signed when Russia broke the terms by taking possession of the Crimea and the entire country east of the Caspian Sea, and compelled the Sultan, in 1784, to acquiesce in this action. It was, however, Catherine's fixed plan to drive the Turkish Power out of Europe and restore the Greek kingdom, by placing her grandson on the throne of Constantinople. Aware of the scheme, three years later the Sultan resumed hostilities against his Russian foe. A year later Joseph II. of Austria heartily entered into Russia's plan for the conquest and final dismemberment of the Ottoman Empire. Again Austria was defeated, and this time was compelled to sign a treaty at Sistovia, in 1791. The Russians, however, were too powerful for Turkey. They overran its northern provinces, and dealt a crushing blow to the Turkish fleet. The Ottoman Empire was apparently about to fall, and its very foundations seemed shaken by the victorious tramp of the mighty Russian Bear. All Europe now became alarmed. Pitt formed the Triple Alliance, made up of England, Prussia, and Holland, for the preservation of the European balance of power and the muzzling of the Russian Bear. Notwithstanding such a serious obstacle, Catherine determined to continue her warfare against the Turks until the completion of her cherished designs. To best accomplish this, Russia and Austria again effected an alliance, and the combined armies proceeded against the common adversary. The result was disastrous to Turkey, which was not only compelled to pay a heavy indemnity, but ceded Bucharest, Bender, Akerman, Ismail, and the Crimea and Kuban to the Russians, while Belgrade was given to Austria. The treaty of peace with Russia was signed at Jassey in January, 1792. The Dneister was made the frontier boundary between the two empires. The treaty also recognized the protectorate of Russia over Tiflis. Had it not been for the strong influence of the Triple Alliance, Catherine would have captured Constantinople itself. Indeed, so intense was the feeling of Pitt against the predominant and grasping policy of Russia that he united with Prussia for war against Catherine, and nothing but the strong public opinion against him rendered it impossible for the English minister to carry out his plan.

The far-sighted policy adopted by Peter the Great, the greatest Russian ruler up to his day, was one of acquisition. Constantinople and its straits were his dream, just as Jerusalem was that of the Crusaders. He knew that the Black Sea was the only coast available for the military and commercial enterprises of his people ; and it was but natural that he should take a deep interest in the question of the Straits, the outlet of that body of water which involved the maritime portion of his domain. The position of the Bosphorus and the Dardanelles, and their strategic importance, are doubtless well known to every one of my readers. The only countries bordering on the Black Sea are Russia and Turkey. But for the narrow channel called the Bosphorus, which connects the Black Sea and the Sea of Marmora, the sea would be to Russia simply a great land-locked lake. The Bosphorus is seventeen miles long and at places only a half mile wide, yet it is so deep that it enables the largest ship to anchor close to its shores. Entrance from this to the Mediterranean Sea is made possible by the Straits of Dardanelles, narrow and deep like the Bosphorus, and forty miles long. Close these straits, and Russia becomes an inland region, and its ships in the Black Sea are virtually land-locked. Fortify these straits, and Constantinople is invulnerable from the sea.

A treaty signed in 1807 between Great Britain and Turkey confirmed a right which the Sultan has always claimed, *i. e.*, to exclude foreign war vessels from both straits. However, by a second clause that was inserted in the treaty of Hunkiar-Iskelessi, July 8, 1833, Turkey and Russia effected an offensive and defensive alliance, by which the latter government was granted the right to sail its war vessels through the straits, while the Sultan was bound to keep the Dardanelles closed to all war ships of other powers, thereby shutting out the enemies of Russia from the Black Sea, but leaving Russia's own vessels free passage through the straits. The stipulations of this treaty, to the consternation of the English, made the influence of Russia almost supreme in Turkey, and in turn made the Sultan virtually a vassal of the great Czar. The jealousy of the Powers, particularly of England, became very intense over the advantage gained by their political rival. At length England, at the head of five great Powers, effected a treaty in 1841 by which no foreign fleet should enter the straits in time of peace, and in time of war it should be the Sultan's right to allow the war vessels of friendly nations to pass into the Sea of Marmora for the purpose of co-operation with and protection of the Porte. Thus the navy of Russia was shut up in the Black Sea, which has virtually always been the case. To change this, and give his country an unhampered commercial and military outlet through the straits, Peter the Great had bent all his energies. In his alleged will, which was published for the people, and accepted as genuine,—though now its authorship may be questioned,—he is quoted as having said :

Raise war continually—at one time against Turkey, at another against Persia; make dock-yards on the Black Sea; by degrees make yourselves masters of the Sea as well as of the Baltic; hasten the decay of Persia, and penetrate to the Persian Gulf; establish, if possible, the ancient commerce of the East by way of Syria, and push on to the Indies, which are the *entrepôt* of the world. Once there, you need not fear the gold of England.

So thoroughly did this supposed will of Peter the Great represent the attitude of Russia that the people believed it their duty to follow its commands, as they are doing with great patience and zeal. England, of all the Powers, has been most jealous of the encroachments of Russia in the East. Her officers and emissaries continually report that evidences of Russian intrigue in central Asia are apparent; and it is known that the policy of England, even in Afghanistan, was

CONSTANTINOPLE AND THE GOLDEN HORN.

directed and influenced by the representations of the Czar.

Emperor Nicholas had made up his mind that the Ottoman Empire should be speedily extinguished. In order to put his plans into a definite course of action, he visited England in person, in 1844, and there plainly outlined his design, and exchanged views with the British diplomats as to the final dismemberment of Turkey. His conversation at the time gave the impression that his loftiest ambition was to consummate a friendly alliance with the British government, as a prelude to dividing the spoils upon the collapse of Turkey, which he believed was impending. In conversation with the Duke of Wellington and Lord Aberdeen, then Foreign Secretary, he spoke with astonishing frankness regarding his views on Turkey, its prospects, and what would probably take place if it were dismembered. When he returned to Russia he caused a memorandum to be drawn up, which he believed embodied the views held alike by himself and Wellington and Aberdeen. It stated that England and Russia were alike in the belief that their common interests were conserved by the maintenance of the Turkish Empire in its existing independence and existing territorial extent. That while they both had a common and equal interest in guarding its safety, yet while Turkey continued to violate its treaty obligations, it was impossible to maintain its integrity. Nor did he speak with uncertain tone when he described the conduct of the Porte. He stated that Turkey relied upon the jealousies of the Powers to secure its immunity in breaking treaties; it believed that if it did

NICHOLAS I., EMPEROR OF RUSSIA.

not keep its engagements with any nation, others would protect it from chastisement. Continuing the memorandum, he said:

> As soon as the Porte shall perceive that it is not supported by other cabinets it will give way, and the differences which have arisen will be arranged in a conciliatory manner, without any conflict resulting from them.

It further contained a clause that dwelt upon the immediate necessity of the Porte's improving the condition of its Christian subjects. It was asserted that on such conditions Russia and England could but desire the preservation of the Ottoman Empire. In the event, however, of the unforeseen disaster, it was, according to the memorandum, desirable that Russia and England should arrive at an understanding as to the course of action to be taken by them.

When the copy of the memorandum reached England it was quietly filed away in the Foreign Office, and was not made public till at a later time, when the Russian press maintained that the British government had for a considerable period of time known the views of Russia regarding Turkey. Up to the time of its publication the Czar had assumed that England consented to his plan, following the theory that "silence gives consent."

On the evening of January 9, 1853, in a confidential talk at St. Petersburg, with the British Ambassador, Sir G. Hamilton Seymour, Nicholas withheld nothing, expressing himself in the most positive manner regarding the future of Turkey and the arrangements it might be necessary for Russia and England to make. It was then that he gave expression to the phrase that is now famous, and has contributed an appellation that will probably attach to the Ottoman Empire as long as it exists—"The sick man we have on our hands."

In subsequent conversations with Sir Hamilton Seymour, he spoke of the guard which treaties gave him the right to keep over the several millions of Greek Christians in Turkey, and said he would not permit a permanent occupation of Constantinople by Russia; nor would he agree to its being held by any other great Power. He said he was opposed to the reconstruction of Greece into a Byzantine empire, and he was even opposed to the subdivision of Turkey into small republics. He asserted his attitude positively, that the existence of Turkey in Europe should cease, and nothing should be allowed to take its place, not even Russia. Servia and Bulgaria might become independent states under his protection. England might take possession of Egypt and Candia; but what he desired was that Russia and England should come to an agreement after which he would be totally indifferent as to what other Powers might say or do.

Despite Nicholas' outspoken manner and apparent good will toward the English government, the British looked upon him as a shrewd schemer and plunderer, and the Czar in turn thought England a faithless accomplice. England replied to his overtures that she did not regard it as customary to prepare for the disintegration of a friendly Power, and that she had no wish to take possession of any part of the Ottoman Empire. Seeing that there was no hope of the English joining him in his project, the Czar retreated somewhat from his advanced position, and would probably have endeavored to maintain a neutral attitude in relation to the future of Turkey. However, the antipathy of the Russians toward the Turks was so intense, on account of the persecutions of their co-religionists, that it compelled the emperor to renew hostilities, if he desired to retain the support of his subjects.

A cause for war was not far to seek. It was to be based upon the contentions of the Greek and Latin churches over the holy places in Palestine. The Latin Church, under the protection of the French government, had, during the reign of Francis I., been given the right of protection in a *firman*, granted as early as 1564, by Suleyman the Magnificent. Later, in 1620, another *firman* has the following:

> The Franks, ancient exclusive possessors of the Great Church of Bethlehem and the Church of the Tomb of the Virgin, have, of their full accord, granted to each of the other Christian communions sanctuaries in the Superior Church; but the inferior portion, the place wherein Jesus Christ was born (may salvation rest with Him!), is the sanctuary of the Frankish monks; no other nation has any right therein, and it is forbidden to each and every nation to usurp hereafter the said place. . . We order that no individual, Armenians or other, be permitted to say Mass in the place where Jesus Christ was born, a place situate underneath the Church of Bethlehem, no more than in the cupola, which is called the Tomb of the Holy Virgin; nor, finally, in the sanctuaries, which, from the old time, belonged to the Frankish monks.

Thus, since the time of the Crusades, the French had the general primacy in the holy places. Later, however, through a religious propaganda of Russia, the Greek Church was granted the same privilege under the protection of the Czar. Each succeeding Sultan gave these capitulations indiscriminately, totally disregarding what his predecessors had done; and, as each church claimed the general care and primacy over the holy places, there was a constant quarrel, each church being naturally supported by its protecting nation.

About this time Napoleon III. installed himself as Emperor of France, and he was anxious to distract his subjects' attention from the disturbed condition of home politics by a brilliant foreign policy. He cared no more for the incessant claims of the Latin monks in the Holy Land than he cared about the existence of Turkey, excepting as they might be turned into political capital. He suddenly became peremptory in his claims that the demands of the monks should be granted. It was his chance to inaugurate the new foreign policy. His action, beyond a doubt, precipitated the Crimean war which followed. It would, however, have occurred just the same had France done nothing.

In the negotiations of Russia with the Sultan, just preceding the Crimean War, she claims the exclusive protectorate of all the Eastern Christians in the Ottoman Empire. An acknowledgment of this right was the lever by which the Czar sought to compass the fall of the Ottoman Empire.

Russia based its contentions upon the seventh clause in the treaty of Kutchouk-Kainardji, made in 1774, between the two governments. At the time when the clause was incorporated it was apparently of no marked significance. However, it was destined to shake the very existence of the Ottoman Empire. The clause declared that

> The Porte promises to protect constantly the Christian religion and its churches; and also to allow the minister of the

Imperial Court of Russia to make on all occasions representations as well in favor of the new church in Constantinople, as in favor of those who officiate therein, promising to take such representations into due consideration as being made by a confidential functionary of a neighboring and sincerely friendly Power.

The church in Constantinople referred to was the one which the fourteenth article of the same treaty gave Russia the right to build in the Galata quarter of Constantinople, in addition to the chapel erected at the house of the minister. Referring to these, the treaty said:

They shall be always under the protection of the ministers of the Russian Empire, and shielded from all obstruction and damage.

While the specific right of intervention was clearly attached only to a single church at Constantinople and its ministers, out of the clause Russia claimed the right of protectorate over all the Christians of the Greek Church in the Ottoman Empire.

Of all the eminent European statesmen, Mr. Gladstone alone accepted the Russian interpretation of the seventh clause. Lord John Russell, in a letter to Sir Hamilton Seymour, recognized the clause as binding, though it is believed thoughtlessly and without realizing the importance that would be attached to his words.

The Czar had sent to Constantinople to represent him in the negotiations for the settlement of the dispute about the holy places Prince Menschikoff. This man was a typical oldtime tyrant, with the fighting propensity of a bulldog; haughty and arrogant, insolent and harsh, he was apparently selected with a view to prevent an amicable settlement. On the same day that the decree settling the dispute appeared, the prince, who had been empowered to settle or unsettle the matter, suddenly forsook the question of the holy places and sought another pretext for a quarrel by introducing a new issue. He demanded that the protection of the eleven million Greek subjects of the Porte be vested at once, and completely, in the emperor of Russia. His demands were imperious, and his language to the Sultan and Grand Vizier was peremptory; and he so insulted the Minister of Foreign Affairs that that official resigned. In negotiating for a treaty between Russia and Turkey, he requested the Turkish ministers to pledge themselves not to reveal to the French or English ambassadors the nature of the documents. This the ministers refused to do. In May, 1853, the Sultan, backed by the English and French Powers, formally declined to recognize Russia's demand for a protectorate of the Greek Christians. Immediately the imperial arms were lowered from the Russian embassy, and Menschikoff, in simulated anger, withdrew from Constantinople, giving the Sultan to understand that he would wait a week at Odessa, and if within that time a note of concession to the Czar's demands was not forthcoming, a rupture with Russia might take place. The Czar acquiesced in the acts of Menschikoff, and, as no note came, the war began. Russia was prepared for the contest, for it was expected. Troops had been massed upon the Turkish frontier. The Danubian principalities were occupied by the Czar, who claimed that this was done to secure guaranty that the concessions due his government would be granted, but which Turkey declared would not be made. In the hope of averting a conflict, the English government advised the Porte to disregard the attitude of the Czar, which was admitted to be ample ground for the declaration of war. A Vienna note was prepared, which, but for the astute statesmanship of Lord Stratford de Redcliffe, would have been accepted. It was so cleverly constructed that the Powers were entirely misled by it. Russia had signified her willingness to accept the note, and the Powers were so delighted with it that they were in haste to agree to it, until Lord Redcliffe, the British ambassador at Constantinople, pointed out that, while apparently not a concession to Russia, it in fact granted to that Power the very point which the Powers were unwilling to concede, namely, the claim to a protectorate over the Greek Christians in Turkish territory. Thereupon the Sultan refused to accept the note unless it was greatly modified. The Russian government would not agree to a single letter of modification, and all hopes of European peace were abandoned.

Actual military preparations were begun by the Turks in October, 1853, and for a few days they were highly successful. Then followed the destruction of their fleet by the Russians at Sinope in the Black Sea. This engagement has ever since been called the Massacre of Sinope, for in it only four hundred Turks out of four thousand escaped death, and all these were more or less wounded. The feeling in England and France was intense. The condition of the Eastern Christians was altogether lost sight of by them in the larger issue raised by Russian aggression, and the Czar was informed that they were determined upon enforcing the neutrality of the Black Sea.

The French and English ambassadors were immediately recalled, and diplomatic relations between the two Powers and Russia ceased. Napoleon III. dispatched a letter to Nicholas requesting him to allow an armistice to be signed and to negotiate a convention with the Porte, to be submitted to the four Powers. If this were not done, Napoleon declared that the matter would have to be settled by war, in which the French and English would be allies. The Czar replied that treaty rights confirmed his claims; that the conditions upon which he was willing to treat were well known; and if driven to arms he was certain that his nation would hold its own as it had done in the war of 1812, of which the burning of Moscow and the disastrous retreat of the French were incidents. The British government, too, sent a messenger to Nicholas with a note which declared that unless the messenger, on leaving St. Petersburg after a stay of six days, bore a communication signifying his intention to completely evacuate the provinces of Moldavia and Wallachia before April 30, war would be declared. The messenger left St. Petersburg without such a note, and several days later England declared war against Russia. The Crimean War was the result. England and France allied themselves with the Sultan Abdul-Medjid, and in the spring of 1854 landed their army at Varna. Austria occupied the Danubian principalities, while the Turks successfully defended Silistria, and the allies transferred their troops to the Crimea. The invasion of the Crimea was one of the most disastrous and one of the fiercest engagements of modern warfare. Only the forces of little Sardinia, under the able direction of Count Cavour, escaped from its destructive results with slight loss of life. Sevastopol fell in September, 1855, and Moscow was set on fire. Nicholas, in chagrin at the defeat and the complete failure of his plans, died, broken-hearted, March 2, 1855. Then the English and French governments stepped in and treated with Russia at once, as the Power which affected their interests more than it did the interests of Turkey. All the way through, during negotiations and war, this principle prevailed, while Turkey, without much exertion of her own, stood by and watched the Western Powers who fought her battles and maintained her integrity.

On the 25th of February, 1856, a congress was called at Paris, where Alexander II. appeared, with England, France, Austria, Prussia, Sardinia, and Turkey. The object of the congress was, of course, to effect a treaty of peace. The treaty was signed on the basis that Russia should give to Turkey the portion of Bessarabia adjacent to the mouth of the Danube, and abolish its exclusive protectorate over the Danubian principalities. The Black Sea should be made neutral; while its waters were to be open to merchant vessels of all nations. Neither Russia nor Turkey should maintain warships or create arsenals there, and each should keep but ten lightships to watch the coast.

The signing of the Paris Treaty, March 30, 1856, by the above-named representative Powers, formally ended the war. The independence and territorial integrity of Turkey seemed assured, and the controversies about the Christian provinces, the Straits, and the Black Sea were thought to be settled.

Meanwhile the Sultan issued a *firman* granting perfect religious equality between Christians and Mohammedans and designed to ameliorate the condition of his Christian subjects. That such a promise on the part of the Porte is a sham, and simply designed to throw dust in the eyes of Europe, is obvious from the very fact that the Turk holds the Koran above the Sultan, and the Koran recognizes no possibility of equality between an infidel and a believer in Mohammed. Therefore the Turks could not be made to obey the decree of their ruler declaring such equality. One of the most foolish stipulations of the treaty was that the concert of Europe should have no right to interfere, either collectively or separately, in the relations between the Sultan and his subjects. This clause of the treaty really committed the Christians to the tender hands of the unspeakable Turk, who has always held them in bondage. The relations between the Porte and its Christian subjects could mean nothing less than acts of outrage and murder on the part of the Turks. Such has always been the character of those relations. It was provided by this treaty, however, that the Christian Powers should fold their arms and stand by, giving the Turk a free rein for all sorts of barbarity and carnage, which have ever characterized his relations with his subjects. When Lord Stratford de Redcliffe, that man of great diplomatic craft, heard of the Paris Treaty, he said :

"I would rather have cut off my right hand than have signed that treaty."

In a letter written at that time, he said:

> How are the Sultan's reforms to be carried through—the allied troops all gone, and no power of foreign interference reserved? How is the country to be kept quiet if hopes and fears, equally excited in adverse quarters, have to find their own level? What means shall we possess of allaying the discordant elements if our credit is to decline and our influence to be overlaid by the persevering artifices of a jealous and artful ally? How can we hope to supply the usefulness derivable from our command of the Contingent and Irregulars, if they are to be given up? In short, when I hear the politicians of the country remark that the troubles of Europe with respect to this empire are only beginning, I know not how to reply.

Indeed, in subsequent years the isolated intervention of the Powers, under the ignoble spirit of low jealousies, has proved the death warrant of the Christians under Ottoman sway. Only four years after the Treaty of Paris, the Sultan celebrated his reforms with the massacre of over ten thousand Syrians at Lebanon.

In 1875 the Christians in Bosnia and Herzegovina were forced to take up arms to protect themselves from Turkish oppression. The insurrection spread to such an extent that the Turks were unable to cope with it. Austria sent the famous Andrassy Note, demanding immediate reforms in the Balkan Peninsula; then the Porte played its old game, and promised that the religious equality of its subjects should be maintained. It also gave the assurance that the farming of taxes would be abolished and that the tax money levied in the rebellious provinces would be expended there. The insurgents, however, placed no confidence in these promises, and joined with Servia in declining to accept the terms.

In 1876 the Turks, acting at the suggestion of the English Foreign Office, made a determined effort to restore quiet in the perturbed provinces, by a severe enforcement of military law. It was sought to intimidate the insurgents by an exhibition of rigorous military law. Bulgaria was to be made an object lesson.

Then followed the massacre of Bulgarians by the wholesale. They were tortured with nameless cruelties. At the churches, whither they had fled for refuge, they were found dead in heaps. Women were outraged, and such infernal tortures as only the Turk can devise were inflicted upon unresisting and helpless Christians. Only the massacre of the Armenians of to-day, a description of which will be found in a subsequent chapter, can give an idea of the barbarity and cunning of the Turks during their campaign of butchery among the Bulgarians. In all the preceding and subsequent massacres of the Christians the Turk simply acted in accordance with the relations between himself and his subjects which the Powers have maintained and respected.

The horror of these acts caused a revulsion of feeling which rose to fever heat in England, and sympathy for the Turks apparently waned. Mr. Gladstone, then in the zenith of his power, put himself at the head of the loud uproar that spread like wildfire through the country: "Better the Russians on the Bosphorus than the Turks in Europe." The policy of protecting the Sultan from the vengeance of his subjects was not only relinquished by England but by the Powers at large; and this very situation presented exactly the opportunity that the Emperor of Russia desired, for he was not the man to lose his chances when he had the advantage of the British sentiment. He, therefore, claimed again the protectorate of Christians, and informed the Powers that if they would not co-operate Russia was prepared to end the Turkish misrule alone. The diplomatic corps of Europe, headed by the British ambassador, hastened to the Porte, and remonstrated with the Sultan, urging him to accept their advice concerning immediate reforms for improving the situation; and, as the basis of their policy for reform, they simultaneously prepared a precise programme and insisted upon the Sultan, in all possible ways, assenting to its terms, if he wished to avoid a serious rupture with Russia. The Sultan, however, baffled the Powers in their clamors for reform, and refused to yield to the counsel and entreaties presented. Thereupon, their patience was exhausted. Even Lord Beaconsfield, the great supporter of the Turks, was obliged to remain neutral.

In April, 1877, war was declared by Russia. It was a short contest, lasting only about nine months, and resulting in the overwhelming defeat of the Turks. Their tactics during the war were sanguinary in the extreme. So great was the fear of the Czar's officers of the fiendish inhumanities of the Turks that many were careful to be in possession of poison, so that, in the event of their being taken alive by the enemy, they might end their miserable existence. Throughout the war the Russians were very considerate in their treatment of Turkish prisoners.

The story of the war need not be related here at any length. The Russian army, over two hundred thousand strong, crossed the Danube. Osman Pasha made a heroic defense at Plevna and stormed the Shipka Pass. However, the Russian soldiers unflinchingly advanced through the Balkans, entered Bulgaria, captured Adrianople, and were within the very outskirts of Constantinople, when a halt was called. The British fleet had appeared outside the Dardanelles and anchored in Besika Bay. At San Stefano a treaty of peace was concluded. By the terms of this treaty Russia received the portion of Bessarabia which she had lost in the Crimean War, together with Dobrandja, Kars, Batoum, and the adjoining Asiatic territory. It also recognized the establishment of Bulgaria into an autonomous principality; a territorial compensation or payment of a heavy indemnity; the absolute independence of Servia, Roumania, and Montenegro, with extended territory; the introduction of needed reforms by a European commission in Bosnia, Herzegovina, Crete, Thessaly, and Epirus. Added to these stipulations of the treaty, the Czar and the Porte had come to a final understanding in regard to the Straits and the evacuation by the Turks of the Danube fortresses. These terms of the San Stefano Treaty caused a great alarm in the diplomatic circles of Great Britain, and her fleet returned in haste through the Dardanelles and anchored at Princes' Island, and there made a vigorous demonstration for war. Meanwhile England and Austria announced their refusal to give their assent to the conditions of peace, because of the advantages Russia had secured for herself, in violation of the terms of the Paris Treaty, and demanded that the Powers should be given a fair chance to reconsider, so as to discuss, ratify, or annul the terms of the Treaty of San Stefano. Russia reluctantly consented to disgorge her conquests and to submit the treaty to a European conference. Meanwhile England made a secret treaty with Turkey, in which Great Britain undertook to defend the Porte by force of arms, in the event of Russia's making a future attempt to take any more than Batoum, Ardahan, and Kars of the Sultan's possessions in Asia. In return, the Porte assigned the island of Cyprus to be occupied and administered by England, and promised to introduce reforms looking toward the amelioration of the condition of the Christian subjects.

The proposed conference assembled at Berlin in July, 1878. It was perhaps the most notable concourse of European diplomats in modern history. The British jingoism which was robbing Russia of the principal results of her war with Turkey, by forcing this conference upon the court of St. Petersburg, had as its chief representative Disraeli, a man of keen and shrewd diplomacy. So superior was he in craft to his right-hand man, Lord Salisbury, that he evoked the historical remark of Gortschakoff to Bismarck. "Salisbury," said the Russian plenipotentiary, "is a lath, painted to look like iron, but," referring to Disraeli, "oh, that d——d Jew!"

Disraeli had carried his point in triumph. Not only the Treaty of San Stefano had been thrown aside, but the Porte recognized in the English its greatest friend and ally. At the conference a new concert was agreed upon between the seven great Powers—England, Russia, Germany, Austria, France, Italy, and Turkey. The Berlin Treaty consists of sixty-four articles. Bulgaria, north of the Balkans, was made a principality paying tribute, but exempt from Turkish rule. South of the mountain range was formed the province of Eastern Roumelia, ruled by a Christian governor general, but nominally under the Sultan's political authority. Roumania and Servia were formally declared independent. Herzegovina and Bosnia were given to Austria. Besides Bessarabia, Russia acquired Batoum, Kars, and Ardahan, in Asia.

That the decision of the Berlin Congress did not settle the Eastern Question is plain, in the light of subsequent events. It must be remembered that in receiving Cyprus for her part England made a pledge to enforce good government in Armenia, and the Sultan made the following specific and solemn promise in the sixty-first article of the treaty:

> The Sublime Porte undertakes to carry out, without further delay, the improvements and reforms demanded by local requirements in the provinces inhabited by Armenians, and to guarantee their security against Circassians and Kurds. It will periodically make known the steps taken to this effect to the Powers, who will superintend their application.

This article of the treaty not only gave a guarantee of security for the property, life, and liberty of the Christians, but it gave the signatory Powers, particularly England, the right to take action. Yet the lethargy of the Powers in general, and of England in particular, is hard to realize, still harder to explain. Actuated by mutual distrust and jealousy, the diplomacy of the Eastern Question has been a game of blindman's buff with every player's eyes bandaged. The effort to maintain the European concert seems to be impossible, in view of underground and entangling alliances. Bismarck's recent revelations, for instance, disclose an example of such mischievous trickery of diplomacy as to prevent the effective action of the nations concerned in the European balance of power.

When Christian nations do not combine to put down the evil acts of the Turks, the inference becomes obvious that either the evil of the Turks is not very bad, or the Christian nations hardly deserve their name. What is clear, in the light of actual conditions in the Ottoman Empire, is that the Turk is an absolute incarnation of evil. He has always broken his solemn pledges and promises of decent government, and has made the lives of his Christian subjects a veritable hell on earth, with outrage, robbery, and wholesale massacres; and certainly he has falsified all excuses for his political existence. However, he understands the Powers to perfection, and uses the advantage derived from their mutual jealousies over his possessions in playing one Power against the other, in which art he has become an expert from years of practice.

If there is any Power in the world responsible above others for giving the Turk such an advantage, at the expense of the blood of many thousands of Christians, it is England. For about a hundred years Great Britain has made the Turkish Power a pawn in the game of her imperial politics. She has frequently stepped in and helped the Turkish armies when they were on the verge of annihilation; and, by so doing, has enabled the Turks to continue their career of blood.

Since the Crimean War, particularly, there has been

an increasing feeling of hatred against the English on the part of Christians in Turkey. These plundered and outraged subjects of the Porte, when they were in a position to raise a formidable revolutionary opposition, were intimidated or repressed by force of English arms. For instance, in 1862, the Servians, after the bombardment of Bulgaria, made a determined attempt to supply themselves with munitions of war. They were just about to secure good arms through an English firm, when the British government stepped in and prevented the deal from being carried out. In this way the Servians were unable to secure efficient arms. When at last they secured some second-hand Russian arms, they did so against the direct opposition of the English consul general, who at the same time aided the Turks in every possible way. Again, in 1876, when the Bosnians were striking a blow for freedom, Great Britain did all she could to discourage the insurgents and to aid the Sultan. Mr. Holmes, the consul general in Serajevo, acting in accord with the position taken by the British Cabinet, urged upon the *vali* to take steps at once to sweep the insurgents out of Bosnia. England has thus nearly always aided the Sultan, to the detriment of the Christians. She has done this, not because the Sultan has her good wishes, but because in her perpetuation of his present control of the Straits, lies the most apparent safety of England's commercial intercourse with her vast Indian empire. And she is determined that Russia, her naval rival, shall not get an inch of advantage over her in Turkish waters. Other commercial considerations also have weight; for the merchants of the English nation hold the chief share of trade through the Bosphorus, up the Danube, and with Black Sea and Sea of Azof ports.

Should Russia or any other hostile power hold Constantinople and its straits, it would endanger this trade as well as threaten the Indian commerce and communication. The financial consideration, too,—the many millions of Turkish pounds of which the English are bondholders,—enters into the issues of the English policy on the Eastern Question. Morever, the Sultan is the visible head of the Mohammedan religion, and England could not oppose him without deeply offending more than half her subjects in India. If the Sultan is friendly to England, she has a powerful ally whose influence in a crisis in India would mean considerable. On the English policy in the Eastern Question, Mr. John Bright, in an address, has made the following straightforward utterance:

England imagines that some great danger will happen to her; that she will lose her predominance in the Mediterranean, or that her route to India will be in some degree molested, if a Russian ship of war should come through the Straits, and therefore England is anxious to maintain Turkey in its present position, holding the key of the Straits, and forbidding any portion of the Russian navy to pass from the Black Sea to the Mediterranean. Now, you see, England,—I speak of England as it has been, and England as represented by the present administration—England is afraid that if the Turk went out the Russian would come in, and therefore we are driven to this dreadful alternative, that we must support the Turk, with all his crimes, and with all his cruelty, and we must support too, as we did practically support, the Mohammedan religion throughout the whole of that portion of the world. We give Bethlehem and Calvary and the Mount of Olives, through the blood and treasure of England, and the power over all those vast countries, which are almost a wilder-

LORD SALISBURY, PRIME MINISTER OF GREAT BRITAIN.

ness and a desert under the Turkish scepter—we do all this for the simple purpose of preventing Russia passing by any ships of war from the Black Sea to the Mediterranean.

Even Lord Salisbury himself in a mild tone admitted the ignoble character of the policy, in his assertion in 1858, that

> . . . The consequence was that on the continent of Europe our claims to be regarded as the champions of liberty were looked upon as hypocritical boastings; for while we were loud in our professions we were lax in our practice.

The Armenian massacres of to-day have once more brought the Eastern Question prominently before the world. While these massacres have virtually the same leading features as the previous ones, they have given a different complexion to the Eastern Question. England and Russia have exchanged positions in their traditional attitude toward the Turkish government. England has come to the conviction that the Ottoman Empire is hopelessly corrupt and that it had better be ended than mended. With this conviction, Great Britain appeared ready and anxious to treat with the Powers for Turkey's destruction. To prove that this was not idle talk, she sent a fleet to the Dardanelles and threatened to send it to Constantinople. Indeed, at one time it appeared as though the Powers were united with England in this aim and conviction, and were really acting together in earnest for a common object. Squadrons sailed under six flags on their way to make a demonstration, and the most powerful fleet ever gathered together assembled at Salonica Bay. Nobody seemed to know which way the storm was coming, and there was no little guessing in regard to the direction of its blast.

The most expert students of the troublesome Eastern Question are still at a loss to imagine what will be the next chapter of its tedious history. There was suddenly a hitch in the understanding arrived at between the Powers. The European concert was broken; for while they were advocating peace, each Power was trying to get ahead of the others in securing the largest possible slice of Turkey. Meanwhile the massacres went on. Although Russia and France are in alliance, yet they appear diametrically opposed in case the partition of the Sultan's domain be effected. France wants Syria and Palestine; while Russia wants Constantinople, to which the French are unalterably opposed. The Czar dare not let the Holy City fall into the hands of a Roman Catholic nation, for it might cost him his throne. Austria would not consent to Russia's possessing Constantinople and the Balkan Peninsula. The question of Macedonia also enters into the issue and makes more complex the solution of the problem. It was these and other underhand complications that proved too strong to allow of joint action in the East. The Sultan, a perfect master of the situation, has become convinced that his country is safe from any external interference; so he continues to oppose and ignore the demands and threats of foreign Powers, and was even quite indifferent as to the fortifying of his domain for the remotely probable necessity of a defensive stand. The consequence of this resolute attitude on the part of the Porte was that the governments of Europe quickly withdrew their ironclads, with the unpleasant consciousness that a very large mountain had brought forth a ridiculously small mouse.

The latest events clearly indicate that Russia, after the lesson taught her by the Berlin Congress, and the preceding events, that no power should step outside the European concert to deal with Turkey by force of arms, persistently declined forcible interference, and entered into an alliance with the Sultan on the lines of the Hunkiar-Skelessi, and gave it to be clearly understood that she will not tolerate it on the part of others. Meanwhile the Czar has turned his attention from European Turkey to China.

The scope of the Eastern Question has enlarged of late. While it originally related to the troubles that arose between the Greek Christians and the Turks, to-day the question virtually is: " Who shall have controlling influence over all of Asia—England or Russia ?"

The Armenian massacre is but a little incident when compared with the tremendous issues involved in this greatest of international agitations. Indeed, centuries will pass, and millions of lives be sacrificed, before the Eastern Question will be settled. However, it is not within the province of this volume to engage extensively in the discussion of it. The following chapters will be occupied with the internal commotions prevailing in the Turkish Empire.

THE CHRONIC CONDITION OF ARMENIA, AND THE CAUSES OF HER TRAGEDIES.

> "They are slaves who fear to speak
> For the fallen and the weak;
> They are slaves who will not choose
> Hatred, scoffing, and abuse,
> Rather than in silence shrink
> From the truth they needs must think;
> They are slaves who dare not be
> In the right with two or three."
> —JAMES RUSSELL LOWELL.

THAT my reader may the more fully comprehend the extent of the calamity at this moment threatening our unhappy people, it is necessary that I should give some account of the chronic condition of the Armenian provinces.

Many years before the recent massacres, and more particularly since the accession of the present Sultan, the general condition of the five southeastern provinces,—Van, Bitlis, Moush, Bayazed, and Diarbekir,—which in the main comprise our lost country, has been one of deliberate misgovernment and of uncompromising outrage. There has been an almost uninterrupted reign of terror, with daily increasing evidences of unlawful depredations, and the moral effect has been to place the life and property of the Armenians at the mercy of every Moslem.

The Kurdish tribes of the bordering mountains—unmitigated rogues, thieves, and cutthroats by birth—were deliberately cut loose by the Turkish government to prey upon the Armenian peasantry. The Kurds, in turn, ever true to their natural instincts of plunder and robbery, sharing to some extent the Moslem antipathy for the Christian, kept up a systematic campaign against their peaceable Armenian neighbors, who had no greater desire than to be let alone to enjoy the labor of their hands and the worship of their ancestral religion. The poor victims, disarmed by the Turkish government, were hopelessly incapable of anything like self-defense. In order to remove all possible danger, not only were the Kurds exempted from taxation, but, in the year 1891, the Sultan hit upon the policy of making them over into a kind of irregular Turkish army; and, equipping them with the best of modern weapons and ammunition, in place of their ancient flintlocks, he let them loose in their mountain homes, instead of keeping them in regular service. Under such an organized brigandage all the fiercest barbaric passions were set free, unbridled and unchecked, while the Turkish officials watched with happy satisfaction the rapid devastation of Armenian industry. Midnight raids upon Armenian villages, looting houses, attacking caravans, carrying off crops, lifting cattle, burning corn and hay, kidnaping children, dishonoring women, became a sort of pleasant and profitable pastime with the Kurdish *aghes*. Not only did the Turkish government place no restraint upon the Kurds, but it actually incited them with rewards for excess in ferocity. It is considered presumption and insolence for an Armenian to complain to the officials for wrongs done him by the Kurds and Turks, and his protests are not only utterly disregarded, but he is thrown into prison to be tortured and outraged. Such has been the fate of hundreds of Armenians, particularly in the *vilayet* and city of Bitlis; and when once in the noisome dungeon, nothing but death or the payment of large bribes could secure their release. Truth may sound stranger than fiction, yet there are still stranger truths of Turkish brute tyranny of which I dare not speak, for their meaning could be found nowhere but in the regions of hell.

Bad as the Kurd is, in justice let me say he is not half so bad as the Turk. To the truth of this assertion any Armenian who has lived in his neighborhood can wholly subscribe. It is true that the Kurd loots houses, plunders property, and, when resisted, commits murder; but he has some little sense of pity and humanity, and some regard for the truth, which is more than can be said of the Turk. The Kurds plunder and murder for the sake of booty, while the Turk regards the plunder and murder of non-Moslems as a religious privilege and duty. It is the Turk who holds the reins of the government, and it is he who is the real aggressor every time, while the Kurd is simply a tool in his hands to carry out his deliberately planned policy of exterminating the Armenians. In him are combined the pugnacity of the bulldog, the ferocity of the tiger, and the cunning of the fox. Allured by the prospect of a paradise of voluptuous pleasure, he is eager to fling himself into the fight against the infidel in the name of Allah and the Prophet.

The Turk's increasing intolerance towards the Christians has by no means been confined to the Armenian provinces. In the summer of the year 1889, while in

MOSLEM CUTTHROATS IN ARMENIA.

Constantinople, I visited the Turkish prison in search of an intimate friend and schoolmate, who was on trial for his life for having written an essay on Mohammedanism. The indictment was based upon the following words, with which the unsuspecting schoolboy had closed his ambitious literary effort: "May the happy day soon come when the cross of Christ will triumph over the crescent of Mohammed." While in a Turkish dungeon, to my dismay I found many Armenians, mostly of the higher classes, who were imprisoned on baseless and often most ridiculously absurd political charges. I saw there a venerable priest of our national church, whose mild and fatherly countenance was overshadowed with the gloom of despair, as he sat meditating upon his impending doom. His crime was a pious entreaty to his flock to gather under the banner of Christ Jesus. This purely religious sentiment had been interpreted as a seditious utterance against the Turkish government. Such a thing may perhaps appear incredible to a freeborn American, yet one needs only to know the Turk in order to learn how excitable is his imagination, and what a wonderful capacity he has for creating pretexts out of the veriest trifles to enable him to carry out his nefarious plans.

Here are a few examples of the prohibitory edicts which have gone forth: No dictionary shall be allowed to circulate which contains such words as "liberty," "equality," "evolution," "insurrection," "war," as such words might incite the minds of the people. The translation of the hymn,

"The children are gathering from near and far,
The trumpet is sounding the call for the war,"

is forbidden as being revolutionary. In the Lord's Prayer, "Thy kingdom come," and all similar passages of the Scriptures suggestive of dominion, power, and battle; and such phrases as "Kingdom of Heaven," "Kingdom of Christ"; or such words as "According to the law of the Jews," are strictly forbidden. Even the word "Armenia" has been stricken out of every book. Should papers and books published outside of the Ottoman Empire displease in any way the Turkish censors or the press, the mere possessor of them, if detected, is at once placed behind the bars and dealt with according to Turkish justice. I have known of persons who, having once been thrown into prison upon such trivial accusations, have never again been allowed to see God's free sunshine. Of late years the Armenians have hardly been allowed to breathe without being accused of unheard-of crimes and locked up.

The bitter hostility of the present Sultan to the Christian element of his population has become more and more manifest every year. One of his first acts, after his accession to the throne, was to replace Armenians by Turks in all the high official positions of the state which the competence and integrity of our people had secured for them during the reign of Abdul-Aziz. That a few Armenians still hold high governmental posts is due to the fact that there is not competence enough among the Turks to warrant their removal.

Early in 1893 it appeared as though the crisis had been reached and the gathering storm was soon to burst from western Turkey instead of from the Armenian provinces; but the storm passed off at the time with comparatively little damage to the Christians, yet with sufficient indications that it would break over the Armenians sooner or later.

THE CITY OF MARSOVAN.

On the night of the 5th of January, 1894, in my native city Marsovan, and in Yuzgat, hundreds of placards were posted in public places with words of bitter denunciation of Turkish corruption and oppression. This created a great excitement among the Turks and occasioned the wholesale arrest of hundreds of Armenians in the province. Some of the prisoners were tortured into insanity, and false witnesses were produced by the Turkish authorities to implicate the entire Armenian population in a plot for the posting of placards in the two cities and then order a general massacre. The fact of the matter is that it is still a profound mystery as to who was the author or the publisher of the placards, whether it was done by the Armenian Huntchagians or by the Young Turkey Party, which is equally hostile to the existing administration.

Among those arrested were two of my former teachers, Professor Thoumaian and Kayayan of Anatolia College. While there was not sufficient evidence of their connection with the issuing of the placards to warrant their arrest, nevertheless they were put into close confinement, bail was refused, and no one was permitted to visit them. Meanwhile lawless Turkish mobs committed all sorts of outrages in Marsovan, Yuzgat, and Cæsarea. One of the buildings of the Young Ladies' Seminary at Marsovan, which was in process of erection, was burned to the ground. The guilt of the Turkish officials in setting fire to this American property having been conclusively established, the United States, with firmness and resolution, demanded indemnity, and finally secured it, together with a permit to rebuild.

When the trial of the professors came on they were condemned to death, with fifteen other Armenians. The trial was from start to finish thoroughly in accord with Turkish ideas of justice. Lord Rosebery, upon reviewing the case, declared that "all the evidence which has come to us from impartial British officials in Asia Minor, from the neighborhood of Angora, made it perfectly clear that the trial was not a fair trial; that the evidence of the prisoners did not receive sufficient weight even when it was admitted."

While on appeal the death sentences were confirmed, yet the rank and the influence of the professors had a useful result in making their case known in Europe. Professor Thoumaian was an alumnus of Luzern University, and his wife, a high-bred and accomplished Swiss lady, was in Europe at the time. She, with the assistance of friends, aroused popular sentiment in England, and, finally, in spite of the verdict of the Court of Appeals, secured the release of these two gentlemen on condition of their leaving the country.

The circumstances attending the trial fill one with indignation. Not only were all sorts of insults hurled at the professors by petty officials, but over twenty forms of diabolical torture were employed to extort confessions incriminating the victims and their friends. Even before their trial the learned gentlemen were subjected to indignities in every respect similar to the treatment of convicts of the lowest order, and were so heavily loaded with fetters as to be utterly unable to walk.

In the summer the state of affairs in the Turkish Empire was verging upon anarchy. The Christian subjects throughout the country were exposed to the most atrocious treatment by the officials. Taxes were levied so heavily that their collection caused unbearable hardships to the already impoverished people. Armenians everywhere were thrust into prison, and, notwithstanding the Turkish law that no tortures shall be inflicted on prisoners, they were subjected to inhumanities of a diabolical nature. Many ministers of the Gospel were driven away, imprisoned, or banished. This has been the fate of the Protestant pastors in Marsovan; everyone that came was driven away, and there is now no regular minister there. One of them, the Rev. G. H. Filian, barely escaped with his life to the United States. The Protestant pastors at Sungurlu and Yuzgat were driven away, and those at Chakmak and Gemerek were imprisoned for no charge whatever but preaching upon religious themes. Many Christian ministers whom I knew and loved while at home are to-day silent for ever; yet their example of martyrdom in testimony of Christ Jesus speaks even louder than their most fervent words of loyalty to Him.

SUMMARY OF CAUSES OF MASSACRES.

Before entering upon the next chapter, on the Armenian Massacres, I shall endeavor to give a summary of the causes which have brought about the crisis.

The first cause that I can assign to the tragedies is the religious antipathy of the Mohammedan Turks, who are taught to slaughter all opposed to their faith, and in whose brutal vocabulary "dog" is a synonym for "Christian." Upon this cause I have dwelt at length in the chapter on Mohammedanism.

The second cause is the racial antipathy. Turkey is not made up of Turks only, but its subjects are of diverse races, religions, and ideas. The Turks have failed in commingling these different races, as the ancient Romans failed in commingling different races into one homogeneous nation. Therefore, these different elements have been at war, and have each maintained different degrees of civilization, different modes of thinking, and different occupations in life; so that each people retains its national characteristics, manners, and customs. And it has been the method of the dominant race, the Turks, to secure homogeneity as it has always tried to secure uniformity in religion, by the edge of the sword instead of by employing the peaceful agencies of civilization.

The third cause is European diplomacy. The vexatious intervention of the Powers in the affairs of the Turks, instead of healing up the difference between them and the Armenians, has aggravated it. The conscienceless shrewdness of the Sultan has noted the cowardice and perfidy of the European governments, and he has made them dance to any tune he chose to play.

The fourth cause is that the Armenians have imbibed the spirit of the nineteenth century, and so have outstripped the Turks in civilization and intelligence. The advancement of our people in learning, science, and commerce has aroused the jealousy of the Turks, who have always stood for the old régime—in other words, for stagnation. The Turks grow more and more intolerant of the Armenians, on account of their supremacy in the march of civilization. All methods to pull the Armenians down to their own level having failed, they have resorted to the summary process of cutting their throats.

The last, yet not the least, cause of the Armenian outrages, is in the well-founded consciousness of the Turks that Anatolia will be their last refuge when they are driven out of Europe and their possessions are taken from them by the Powers; and they are anxious to have this last resort free from complications of Armenian claims. In order to attain this desired end, they have set out to diminish the number of the Armenians by wholesale massacres, and are invoking Mohammedan bigotry and fanaticism in the work of extermination.

The Turkish version of the causes of this reign of terror throws all the blame upon the Armenians, of course. They endeavor to pose before the world as being desirous to preserve the peace. The Sultan at first with unruffled nerve denied the entire affair of the Sassoun massacre; and when it had been too well authenticated to be denied, he came boldly forward and laid all the blame upon the Armenian revolutionists as a justification for his cruelty. I do not deny the existence and the active propagandism of such a movement. I do not even deny that, to some extent, the religious war has been stimulated by Armenian political agitators. But I contend that such a movement, though hostile to the existing administration, was intertwined with the growth of governmental oppression; and that some Armenians,

A GROUP OF ARMENIAN HUNTCHAGIANS.

driven by long years of Turkish barbarity and cruel misgovernment into a frame of mind akin to nihilism, have made it their patriotic duty to preach the policy of insurrection as the only means of calling the attention of the Powers to their grievances and urging them to fulfill their promises of decent government in Armenia. Moreover, while there have been at times overt acts on the part of the Huntchagian revolutionists, for some of which they deserve our condemnation; yet the extent to which they have succeeded in stirring up actual revolution has been grossly exaggerated by the Turkish government. I consider it cruelly absurd to point out the few smoldering fires of revolution as if they were characteristic of the whole nation. The Huntchagian movement is not and never has been a national movement; its membership is small; and for its acts, whether wise or otherwise, none but the society should be held accountable. To make a sweeping condemnation of the whole race, and deliberately bend every energy upon their extirmination for the deeds of a few handfuls of revolutionists, is one of the manifestations of the Turkish sense of justice. Yet the Turk must have pretexts, and throughout his barbarous career he has never been lacking in the fine art of their manufacture.

In Constantinople, for instance, took place one of the most inexcusable of the butcheries that horrified the civilized world in the fall of 1896. Some twenty-four Armenians from abroad had seized the Ottoman National Bank and had insisted upon holding it until the Sultan should grant their demands: To execute the promised Reform Scheme under European super-

SEVEN TOWERS OF CONSTANTINOPLE.

vision; that there be no massacres in the city on account of the outbreak; that the members of the party in possession of the bank be given safe-conduct out of the empire, and that, pending negotiations, the troops be withdrawn from the vicinity of the bank. In case of the Sultan's refusal of these conditions, the Armenians threatened to blow up the bank, with themselves and the whole staff of the establishment. The Sultan not only allowed them safe-conduct out of the country after their exploit, but he furnished each of them with a considerable sum of money when they were put on board for France. Before they had made their triumphant exit from the bank, however, thousands of innocent Armenians in the city, who had nothing to do with the revolutionary exploits,—who did not even have any knowledge of what had happened,—were brutally battered to pieces with heavy clubs. Had the Turkish government held down the mob, and had it taken the bank by storm, limiting vengeance to those actually engaged in anarchical proceedings, it would have been justified in the eyes of Europe. This is representative of many of the cases in which the Armenians are held by unscrupulous defenders of the Sultan to be aggressors. In most of the massacres the Turks took the initiative without having the least pretext for their unspeakable barbarities.

The Armenians, brave and patriotic as they are, are utterly unable to throw off the Turkish yoke by themselves. A general rising of our people against the Turks, such as took place among the Slavonian Christians,—Servians, Bulgarians, Roumanians, and Greeks,

—is impossible. Our people are neither armed nor disciplined, nor organized to proclaim rebellion and openly stand the chances of a civil war. For, in the first place, the Turks greatly outnumber us; and, in the second place, we are not confined to a certain locality like the Bulgarians and others, but are helplessly scattered over the Ottoman Empire—in fact, over all the world. The Slavonian Christians succeeded, because not only were they concentrated in a certain territory, but they had more or less support from their European co-religionists. Our people have no co-religionists in Europe, and we have not the hope of Europe's intervention on our behalf. So our unhappy countrymen are left to their fate, helpless and hopeless.

THE TURKISH CAMPAIGN OF BUTCHERY.

"Caliph, I did thee wrong. I hailed thee late
Abdul the Damned, and would recall my word.
It merged thee with the unillustrious herd
Who crowd the approaches to the infernal gate,
Spirits gregarious, equal in their state,
As is the innumerable ocean bird,
Gannet or gull, whose wandering plaint is heard
On Ailsa or Iona desolate;
For in a world where cruel deeds abound
The merely damned are legion. With such souls
Is not each hollow and cranny of Tophet crammed?
Thou with the brightest of hell's aureoles
Dost shine supreme, incomparably crowned,
Immortally beyond all mortals damned."
—WILLIAM WATSON.

MY reader may now turn to Sassoun, where, as the initiative of a long series of massacres, took place the most outrageous of Turkish atrocities, in September, 1894.

The Sassoun region, situated south of the Moush Plain, forms a part of the long line of terraces in which the Armenian plateau descends gradually to the valleys through which flow the Tigris and the Euphrates, moistening the soil, watering the trees, and nourishing flowers of rare beauty and perfume. The entire region has been for centuries an earthly paradise, blessed with rich harvests, romantic scenery, and a healthy climate. Its inhabitants were mainly composed of Armenian peasants, who peaceably dwelt in the fair valleys of their ancient fatherland, while the Kurdish nomads infested the high plateaus above. Until a few years ago the Kurds were unorganized brigands; but, as we have intimated in the preceding chapter, the Sultan has organized them into an irregular army, partly in order to exterminate the Armenians, and partly, in case of war with Russia, that they may act as a counter-weight to the Cossacks. Of late years the Armenians have practically become serfs of the local Kurdish *aghas*. In addition to the oppressive taxes imposed by the government, the Kurdish chiefs went from village to village and claimed their own share of the tribute. No sooner had one chief departed than another arrived with fire and sword. Some villages have been thus visited from eight to ten times in quick succession in the course of a year.

To whom could our unhappy people appeal for protection and redress, when they were not permitted to have even a penknife for self-defense against those who came upon them armed with the best modern weapons and supported by governmental protection? Where could Armenians turn, when they were thus tied hand and foot and thrown like lambs into the midst of devouring wolves? The insecurity of life and property became so great that many Armenians deserted their homes and property, and fled to the Russian frontiers in search of new abodes within the borders of the Czar's domain.

Early in the spring of 1893 matters were hastening to a crisis. The Armenians of the Sassoun district, who were perhaps the most oppressed in the southeastern provinces, finally lost their patience; and when the Kurds made their usual visit, with larger demands and bolder depredations, the Armenians of Dalvorig banded together and offered a stout and determined resistance. Preliminary skirmishes were followed by a general attack. The united Kurdish tribes of Pakrantzik, Khiyantzig, and Badnktzik made up an army of about seven thousand men, and attacked a mere handful of about one hundred and twenty Armenians of Dalvorig, who were gathered in defense of their rights. Incredible as it may seem, the superior position of the Armenians behind the rocks of Turfurkar, coupled with their indomitable courage, made them more than a match for their adversaries; for only six Armenians fell, while over a hundred Kurds were slain. Such an unlooked-for result so disheartened the Kurds that they retreated, and perhaps would never again have lifted their hands to strike the brave Armenians of Dalvorig, had it not been for the Turkish government, which at this point hastened to the support and defense of the Kurds. The governor general of the province set out with his regular troops and field-pieces, and occupied the region about Dalvorig, but made no attack at the time. In an interview with some of the leading Armenians he questioned them as to why they did not submit to the government and pay their taxes. To this the Armenians replied that they were not disloyal to the government, but that they could not pay taxes both to the Kurds and to the government, and that if the

MOSLEM ROBBERS DIVIDING SPOILS.
(From a Painting.)

government would afford them protection they would not decline to pay the taxes.

The siege continued throughout the winter. Upon the advent of the spring of 1894 the Kurdish tribes were ordered to attack the entire Sassoun district, which included over forty villages. It is needless to say that they responded, coming, to the number of twenty thousand, from every direction. In a few preliminary skirmishes several Kurds fell. The Kurds secured the bodies of two of their slain countrymen, and, after mutilating the corpses, carried them to the headquarters of the provincial government at Bitlis and showed them to the *vali*. "See what the Christians are doing to us!" they exclaimed, meanwhile reporting that the entire province was in armed revolution. The local government of Moush telegraphed the Sultan of the alleged uprising of the Armenians. The Porte, only too glad of such a pretext, ordered the military commander of that province to "exterminate the rebels." Soon re-enforcements arrived, and a general attack followed.

The Armenians, ignorant of the presence of the regular troops, who were kept out of sight, and thinking they had only the Kurds to contend with, fought gallantly, and held them back for nearly two weeks. During this time the characteristic perfidy and cunning of the Turkish soldiers sometimes deceived even the Armenians themselves. Once they came into a village, and, having assured the inhabitants that they had come to guard them against the Kurds, were quartered in Armenian homes. At night, when the people had retired, these alleged protectors arose and fell upon the households of their hosts, slaying every man, woman, and child. It was this event that made it no longer possible for the Armenians to doubt that the government and its forces were back of the Kurds, and that consequently their own doom was sealed.

The Armenians fought with the energy of despair, and the Kurds, after repeated repulses, refused to do any more unless the soldiers aided them. Then began a general massacre, of almost incredible ferocity, lasting from the middle of August to the middle of September, 1894. The Sultan's *firman* ordering the butchery of the Armenians was read to the soldiers by the commanding marshal, Zekki Pasha. The imperial edict commanded them to exterminate the Christians. Before the reading was completed, as if unwilling to delay the diabolical deed, Zekki Pasha gave the order to "smite" the Christians. Then followed a scene too awful to describe. The brutal officer issued commands to the troops of such a nature that some of the better among them, recoiling from perpetrating outrages on unarmed and helpless men, women, and children, begged that they be not compelled to carry them out.

On the last day of August, that being the anniversary of the Sultan's accession to the throne, the duty of loyalty was again impressed upon the minds of the Turkish soldiers, and the indiscriminate slaughter of the Armenians they were taught to regard as a supreme privilege. There was no line drawn between "loyal" and so-called "disloyal" villages. "Down with the Christian dogs!" was the watchword that rang out from Moslem throats and resounded with the boom of their cannon. The air was filled with one great wail of anguish; the earth was all aflame with burning villages. Nor was the ferocity of the Turk satisfied until all the villages of Sassoun were utterly obliterated and the last man, woman, and child had paid the penalty for the alleged uprising against the Turkish government.

It is hard to select specific instances from such an inferno of cruelty, but let me mention the following cases, the truth of which is based upon uncontradicted reports of those on the ground:

In one place about fifty women and girls were locked in a church, and then the commander set the soldiers "free" among them, and when ravishing ceased they were all killed. In another place children were stood up in a row in single file, and then a test was made as to how many little bodies the leaden bullet of a Turkish rifle could tear through in its deadly flight. The soldiers would toss infants up into the air, and catch them upon their bayonets when they came down. Babes were laid in a row before the eyes of their mothers, and then, with a mighty stroke of a Turkish sword, their heads were severed from their bodies. Again, men, women, and children were crowded into houses and the houses set on fire, their attempts to escape the flames being defeated by bayonets.

It would be a grewsome tale to relate the shocking cruelties perpetrated upon women. I have seen of late some Armenian refugees from near the Sassoun region, and their accounts of Turkish inhumanity sounded to me like the echoes from the barbaric past and filled every fiber of my being with infinite wrath.

As I go in thought from village to village, and look upon the ravines filled with corpses of Armenian heroines and martyrs; as I hear the pitiful entreaties of helpless womanhood and childhood, trembling before uplifted daggers; as I gaze upon the frantic faces of fathers and mothers as they behold their infants pierced by Turkish bayonets; as I see widowed motherhood with frozen tears seeking shelter amid the ruins of desolation, my heart cries, "How long, O Lord, how long!"

Some Turkish devices of hellish wickedness my regard for decency and for the conventionalities of civilized speech will not permit me to relate. Indeed, the English language is impotent for the task.

In this massacre it is believed that ten thousand Armenians perished, though it is difficult to obtain even an approximately correct estimate of the slain. The Sultan, in spite of his denial of the entire affair, at once sent one of the imperial guards to carry a decoration to Zekki Pasha for his so-called bravery and his success in the work at Sassoun, while another envoy carried four banners to the four leading Kurdish chiefs who were associated with the military commander in the massacre and who were the instigators of it. Meanwhile the Turkish government made strenuous efforts to suppress all accounts from the scenes of murder and rapine. What could not be concealed was represented in a light very different from actual facts. The magnates near the scene of carnage prepared a document, which they endeavored to compel Christians to sign, purporting to give the judgment of the people that the thousands killed in the Sassoun region met death as their just deserts, and expressing thanks to the Sultan and his officials for their acts.

SUBSEQUENT EVENTS, AND THE MASSACRE AT CONSTANTINOPLE.

Owing to the report of the massacre at Sassoun, which found its way to all parts of Europe, causing a thrill of horror and a storm of indignation, investigations were made by Mr. Hallward, the British consul at Van, and by the British Ambassador at Constantinople. When to their confirmation of the reports was added the admission of the local military commander, Great Britain informed the Porte that better government was necessary in the eastern part of his dominion or steps would be taken to effect the improvement independently. The Sultan's fear of external interference aroused him to at least a show of action. He appointed a commission to inquire into the massacre and propose a means for restoring quiet. That he intended this commission to accomplish nothing except the distortion of the facts was apparent from the men he chose to compose it. They had the confidence of none of the European Powers. The bestowal of a decoration upon the Turkish commander in charge at Sassoun served to increase the doubts of the Powers as to the Porte's sincerity of purpose in creating the commission. The Powers then began to talk of a separate representative commission of inquiry to act independently of the Turkish commission. Americans were invited to representation in the latter commission, but President Cleveland declined the invitation. He signified, however, the willingness of the United States to conduct an individual investigation and selected, after consultation with England, Consul Jewett of Sivas. The Porte did not consent to this and refused to grant the necessary papers to the consul.

In mid-winter, when the weather in that portion of Armenia where the tragedies occurred is exceedingly severe, the commission began its work, and was shortly established at Moush. The Turkish soldiers extorted money from the Armenians in the vicinity by threatening to report them to that body as insurgents, while the Turkish officers threatened the Armenians with death if they exposed the tragedies that had occurred in their midst. Nor did this exhaust the methods of Turkish ingenuity to cover up the facts. Many prominent Armenians, including clergymen, were thrust into prison without just cause or explanation, and were frequently kept in chains and tortures without trial; and even when their innocence was established they were not acquitted. These Turkish prisons, particularly the one at Bitlis, where many Armenians were confined, may well be described as an earthly hell. Indeed, no human imagination can grasp the horrors to which Christians were subjected in these noisome dungeons. I have seen many Armenian refugees, and their descriptions of these places sent a chill of horror through my veins. The tearing of flesh, crushing of limbs, rending of sinews, brandings with red-hot iron, and all manner of lingering tortures surpassed in fiendishness the darkest ages of the Inquisition. The dreary walls of the Bitlis prison echoed day and night with wails of anguish from victims herded together in a common cell in the midst of filth and disease. Death would be a mercy compared with such maddening torments.

Dr. E. J. Dillon, the special English commissioner of the *Daily Telegraph*, who spent some time on the ground and made himself master of the facts, fully corroborates the reports of the refugees in an article in the *Contemporary Review* for August, 1895. In that article, entitled "The Condition of Armenia," he thus describes the Turkish Prison: "If the old English Star Chamber, the Spanish Inquisition, a Chinese opium den, the ward of a yellow fever hospital, and a nook in the lowest depths of Dante's hell be conceived as blended and merged into one, the resulting picture will somewhat resemble a bad Turkish prison."

The commission at Moush, however, was making progress, and its report of the situation was such as to confirm the worst description, and the most heinous details were found to be abundantly verified. Vice Consul Shipley, the representative of Great Britain on the commission of inquiry, reported in a conservative and moderate tone:

> We [Messrs. Vilbert, Shipley, and Prjevalsky, the representatives of France, England, and Russia] have, in our report, given it as our conviction, arrived at from the evidence brought before us, that the Armenians were massacred without distinction of age or sex; and, indeed, for a period of some three weeks, viz., from the 12th of August to the 4th of September (O. S.), it is not too much to say that the Armenians were absolutely hunted like wild beasts, being killed wherever they were met; and if the slaughter was not greater, it was, we believe, solely owing to the vastness of

the mountain ranges of that district, which enabled the people to scatter, and so facilitated their escape. In fact, and speaking with a full sense of responsibility, we are compelled to say that the conviction has forced itself upon us that it was not so much the capture of the agitator Mourad, or the suppression of a pseudo-revolt, which was desired by the Turkish authorities, as the extermination, pure and simple, of the Gheliguzan and Talori districts." *

It was apparent to the Sultan that the moral sensibilities of the Christian Powers had been so outraged that the nations were on the verge of aggressive action. The English government emphatically announced its intention to afford protection to all Christians throughout the Ottoman Empire. The result of this was a few transitory reforms with which the Sultan hoped to appease the Christian governments. He caused the release of many imprisoned clergymen, and highly incompetent Turkish officials were relieved from office. Meanwhile Great Britain, France, and Russia in a joint note informed the Porte that certain reforms must be carried out, with the following provisions:

A high commissioner, appointed with the assent of the Powers, is to have general supervision over the whole empire, with the assistance of a commission sitting in Constantinople; the provinces of eastern Turkey are to have Mohammedan or Christian governors, according to the preponderance of population, the vice governor to be of different faith from the governor; taxes are to be collected by local and municipal agents instead of by soldiers or treasury agents, and the provinces are to retain enough funds for their administration and send the balance to Constantinople; there is to be a general amnesty for crimes and

* "Blue Book," Turkey, 1895, No. 1, Part I., p. 206.

offenses other than those against the common law; pending political trials are to stop and the prisoners are to be released; imprisonment without special warrant is forbidden and speedy trial assured, together with release in case of acquittal; the number of Christian judges is to be increased in proportion to the Christian population; Christians are to serve equally with Moslems in the gendarmerie; conversion to Islam by force is forbidden, and general freedom of religious confession is to be secured; the powers of magistrates are to be extended, and the local courts are to be under the supervision of a delegation from the Court of Appeals.

These proposed reforms would render Armenia practically independent, and differ very little from the demands made by Russia in 1876 on behalf of Bulgaria, which led to the Russo-Turkish War. The Sultan knew that the difficulties which beset him were great, and he at once altered the ministry and appointed an intensely anti-English Grand Vizier. Meanwhile the president of the commission to investigate the Sassoun massacres was made the Minister of Foreign Affairs. Under such conditions there was a manifest unwillingness on the part of the Turkish government to comply with the reforms as suggested by the Powers.

Of all the Powers, England was apparently the most firm in its demands for immediate adoption of the measures. The Sultan hesitated much. His Mohammedan subjects opposed every letter of the European proposals. At this critical point the Liberal Party of England was overthrown and the Conservative placed in power. The policy of the latter party toward Turkey had always been aggressive, and many hopes were built upon its being true to its tradi-

	Signor A. Pansa, Italy.		Mons. Nelidoff, Russia.	
Mons. P. Cambon,	Baron Calice,		Prince Radolin,	Sir Philip Currie,
France.	Austro Hungary.		Germany.	Great Britain.

THE AMBASSADORS OF THE GREAT POWERS AT CONSTANTINOPLE.

tions. Even the Sultan became alarmed at the accession of the new party and felt that he was at least in a position where he could no longer trifle with the demands of Europe. He straightway promised to effect the reforms, demanding, however, an extension of time. This apparent concession to foreign pressure greatly incensed the Turks, whose sense of national dignity was wounded, and they threatened the Sultan with a Moslem insurrection. Particularly the Young Turkey Party were very active in their expressions of hostility against the existing administration; for they had come to the conviction that it was not the Christians alone who suffered, but that their Moslem brethren also were victims of the Porte's inefficiency under the administrative policy of the Old Turkey Party.

We must not omit an event which was of no little assistance at this time to the Armenian cause. On December 29, 1894, the occasion of the eighty-fifth birthday of the late Mr. William E. Gladstone, in response to our deputation the Sage of Hawarden raised his voice for justice in behalf of our oppressed people, and denounced in the strongest possible language the barbarity of the "unspeakable Turk," expressing the hope that the government of the Queen would do its duty in establishing peace and justice in Armenia.

The Sultan's insincerity regarding reform was more and more impressed upon the Powers, for not only did he delay their practical application, but fresh outrages were going on as usual and even to a more alarming extent. England made a naval demonstration at the Dardanelles and threatened the dismember-

THE LATE RT. HON. W. E. GLADSTONE, THE GREAT ENGLISH FRIEND OF
THE ARMENIANS.

(From a Painting.)

ment of the Ottoman Empire; and for a time it appeared as though the other Powers were in accord with Great Britain's policy of employing coercive measures in order to bring the Sultan to terms. It was soon discovered, however, that the Powers had agreed to disagree. Even England receded from her advanced position, and the whole scheme of reforms vanished in the air. The attitude of the Powers reassured the Sultan that as long as the governments of Europe are divided among themselves he is safe in his position, and he therefore proceeded to indulge in a massacre in Constantinople itself before the very eyes of the European ambassadors who a short time before had been considering the partition of Turkey.

It is an ancient Turkish custom, in case of oppression or national needs, to petition the government for redress, and, therefore, on Monday, October 1, 1895, about two hundred peaceable Armenians marched in a body to the Imperial Government offices to present a petition to the Sultan, asking relief from persecutions. It might appear a foolish thing for the Armenians to do, considering the excited state of feeling that prevailed all over the empire, and they were advised against their action by our Patriarch. Yet it is the constitutional right of the Armenians to present petitions, and in default of free speech or a free press it is the only mode of obtaining redress for grievances. To say that they went there to get themselves butchered in order to draw attention to their wrongs is against reason. But the Turkish authorities are well versed in the art of giving a peaceful constitutional proceeding like this the appearance of a riot. The government ordered the police to disperse the Armenian petitioners. In some unknown way firing began, and after many of the petitioners had been killed, the homeward march was broken up. The butchery, however, did not stop here, but spread throughout the city as enraged bands of *softas* went from place to place, clubbing every Armenian who appeared on the street. The rioting continued over Tuesday, and during Tuesday night quiet, peaceful homes were attacked and some eighty innocent people were slaughtered in cold blood, making a total of about three hundred victims.

MASSACRES AT TREBIZOND AND ERZRUM.

The next scene of Armenian carnage was at Trebizond, situated at the eastern end of the Black Sea, and occupying a position that formerly gave it much commercial and political importance. It is this city the declining Christians of western Europe made their stronghold in the thirteenth century, keeping part of the northern coast of the Euxine, while the interior was held by the Turks.

Owing to its being a fortified stronghold within a short distance of both the Russian and Persian borders, all strangers at the time were regarded with more or less suspicion, particularly as the Turkish authorities were then thoroughly inflamed and were on the lookout for Russo-Armenian agitators, who, they supposed, were smuggling arms across the frontier. The population of the city is about fifty thousand, there being nearly as many Armenians as Turks, with quite a representation of Greeks. Early in October, 1895, after the troubles at Constantinople, Bahri Pasha, former governor of Van, who had been called to Constantinople in disgrace, because of pressure brought against the Turkish government after the Sassoun massacre, was assaulted by an Armenian, who only succeeded in slightly wounding the man he tried to kill, though he fired six shots from a revolver. Unfortunately, he did mischief he never intended, One shot wounded a Turkish boy, who died the next day ; another wounded the hand of the *vali* of Trebizond, who was in company with the disgraced officer, while still another struck an Armenian lad. The attack of the would-be assassin, who escaped, was purely a personal matter and should not have had any significance for Turks in general. The latter, however, were ready and anxious to believe that it was the initial step to an occurrence similar to that at Constantinople, and pretended that a concerted move was to be made against them by the Armenians, declaring themselves to be in fear of an attack. In the street at night there were menacing demonstrations by the Turks. Armed bands of lawless and unrestrained Moslems lounged about the corners, or with brandished swords and frowning looks patrolled the streets.

The European consuls, alarmed at the situation, held a consultation and besought the governor to restrain the leaders who incensed the people. He declared he would do what he could to restore peace. The turbulence had seemed to subside, when on Monday, October 7, the son of a leading Turk of the city died from injuries received while in a drunken brawl, fighting with a comrade. The Turkish population was ready to believe that he had been murdered by an Armenian whom he was trying to place in custody. The excitement became intense, and a massacre the same night was

AN ARMENIAN MASSACRE.

only averted by a heavy fall of rain which dispersed the mobs.

The following morning, as there was no indication of disquiet, after a brief suspension, the Armenians reopened their shops and resumed their daily occupations. At about noon on October 8, when the streets of the city seemed as peaceful as possible, a cannon was fired somewhere in the eastern part of the city, as the signal of the authorities for the massacre to commence. In the twinkling of an eye the pent-up fury and enraged fanaticism of the Turks were let loose like a deluge of hell. In blind and unopposed fury the Moslems descended upon the unsuspecting and unarmed Armenians.

When the bloody violence was somewhat abated the plundering began. Doors and windows of houses were broken in, the better to facilitate the rapacious hunt for articles of value. Such things as were not desired by the despoilers were ruined beyond repair. The actions of the Turks seemed to indicate that they were bent upon the utter annihilation of the Armenians. Far from restraining the fiery Turks, the soldiers and police took part in the massacre, and were found distributed among the murderous crowds.

The next day the Turks spread reports to the effect that the Armenians from the adjoining village, thoroughly organized, were advancing to attack the city. The truth of the matter was that the massacre was extending to the village, though the Turks endeavored to make it appear that they were quelling an uprising. After the massacre those Armenians who escaped were thrown into prison for no cause, while perpetrators of the horrible outrages were let loose to continue their work to their hearts' content. The wave of murder and despoliation spread southward from Trebizond along a road that had been built to Erzrum in former years with a view to retaining the commercial importance of Trebizond, which was fading because of the diversion of trade to Batoum after the Treaty of Berlin and the occupation of Batoum by the Russians. The city of Sumushkhane, famous for its silver mines, whence its name, was the first place raided. As in most mining

THE COSTUME OF A TURKISH HIGHWAYMAN.

towns, the population was easily excited and quickly aroused. Christians were murdered in their places with as much heartlessness as at Trebizond, and the town in which they lived was practically destroyed. At Baiburt, a prosperous city of about fifteen thousand inhabitants, famous for their intense national feeling and vigor of character, the black cloud of rapine and destruction next fell. Upon this most-hated community of Armenians, with a ferocity that beggars description, the Turks fell, flushed with the excitement of their murderous work which had begun at Trebizond five days earlier. Authorities differ as to the number of persons killed, but the most reliable estimate is placed at one thousand. The carnage was terrible; and, when the Turks had finished their bloody work, Baiburt was but a forlorn and barely recognizable pile of ruined buildings.

All eyes were now turned upon Erzrum, which throughout the rule of the Turks has been the most powerful and important commercial city of eastern Turkey. It is the point of divergence for the various routes from the eastern end of the Black Sea to Persia, Bagdad, and central Asia Minor. The various European governments concerned in eastern Turkey maintain consulates at this city. It has an altitude of six thousand feet above the sea, and is surrounded by high mountains. Its climate runs to extremes of heat and cold, while its close proximity to the Russian border made it a favored point of attack to the Russians in the different Russo-Turkish wars. Twice Erzrum has fallen into the Russians' hands, and as many times has been released by special treaty stipulations. The population of the city is fifty thousand, and is composed, to a great extent, of Turks, though the Armenians were strong numerically and still stronger financially. The arrival of some of the leaders in the Trebizond and Baiburt massacres, and their glowing accounts of Moslem outrages, aroused the Turks to a high pitch of excitement. The police apparently endeavored to maintain peace, and as the time for an attack had several times been set, without anything taking place, the Armenians concluded that the talk of the Turks was meaningless.

The Armenians were therefore in their accustomed places on Wednesday, October 30, totally unconscious of the storm that was about to break. About noon the crack of musketry was heard in the direction of the market-place. Turks, armed to the teeth, appeared rushing towards the market, firing at random into the houses of Armenians along the way. In some instances the fire was returned. Some of the more wealthy Armenian merchants had stored most valuable goods in the mission building for safety. The resident American missionary, Mr. Chambers, had just dispatched a telegram to the Americans at Bitlis to inform them that all was well at Erzrum and to inquire of their condition. As he was returning to the mission building he noticed a spirit of unrest along the one straggling market. An Armenian came rushing by, shouting to his brethren to prepare for the onslaught of the Turks. Shops were being hurriedly closed and locked, while some merchants endeavored to hide their wares. Shortly the firing began. Mr. Chambers made haste to regain the mission building, where safety was assured. Bullets began to fly thick and fast, and the din in the vicinity of the bazaar was terrifying. To add to the general confusion a large fire had started in the extreme western part of the city, and continued for nearly twenty-five hours. The attack was made in different sections of the city simultaneously, and woe betide the Armenian who exposed the least part of his body to the merciless fire of the Turks! Murder and plundering followed. The soldiers were most aggressive. In order that they might carry away more plunder, Turkish women accompanied them, and lugged off bundles of cloth, furniture, and jewelry. Great pains were taken to destroy or render useless the food that might keep off starvation. The Turks continued their work through the following day, and then quiet reigned once more. After waiting several hours some of the more fearless, who had escaped the Turks by hiding, stole forth to seek their homes, which were, in most cases, found to be ravished and uninhabitable.

The next day, Friday, was the Moslem's Sunday, and although Thursday night there had been no violence the fears of the Armenians were again revived. To add to their apprehension, the Turks and soldiers had openly boasted that they would renew their ravages on this day. Over five hundred terrified people crowded into the mission building and its surrounding grounds, and they could in no way be induced to go home. As night drew on and hostilities had not been renewed, many gained courage and left for their homes, thereby reducing the number to about two hundred. Nothing occurred during the night, and Saturday morning the work of burying the dead began. It was a sickening sight that met the people engaged in this work. Of one thousand killed all were Armenian men, with the exception of three Armenian women and a number of children, besides thirty young men scarcely out of their teens. At the Armenian Gregorian Cemetery a trench 150 feet long and twenty feet wide was dug, and in it were laid hundreds of bodies of dead Armenians. Nowhere could a dead Turk be found. Many of the bodies were burned, others were mutilated beyond recognition. A body was found with the head attached but arms and legs missing. The corpses were nearly naked, and in some cases quite so, for the Turks had stolen everything worth stealing.

After the massacre had subsided the English and Italian consuls, accompanied by Tewfix Bey of Shakir Pasha's suite, and Mr. Chambers, inspected the Armenian quarters, or rather what was left of them. At one place they found the naked bodies of two young women who had been brutally murdered. A man with sixteen wounds was attended by Mr. Chambers, and another whose wounds he helped to dress had three awful wounds about the head, two sword incisions in his back, and a bullet through the left hand. In justice to some of the Turks, it must be said that there were a number of cases where Turks attempted to save their Armenian friends, and several instances of heroic rescues are recorded.

Instances were not only shown at Erzrum, but during the massacre in my native city, Marsovan, there were found a number of Turks who, at the risk of their own lives, protected their Armenian neighbors and friends. My own grandfather, while returning from the country on that fatal day of the massacre in Marsovan, was seized by the Turkish mob, who were like tigers, roaring for blood. They tied him hand and foot, and were about to strike the fatal blow, when a Turk to whom my grandfather had done many deeds of kindness rushed to his rescue, and after a heroic struggle managed to save his aged Armenian friend and conducted him safely home.

As intelligence of the massacre at Erzrum was spread abroad there was a profound sensation. It seemed impossible that such a thing could occur in a city containing Russian, English, and French consuls and important Turkish officials, but such skepticism will vanish in the light of later events. In August, 1896, in Constantinople itself, before the very eyes of all the European ambassadors and consuls, over four thousand Armenians were massacred within a few days. The Turks endeavored by every subterfuge to make their horrible work seem justifiable. They spread ludicrous reports of an Armenian revolution that they had quelled, and told of vast stores of arms and amunition that the revolutionists had in hiding. When these alleged places of hiding were found and searched there was nothing to substantiate the outrageous charges of the Moslems.

The city of Harput is 200 miles southwest of Erzrum, and about 20 miles east of the Euphrates. Its chief importance lies in its position, for it is the center of a large number of villages covering an extended plain and constituting the only section of Armenia where the Armenians can fairly claim to constitute a majority of the population. Although the city itself has only 1500

Armenians against 3500 of Turkish population, yet the surrounding plain is almost entirely Armenian. The massacre at this place, which made the entire province the center of the greatest suffering with over 100,000 destitute and perishing people, was, like most other Turkish butcheries, premeditated and prearranged. " Eat and drink while you may, for within eight months you will be killed," was the warning of a Turk to an Armenian family which had just arrived in this country from the scene of blood and fire.

If the massacres are provoked by revolutionary agitators, as the Turkish government persistently claims, no massacre should have ever occurred in Harput; for throughout the district the people are quiet, peaceful, and submissive folk, while self-restraint and intelligence are prominent among their characteristics. The missionaries of the American Board, who have made the city the center of a large mission and educational work, had always been on friendly terms with the government officials, and felt assured that they were removed from any possible danger or disturbance.

The Kurds, however, gathered together in great numbers and descended upon the peaceful plain; and the villages were destroyed and their inhabitants scattered or killed. The marauders did not at once attack the city, although, when the villages had been plundered, they turned to it with avaricious eyes. They were emboldened by the co-operation of the Turkish rabble of the city and villages. The situation became quite alarming, so that the Armenians were doubtful of their safety in spite of the repeated assurances of the Turkish officials that no Kurd would be allowed to enter the city.

Soon from the city the plain presented a sad view of desolation and ruin. By day bands of Kurds rode fiercely from village to village, brandishing their weapons and in many instances shooting down Armenians in cold blood. At night the sky was illuminated by burning villages, and the glow of red that hung upon the horizon seemed a portent of the redder blood that was to flow in the streets of Harput. It was not safe for any Armenian to leave the city, which was virtually in a state of siege. The cordon of fiendish savages was drawing nearer the city.

On Sunday, November 10, the worst element among the Turks in the city began a noisy demonstration, and it was plain that the crisis was not far off. The next day a village on the plain, only a short distance from the city, was attacked. After two hundred had been murdered, and as many wounded, the savages advanced to a position near an old fortress in the eastern part of the city. Turks from the city met them, and the impression was given that a council was being held. Apparently the invaders were forbidden to attack the markets, from which it was known that all the merchandise had been removed. The deception was carried still further by a sham battle, which made it appear that the soldiers had resisted the invasion of the city. The firing had not continued long before a signal cannon was fired, and instantly the raiders began their work of murder and pillage all over the city. Amid flame and smoke, shout and groan, and saber strokes and death-shots falling thick and fast as lightnings from the mountain cloud, the refugees sought safety at the school and mission-buildings and churches. The soldiers protected the Kurds, and the Turkish military forces did not make the slightest move to repel them, but stood by and saw American property destroyed and plundered and American citizens fired upon without lifting a finger to prevent. It was not incendiarism but official destruction. Nearly one hundred houses in the vicinity of the educational and missionary buildings were burned, and then those buildings began to burn. It was evident that the plan of the marauders was to destroy these, so that the Americans and refugees would have no shelter. The missionaries, with their several hundred people, were driven from one place to another by the fire and the whistling of bullets. The savage horde shot down and tortured to death those who would not abjure their Christian faith. Quite a number of Armenians fled to a church in the vain hope that its sacred walls would furnish a shelter against those who were raving for Christian blood; but the doors were soon battered in with heavy axes, and as their Moslem captors appeared, with raised daggers, the shrieks and cries of the helpless women and children rose louder and louder. Their captors dragged them out of the church one at a time, and, upon their firm refusal to accept Mohammed, they were killed with horrible tortures. The Protestant pastor of the church was the first victim, and as he was dragged out he exhorted the others to die like himself —a Christian martyr.

In the cities of Arabkir and Malitia the Armenians offered resistance to the ravishers, but only succeeded in stirring the Turks to greater deeds of violence. They suffered terribly, while the Turks lost only a few of their numbers. At Malitia five thousand Christians were murdered, and at Arabkir two thousand, while it is estimated that not more than four hundred Turks were killed. A reliable estimate of the number of Christians killed in this region in one month alone, commencing with the latter part of October, 1895, is 12,710. The houses destroyed numbered 5064. The total number killed in the *vilayet* of Harput is estimated at 40,000, including those who perished from hunger and cold; wounded, 8000; houses burned, 28,789; forcibly converted to Islam, 51,180; raped, 5530; married by force to Turks, 1530.

It is needless to enter here into a detailed account of all the massacres. The wave of carnage that swept over the empire, from Trebizond, southward into the valley of the Euphrates, westward to Marsovan and Cæsaria, and out to the Mediterranean Sea, and even Constantinople itself, carried in its overwhelming tides death and destruction. Sword, fire, famine, and pestilence have accomplished the infernal design of the oppressors. Thousands of Armenian women were violently carried off to the harems of their persecutors, while many men of the productive classes are doomed to languish in Turkish dungeons, arrested on unexplained charges and given no opportunity to vindicate themselves. Their property was stolen or destroyed, and in many instances their lands and title deeds were forcibly seized by the officers of the government. In the face of the misery which befell unfortunate Armenia, one can easily imagine the harrowing prospect of the winter season in that cold region, when many thousands of innocent

ARMENIAN CHILDREN.

orphans and widows, stripped of everything which makes life comfortable, were turned over to exposure and famine. Nowhere have childhood and motherhood seen darker days than in Armenia.

As to the nature of the massacres, it is obvious that

they primarily started on political issues, but soon the religious element overpowered the political. Indeed, it became the leading issue among Moslems whether Christians should longer be tolerated in a land where the Caliph of Mohammed has the sway of the government. It was on this very principle that the Sultan ordered a general massacre soon after he had promised the Powers to accept the proposed reforms giving Christians within the six *vilayets* rights that depended on their number. The massacres have been chiefly confined to these *vilayets*, the object being so to reduce the number of Christians as to give them no possible claim to any influence. The work of extermination—pillage, rapine, and murder—proceeded systematically.

The Turkish Question as it now stands is distinctly religious, and stands above humanitarian and political considerations. "Mohammed or the sword" has been the cry in all the scenes of the massacres, yet the Armenians have asserted the same firmness in their adherence to Christianity as they had through the vicissitudes of long centuries. The Rev. Dr. Cyrus Hamlin, who above all living Americans has made himself master of the facts, by long years of toil and achievement in the Ottoman Empire, corroborates my assertion at this point when he says:

> But there is one noble trait that has come out in this terrible persecution which has astonished the world and has enraged the bloody persecutors.
> It is the firm refusal of men and women—of young men as well as of old—to save life by professing Islam. The confession is very brief. Only say: "There is but one God and Mohammed is

his Prophet," and wear the Moslem turban, and your life is spared.

The eighty to one hundred thousand who have perished might have saved their lives by this confession, and by then adopting the Moslem dress and worship and trampling upon the Cross. They have died the death of martyrs. Many have saved their lives by this confession, it is true, but most of these acknowledge their present extreme wretchedness, and some have been killed for showing this keen regret.

There is now an immense number of sufferers scattered through all the regions where massacres have occurred, who have lost fathers, brothers, property, dwellings, and who are simply fighting for life. Many thousands of them will perish of cold and famine next winter. Their number is estimated at from three to four hundred thousand. They suffer for clothing, for food, and for shelter. As all their tools have been destroyed or stolen, their miserable "dug-outs" resemble the lairs of wild beasts.

And yet all this they endure rather than deny the faith. They suffer "scourgings and cruel mockings, yea, moreover, of bonds and imprisonments—they wander about in sheepskins and goatskins, being destitute, afflicted, tormented."—Heb. xi. 36, etc.

All these can escape their misery by professing Islam. They, as well as the thousands slain, are martyrs of Jesus. They may be much less enlightened in Christian doctrine than we, but they have a faith that enables them to "resist unto blood." They suffer the most cruel torture and death rather than say Mohammed is Lord and not Jesus of Nazareth.*

The failure of Christendom to protect its co-religionists has proved a great moral disaster, for not only have the Christian victims lost faith in the sincerity of the great nations who profess Christ, but the Moslem world has taken it as an acknowledgment that Christianity is inferior to Mohammedanism.

* From an article entitled "The Lesson of Armenia," in the *Presbyterian*, for November 4, 1896.

Christians do not believe in the propagation of their faith by force of arms as do Moslems. But Christians have the right to insist that the powers of their government should be used for the protection of those who hold the Christian faith.

But the Armenian appeals to Christendom for protection and freedom are not simply based on their religious affiliation and unity of creed; for the Mohammedan Turks have just as much right to rule over the Christian population in Armenia as the Christian English have to rule over the Mohammedan population in India. But when our people are singled out on account of their religion and robbed and tortured and killed, there we find a legitimate ground on which to call for interference on the ground of common humanity.

Cold indeed must be the heart that is not touched by the story of the atrocious deeds of the Turk. The tales of the dead are sad, those of the living more sad. Thousands of them have been deported, and those who remain are terrorized into silence. But the history of those awful days, when the tides of massacre, lust, and rapine raged throughout the cities and plains of our unhappy land, has been ineffaceably written, and the blood of her hundred thousand martyrs still cries aloud from earth to heaven.

The thought of home and native land fills my heart with mingled feelings of gloom and rage. Many a youthful friend and schoolmate with whom I had spent the happiest days of my life in walks and talks and sports under the arching trees of my father's vineyard—many a bright boy of marked future possibilities with whom

I had dreamed by the babbling brooks the dream of youth—lies to-day in an unknown grave.

WHAT IS TO BE DONE?

There seems to me only one possible course of action for my people to take, especially for the young, and that is to seek in other lands and among liberty-loving people new homes and new hopes of enterprise; to seek some land where they can work and receive the benefits of their toil, where they can worship Him who has granted them freedom of conscience; a place where they can own themselves, where honest thought and labor make vantage ground from which their posterity may climb to nobler heights. This newest Land of the Free, which, from the early advent of its Pilgrim Fathers, has been an asylum for the oppressed and persecuted from every clime—why may it not open its hospitable doors and extend its welcome to the oldest remnant of early Christianity to share the heritage of freedom within its borders? Utterly hopeless and helpless in the midst of everlasting oppression, the young Armenian looks to America as his ideal Utopia. No doubt there are many, particularly those advanced in years, who would cling to their fatherland, no matter how dark the adversity. Yet there are many, particularly the younger element of the Armenians, who, though with much regret, are being led to desert their homes and firesides.

Quite a number of Armenians have already come hither, and still larger numbers of them will come if they are encouraged with employment and practical sympathy. Of course it is not an easy matter for the Armenians to get out of the country that has cursed them. The refugees are restrained by the vigilant Turkish authorities, who, like Pharaoh's hosts in dealing with Israel, would rather slay them than to permit them to go.

Only recently two of my younger brothers came to this country. The first to arrive here was shot at while in the old country, and doubtless would have been killed had he not been careful and speedy in his flight. He was actually smuggled over to this country. He was living at the time in Samsun, one of the ports of the Black Sea. After much planning and trial he managed to evade the vigilance of the Turkish officers, and boarded one of the European steamers, where the captain kept him over a week in the hold of the ship, until the steamer finally left Turkish waters. This instance serves to show why more Armenians do not leave Turkey. My brother's case was a very easy one. He did not have to contend with difficulties to secure a passport, an almost insurmountable difficulty to the average refugee. Cannot the United States government effect an understanding with Turkey by which Armenian emigrants to American shores may have a safe-conduct through the Sultan's domain?

There are now upward of ten thousand Armenians in this country—all good citizens and peaceable, sober, and orderly members of society. There are among them even professors and teachers in American schools and colleges, as well as ministers of the gospel. I have watched the career of many an Armenian refugee within the past two or three years, and I can truthfully say that their industry and behavior have been for the most part a credit to the race. Once in a land of freedom, they have, in grateful acknowledgment, made it their duty to advance the interests of the country to the best of their knowledge. Being of a kindred race and religion, they readily conform to the institutions and ideas of their new habitation. To say that the Armenians are a law-abiding people is a trite assertion. Scarcely ever have the criminal courts had any dealings with our people.

Several years before the massacre I began in my public lectures to firmly advocate Armenian emigration and colonization in the United States. I knew the sufferings and outrages to which my people were subjected in the Old World, and I could predict for them a better existence in the New. I was led to this conviction not only by my high esteem and love for the American people, but by the happy and, for the most part, contented disposition of my countrymen who were scattered around me. Particularly when the recent massacre in Turkey came on I felt most keenly for the flower of Armenian manhood and womanhood who perished there, and who might have been saved here for higher usefulness.

In the preceding pages I have endeavored to present the history and portray as accurately as possible the conditions of my beloved race.

As I pen these last few words my mind instinctively turns to my countrymen, zealous in the faith, constant to the right—the type of a fearless, honorable race.

Providence has so ordained that the people of the earth should be divided into nations, the governments and laws of which are as diverse as the ideas peculiar to their originators. We may be united in civilization and common sympathies, but the patriot is ever proud of and partial to the land which has given him birth.

Christianity is broader than any constitution, more effective than the most wise laws of men. Its kingdom is confined to no territory and has no limitations to its power. We are all patriots of that kingdom, and it is not only loyalty to my country but loyalty to the broader, more glorious kingdom, that prompts me to turn my purposes and energy to her welfare.

The light of morning already tints the eastern sky, but the mists still rising from man's ignorance and superstition obscure the rays and hide the sun. When, rising over hill and valley with its glorious splendor, God's own light shines in the zenith of the heavens, the obscuring mists all cleared away, then, and not till then, will the soul of man be fully illumined and his destiny made clear.

THE END.

www.ingramcontent.com/pod-product-compliance
Lightning Source LLC
Chambersburg PA
CBHW050850300426
44111CB00010B/1197